IMAGES
of America

JERSEY SHORE

On the cover: Please see page 59. (Courtesy of the Jersey Shore Historical Society.)

IMAGES
of America

JERSEY SHORE

Wayne O. Welshans for the Jersey Shore Historical Society

ARCADIA
PUBLISHING

ISBN 978-0-7385-4641-4

Published by Arcadia Publishing
Charleston, South Carolina

Printed in the United States of America

Library of Congress Catalog Card Number: 2006927854

For all general information contact Arcadia Publishing at:
Telephone 843-853-2070
Fax 843-853-0044
E-mail sales@arcadiapublishing.com
For customer service and orders:
Toll-Free 1-888-313-2665

Visit us on the Internet at www.arcadiapublishing.com

Contents

ACKNOWLEDGMENTS

This book provides a brief photographic journey into the history of a small town in north central Pennsylvania called Jersey Shore. Many of these photographs are held by the Jersey Shore Historical Society and are the product of the town's early photographers. Fires, floods, and indifference have eliminated most of their work, but what is left presents an interesting story of Jersey Shore in its golden years, roughly 1860 to 1930. John Nice and Jonathan Potter were our photographers of the Civil War era and were followed by William H. Garman, D. Vincent Smith, Joseph Mick, Nelson Caulkins, and Charles and Robert Harer. The majority of the following images in this time slot are attributed to Joseph Mick. Also, the following people are recognized for their time, contribution, and encouragement: Mary Teufel, Harold Bachman, Donald Dietzel, Jane Spangler, and Fred Mick.

The *Jersey Shore Herald,* which began publication in 1860, has provided interesting local information concerning our area. Special mention should be made of the historical writings of Joseph Cox who worked for the *Jersey Shore Herald* from 1946 to his death in 1972. The title of his column was "Shore Lines." Other sources of interesting information came from borough council minutes dating back to the 1850s, numerous church records, the writings of Helen Russell, historical records held by the Jersey Shore Historical Society, and from the memories of older citizens of Jersey Shore who are deeply proud of their hometown.

FOREWORD

It is a familiar American story. Historically a spot along a river becomes the focal point of interaction among a few pioneering adventurers. They bring families, and the spot gets bigger as it gets safer. Eventually someone qualifies it for a dot on his map. An emergent culture begins to characterize a huddled village. Location, natural resources, and such accidents of history as the concomitant development of places nearby enable the success of local enterprise. The village becomes a town.

Somewhat ploddingly, over decades, the town goes its own way, does its thing as we say. Then one day the world comes knocking. With dramatic suddenness the community is transformed from without. Its economic, social, and cultural attributes undergo an upheaval that leaves almost nothing unchanged. The town grows bigger, busier, noisier, and equates prosperity with progress. After more years of growth and optimism, with even greater suddenness the world goes away again. Progress was only change after all, and the town must change again.

On the West Branch of the Susquehanna River in Pennsylvania, the small town of Jersey Shore was spurred to prominence with the arrival of the railroads. The town was made pivotal in the operations of the New York Central rail system. For half a century Jersey Shore was a railroad town. The railroads supported industry, commercial sprawl, and a vibrant diversity of new citizens who required infrastructural accommodation. With the subsequent dissipation of the railroads, Jersey Shore had to redefine itself on a diminished scale.

Jersey Shore is, however, a success story, and representative at that. The following pages are not just another story of the comings and goings of the railroads. Rather it is a record of a community, a cultural unit, forced into changing its culture. What was here before the railroads? What came with them? How did it happen? What remained to build upon when they left? Is Jersey Shore really typical? Is it unique? Could it be both?

The marvelous photographic record presented here is from a definitive collection compiled and researched by author-editor Wayne Welshans. His vision of that record links the culture of a locality, its survival or demise, its metamorphosis, with crucial turning points in its history. Anthropologically the term culture is of sweeping application, encompassing every aspect of human life. Its totality, however, is nothing more than just people together engaged in their daily living. Welshans gives us something of that broad sweep, while inviting us to recognize and even rejoice a little bit in our connectedness with what has passed in one small town.

—Harold Baughman, April 2006

INTRODUCTION

The first known European to travel near this place was the Frenchman Etienne Brule, who traveled the length of the Susquehanna in 1616. It was more than 100 years before other white men (missionaries) reached the site of present-day Jersey Shore. These were the Reverends Brainard, Zeisberger, and Mack who traveled here in the 1740s. There were few settlers at this place before the Revolutionary War and this land did not "open up" until the Indian Treaty of 1784, one year after the Susquehanna was declared a "public highway." Although the first six legal land warrants, surveys, and patents were established in 1785, there were only four houses in the town by 1800.

The little community grew significantly after this. A road was built from Level Corners, and a dozen or more businesses were established by 1802. A post office was established in 1806, and this postal village was called Waynesburg. Surveyor William B. Smith established a street plan in 1812, showing the town developing along the river with Walnut Alley (Broad Street) at the western edge of town. A stagecoach run was extended to Jersey Shore from Williamsport in 1814, with fare at 6¢ per mile, and the Antes Ferry crossed the river near the mouth of Antes Creek.

During the 1820s the name of the post office reverted to Jersey Shore and the town was legally organized on March 15, 1826. The first newspaper printed was the *West Branch Courier*, edited by Daniel Gotshall; and the Lafayette Masonic Lodge No. 199 was established. The following decade, the 1830s, brought the establishment of the first cemetery (Richmond Park today), Nice's Excelsior Carriage Works (at the corner of Main and Smith), the first Methodist Episcopal church (where borough hall stands today), and the Washington House Hotel (where the Moose Club is today). Cement was mined from Cement Hollow for the building of the locks and aqueducts of the new West Branch Canal that entered Jersey Shore in 1834. Commercial rafting on the Susquehanna began in 1835, and the last spar timber, for masts of ships, floated down in 1865. Nine-passenger stagecoaches stopped at the Franklin House Hotel, where the Carpenter and Harris law office is located. The first set of covered toll bridges was built in 1838, and a distillery was established near Broad and Locust Streets. During the 1840s, cook stoves began replacing fireplaces, and Jersey Shore is first mentioned in a book by Sherman Day, the population was set at 525. The First Baptist Church was built in 1844, and the first three-story building, Crane's Arcade, was built next to the bridge. The following year brought the first free school in town run by Elisha Parker and the organization of the Independent Order of Odd Fellows (IOOF), Lodge No. 101, the oldest such lodge in Lycoming County. The First Methodist Church was built in 1847 with logs floated down Pine Creek from English Center. Envelopes and postage stamps came into common use. In 1850, Jersey Shore had a population of 608 (112 families) and the First Presbyterian Church was built on Main Street, across the alley from the Water Company. Also at that time the West Branch High School was established in the old seminary that housed the Baptists and Presbyterians in 1832. The Larrys Creek Plank Road was built in 1850, and the Susquehanna Log Boom was built the following year. The Jersey Shore Cemetery, Mount Pleasant, was laid out in 1853 by surveyor A. H. McHenry on land donated by Mark Slonaker. J. B. Bachelder produced a beautiful lithograph of Jersey Shore in 1854, and the Philadelphia and Erie Railroad passed through Granville (Antes Fort), stopping at the Jersey Shore station. Soon after 1858, the canals were sold by the state to the Philadelphia and Erie Railroad. The last year of the decade saw establishment of the Jersey Shore Gas Works and a store called L. L. Stearns opening in the Arcade building. In 1860, the first fire company was established with a new engine house located at the end of Smith Street, and the *Jersey Shore Herald* began as a weekly newspaper.

In 1862, Jersey Shore was established as a borough. Borough council met on the second floor of the new engine house and passed a special tax for the maintenance of families and volunteers fighting for the Union. The first borough ordinances were established, with No. 4 "not allowing pigs to run the streets." A special town meeting was held in March 1864 for the purpose of raising volunteers to fill the draft quota. The borough agreed to pay each of 14 soldiers $100 for mustering in. In May, they paid $150 to each man reenlisting in the 8th Pennsylvania Cavalry. In March 1865, the disastrous St. Patrick's Day Flood took out the two covered bridges, and two new ones were built in their place. In 1865, returning Civil War soldiers stopped and signed in at the Washington House on North Main Street. In 1867, there were six schools in Jersey Shore. A female teacher earned $26 per month, and a male earned $50. Average attendance was 263 students with total tax levied at $2,101. Also in that year, St. John's Lutheran Church was organized. Members met in Staver Hall until their building was completed in 1871. In 1868, the Ferguson School House was built, as was the Allegheny House. The following year the first bank in Jersey Shore was established on Main Street as Gamble, Humes, and White. During the 1870s, the first lime used for fertilizer was burned at Bailey's Kiln on Pine Creek. Graduation exercises for the first senior high school class were held in 1876 in the John Staver building at the corner of Bank Avenue and Main Street. The largest hotel ever built in Jersey Shore, the Gamble House, opened in 1877—the IOOF building/Masons are there now. William H. Garman was the photographer of the time, replacing Jonathan Potter. In 1878, the first Clinton and Lycoming County Agricultural Fair was held at the fairground (located between the YMCA and Arby's today). By 1880, there were 23 telephones in town; there were only 595 in the whole county. The Pine Creek Suspension Bridge was built replacing the covered bridge built there by Phelps Mills. It was used until 1924. In 1882, a new stone jail was built on the southeast corner of the Broad Street School property. George Poust built the jail at a cost of $317, and the Pine Creek (Fallbrook) Railroad was constructed. James Bren started a floral business that lasted a century. In 1884, the Beech Creek Railroad constructed shops at the junction in Jersey Shore, and the New York Central Railroad built new ones in Avis starting in 1902. Also in 1884, the Jersey Shore Water Company was incorporated and Robert Camerer began operation of the planing mill in Jersey Shore. Cohick Brothers was founded in Salladasburg, and the *Grit* became a Sunday newspaper.

The Haney Addition was added to the borough in 1885. It ran from Wilson to Staver Street and added 166 new people. Also in 1885, the Women's Christian Temperance Union was organized in Jersey Shore, and the Broad Street School was built, replacing an older six-room school standing on the corner of the lot. In 1886, the Third Ward (Walnut Street) School was built, and the First Trinity Evangelical Church was built at the corner of High and Underwood Streets. The great timber flood of June 1889 carried one billion board feet of lumber downstream and again took out the two covered bridges at Jersey Shore as well as the canal aqueduct over Pine Creek. The first annual commencement of the new public high school on Broad Street took place with a total of 11 graduates.

The "Junction" was annexed by the borough, and eight trains stopped daily at the Jersey Shore Railroad station in Antes Fort in 1891. Sallada Brothers General Mercantile Business opened that year. A charter was granted by the state department in 1893 for the Jersey Shore Electric Heat and Power Company, and another big flood in 1894 swept away the first new iron bridge at Jersey Shore as it had the covered bridges before. The ferry was running again; fare for a foot passenger was 5¢, a single rig was 25¢, and a double rig was 50¢. The water company laid a new 10-inch iron pipe across the river to Aughenbaugh's Gap where an intake dam was constructed. This supply was used until 1902. The First Presbyterian Church burned in 1893, and a new one was built up the street in 1895. The borough of Jersey Shore paid for the new town clock at a cost of $625. The athletic field for the high school was located on the island, and football and baseball were played there in 1895. Also the Epworth Methodist Church formed, and the congregation built their church on the site of the present Jersey Shore Public Library. It burned in 1919, and a new brick building was constructed in 1921. Compulsory school attendance affected students between the ages of 8 and 13. The Gustav Adolphus Swedish Lutheran Church was dedicated in 1897. It was located at the corner of Pine and Locust. On June 25, 1898, the first electric lights were turned on in the town. The following year the Walnut Street Baptist Church began as a mission of the First Baptist Church and was officially organized in 1902. The present borough hall was completed in 1901. The names of the streets were posted, and 33 electric arc lights replaced most of the gas lamps in town. At this same time, the New York Central Railroad built one of the largest engine and repair shops in the east at Avis, just to the west of Jersey Shore. This brought many new people, businesses, and wealth to this community such as had never been seen before. A building boom caused the development and expansion of "uptown" Jersey Shore. This golden era in the town's history lasted until 1931 when the engine repair shops left. The town continued to decline until 1955 when the car shops closed. The population of the town dropped from over 6,000 to over 4,000, and the booming economy of Jersey Shore came to an end.

One

The Early Years

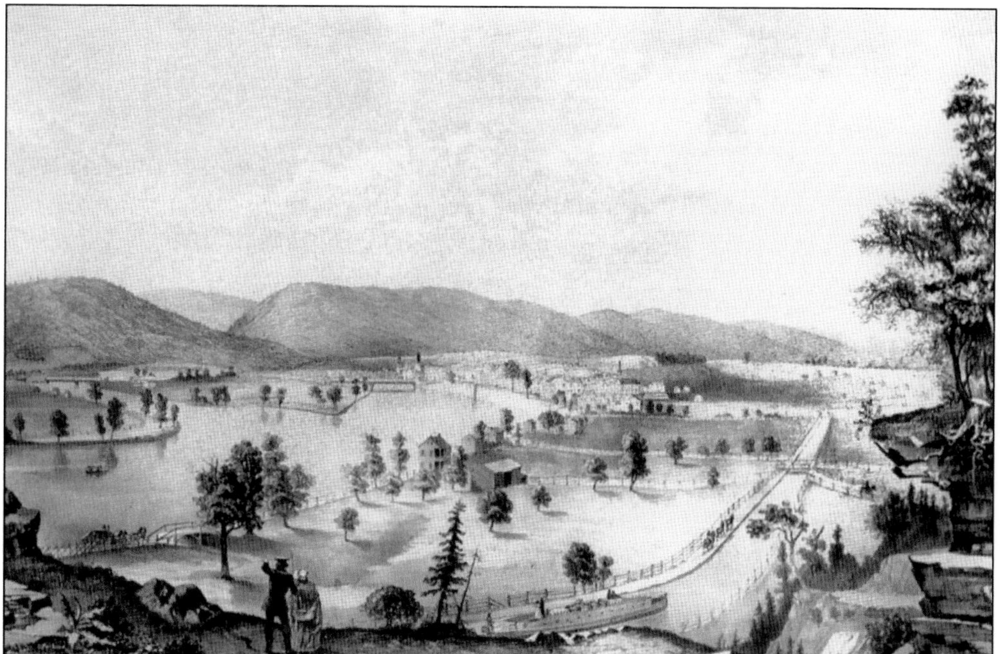

This highly accurate, panoramic view of Jersey Shore was produced by John B. Bachelder in 1854. He was working out of New Hampshire at the time and also produced views of Williamsport and Lock Haven. From left to right may be seen Boat Mountain, Aughenbaugh Gap, Long Island (with covered bridges on both sides), steeples of the Presbyterian and Baptist churches on South Main Street, and the steeple of the old 1832 seminary. The seminary, by this time, was being used as the West Branch High School.

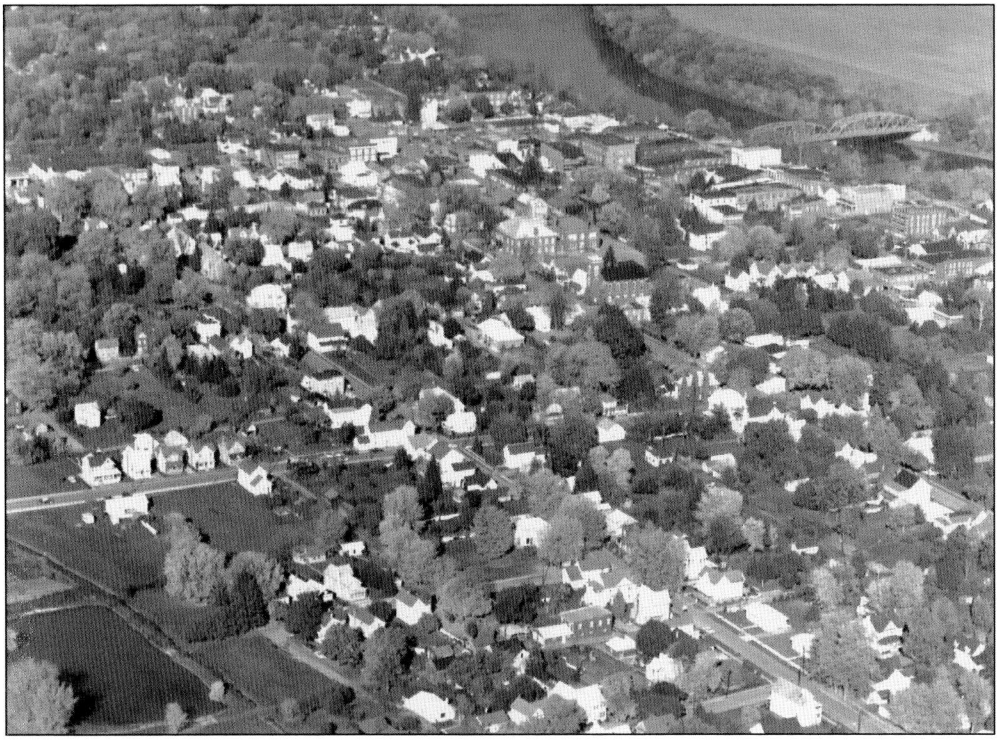

This photograph shows a view of downtown Jersey Shore 116 years later.

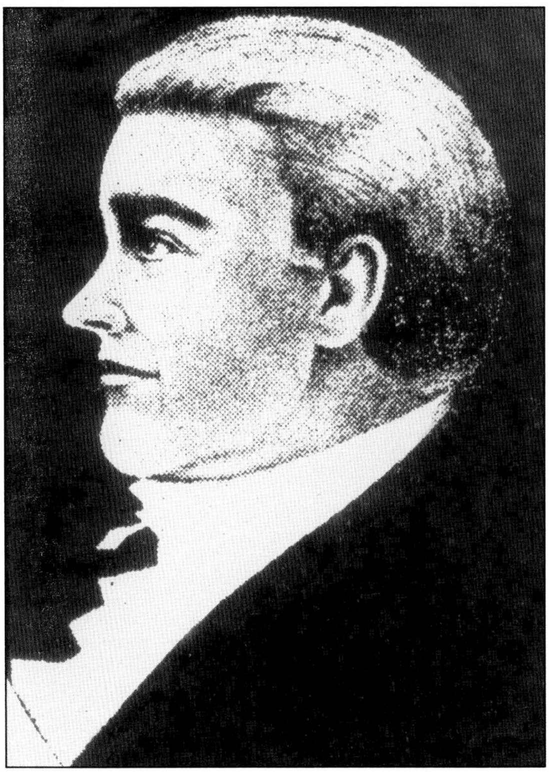

Col. John Henry Antes, who settled near the mouth of Antes Creek in 1773, was a primary defender of pioneers settling in this area. By 1776, conflicts with American Indians caused him to build a small fort on a bluff opposite the site of Jersey Shore. Below it he built a primitive flour mill. These accommodations made a natural gathering place for the settlers to meet and discuss the latest news from Philadelphia concerning the impending war for independence.

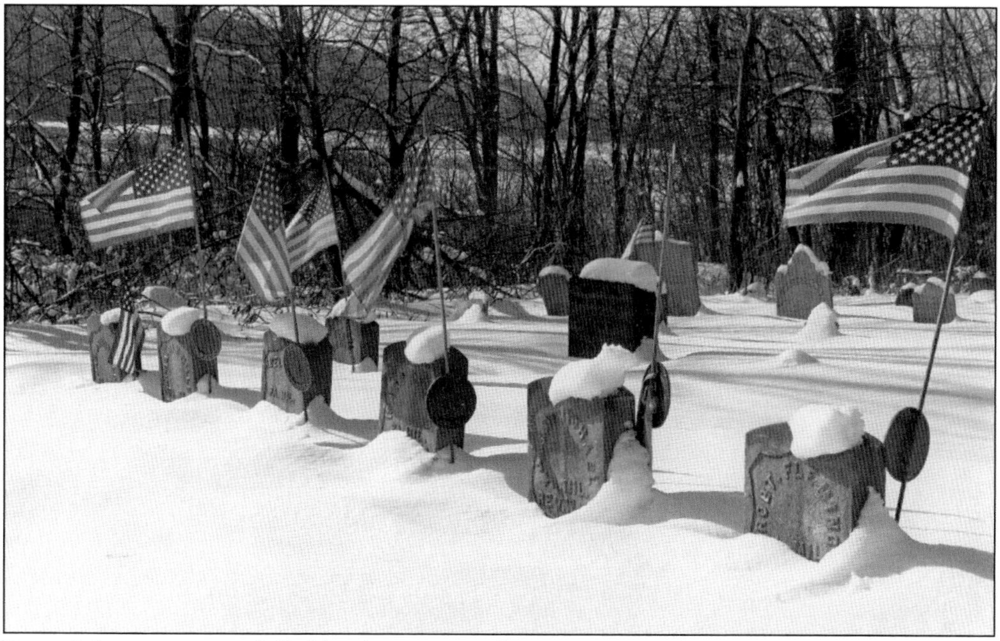

Four of these men were killed by American Indians just across the river from Fort Antes, on a Sunday morning in June 1777 as they went to milk several cows in pasture. From left to right they are James Armstrong, Zephaniah Miller, Abel Cady, and Isaac Bower. The next two graves are James McMichael and Robert Fleming, who were also killed by American Indians in 1778 as they were coming from upriver Fort Horn to secure a flatboat for the "Big Runaway."

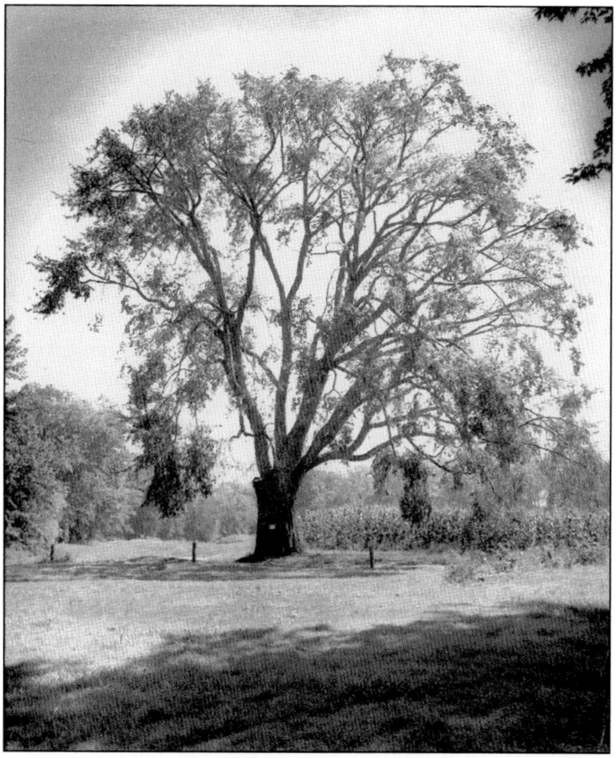

Squatters, known as Fair Play Men, who lived beyond the 1768 purchase line, met under this 300-year-old elm tree, known as the "Tiadaghton Elm" on July 4, 1776. They drew up a resolution declaring themselves independent from Great Britain. This was done before the news from Philadelphia made it to this frontier region. The tree was dead by 1975, but Fourth of July ceremonies are still held at this place every year.

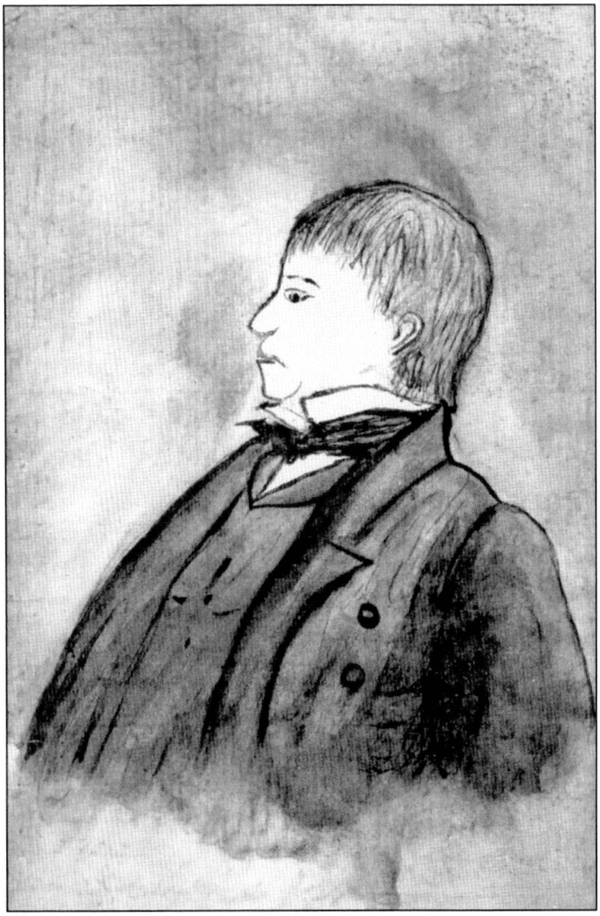

James Davidson, a doctor and prominent citizen of the Jersey Shore area, was appointed surgeon of the 5th Pennsylvania Battalion on April 5, 1777. He took an oath of allegiance before Gen. Anthony Wayne, dined with General Washington at Valley Forge, and served faithfully until the end of the war. It is likely he suggested the name "Waynesburg" for the name of the town and became one of the first associate judges of the newly formed Lycoming County.

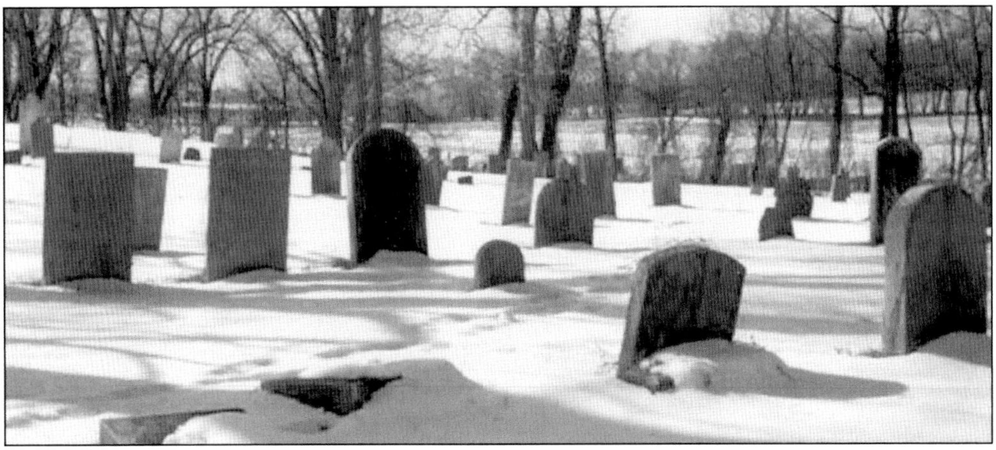

The Davidson, or Pine Creek, Cemetery lies about a mile west of Jersey Shore along the old Pennsylvania Canal and was originally located on the north end of Dr. Davidson's farm. The first interment was in 1794 when a young child of Jacob and Jane Tomb fell out of a canoe as they entered Pine Creek on their way to a new home. The doctor could do nothing for the little girl but offered the parents a burial site. Many early prominent citizens were buried here including 14 Revolutionary War soldiers.

Lt. Robert Davidson, son of Dr. James Davidson, fought in the War of 1812 and was killed on July 25, 1814, at the battle of Lundy's Lane, where Niagara Falls, Ontario, is located. Some 5,000 American, British, and Canadian troops fought at close range for five hours. A letter written to his father stated, "At last sight he had his sword waving and was encouraging his men into battle. The grape-shot was so intense that no trace could be found of his sword, clothing or body."

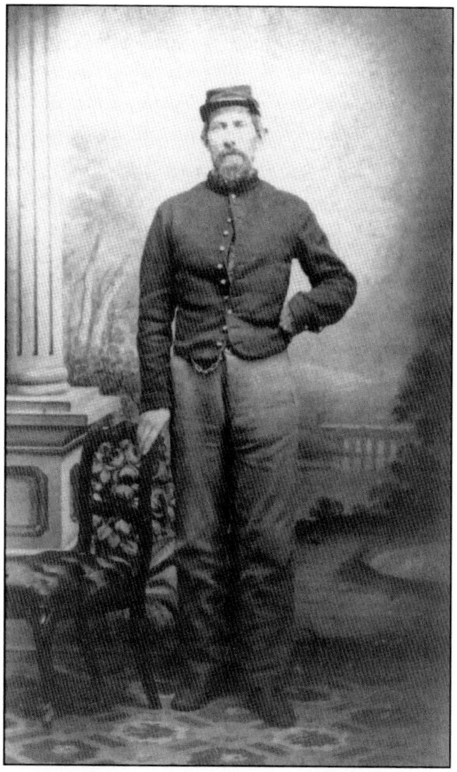

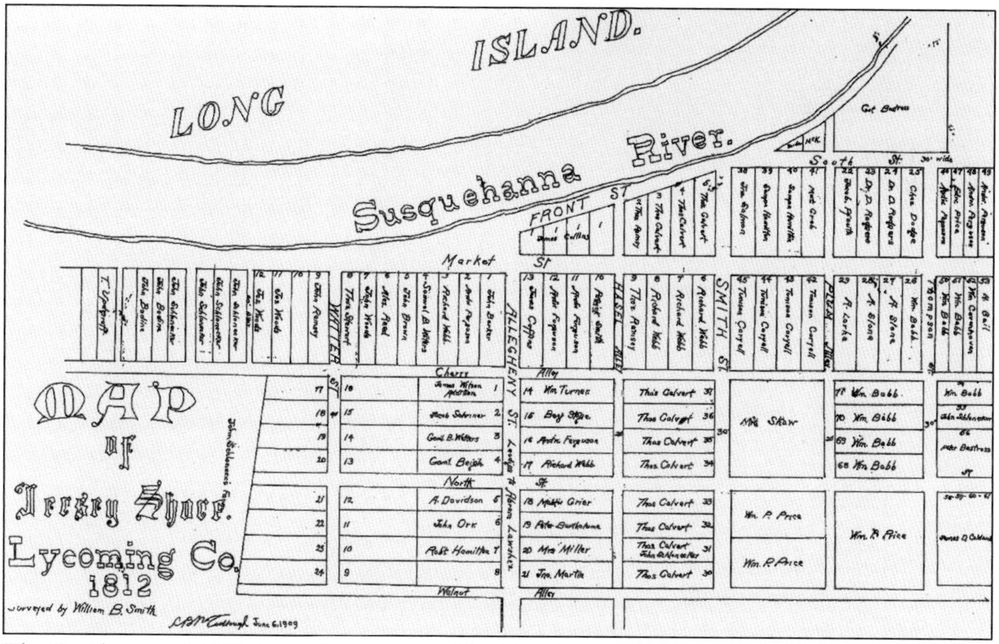

The Smith map of 1812 shows the streets and building lots of downtown Jersey Shore pretty much as they are today. However, at this time, Main Street was called Market Street, Seminary Street was called Watter Street, Pennsylvania Avenue was called North Street, Bank Alley was known as Hazel Alley, and Broad Street was called Walnut Alley and was at the western edge of town.

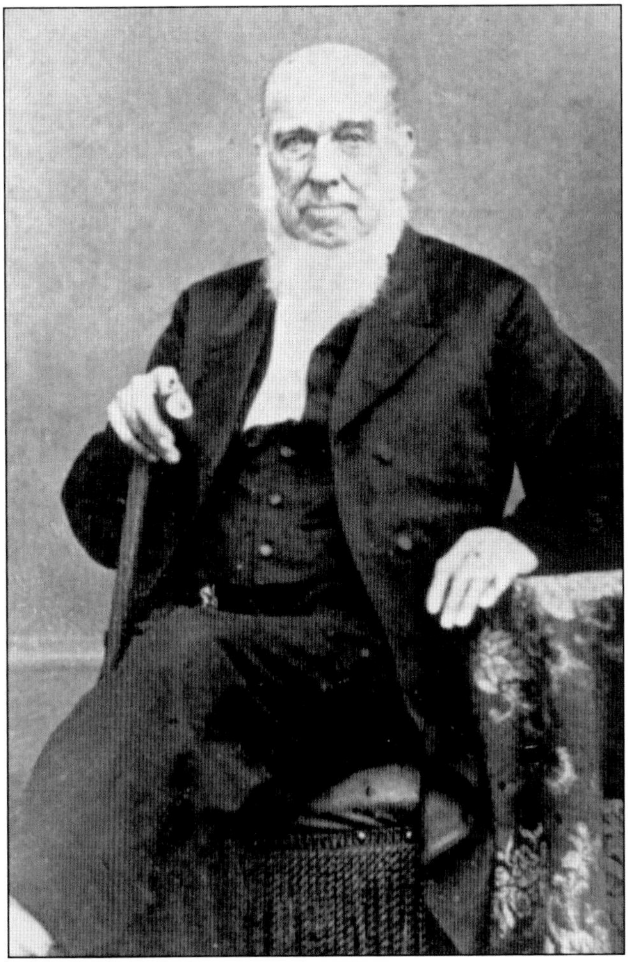

The Reverend John Hays Grier moved to Pine Creek and the Jersey Shore area in 1814 and served as Presbyterian minister here for 37 years. He has been referred to as the "Marrying Parson," as his private records indicate he married some 624 couples by 1868. His first wedding was in Nippenose Valley, above Collomsville, on September 7, 1815. He was married four times.

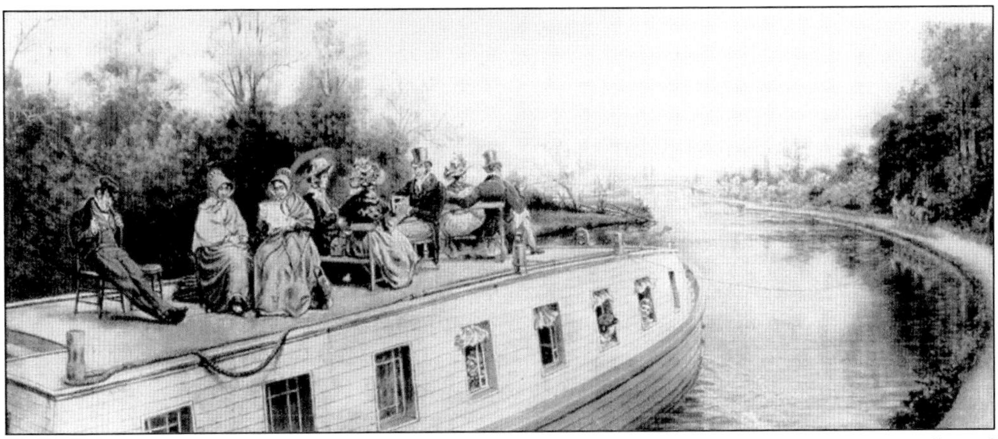

The West Branch Canal operated through Jersey Shore from 1834 to 1889 carrying goods and passengers. Volume I, No. 32, of the *Jersey Shore Republican* newspaper wrote: "The packet boat leaves Harrisburg valley daily at 4 o'clock in the evening and arrives in Williamsport the next evening, and is at Lock Haven the following morning at 4 o'clock." This picture is thought to show such a boat coming into Jersey Shore.

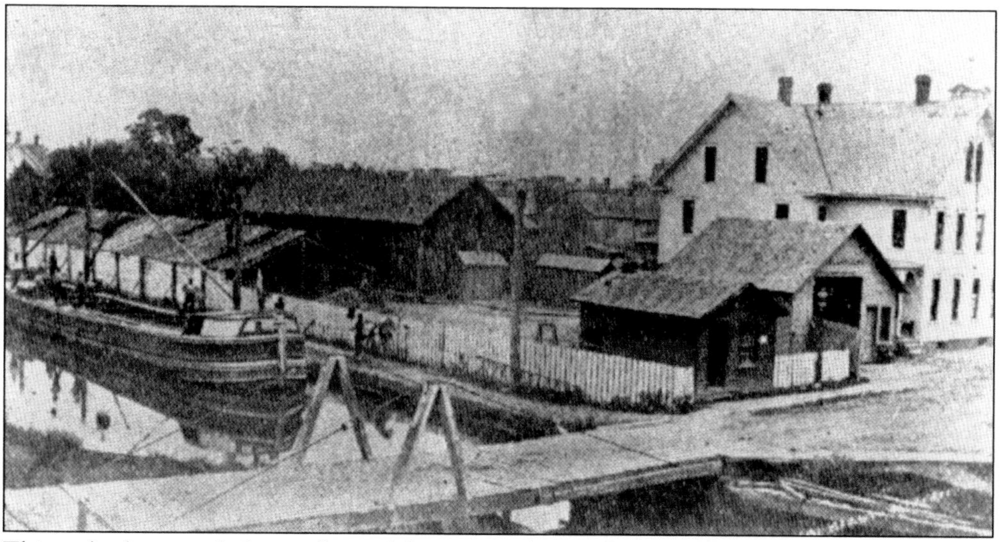

This early photograph shows a barge delivering coal to Wellman Garverick on Thompson Street close to where Hollick's coal yard is today. Just beyond the swinging bridge is a lock that is 69 feet above the water level at Muncy dam, a distance of about 33 miles. The first boat through Jersey Shore belonged to George Aughenbaugh.

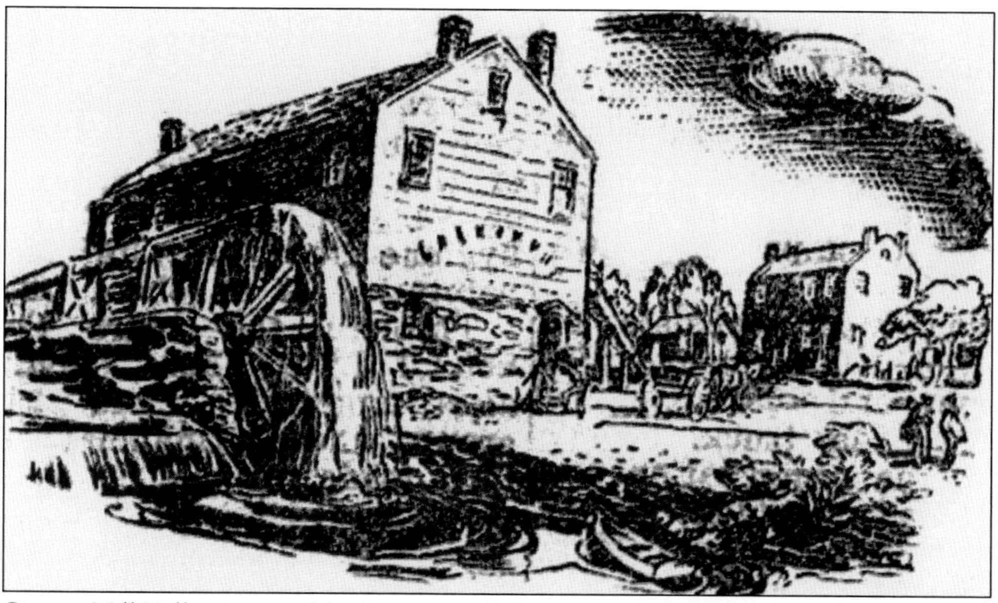

Cement Mill Hollow is named for the stone mill that was used to grind rock suitable for cement. It was found on the King farm. The hydraulic nature of this material was discovered by Robert Faries, chief engineer of the canal project, and was used to build locks, culverts, bridges, dams, and aqueducts. The aqueduct over Pine Creek was over 300 feet long. George L. Sanderson was one of five directors.

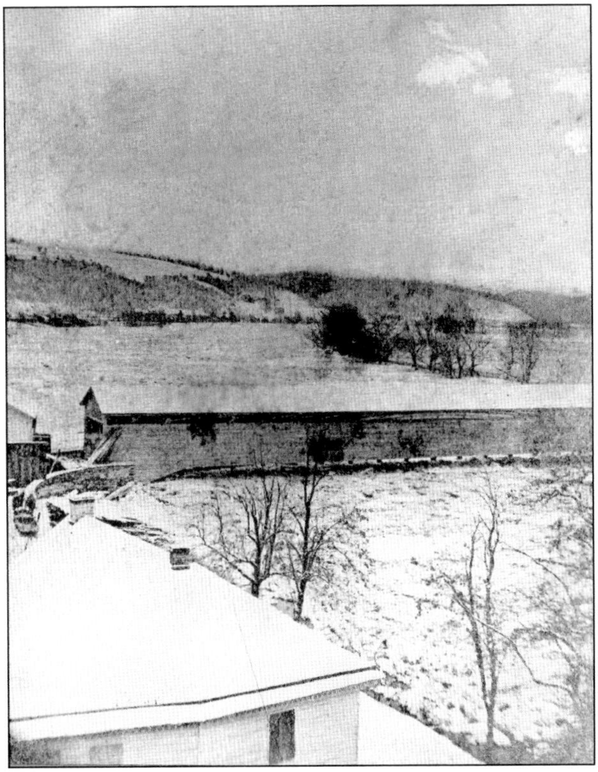

This is one of the first covered toll bridges to cross the Susquehanna at Jersey Shore. It was authorized by an act of assembly on May 14, 1838, and lasted until it was destroyed by the ice flood of March 17, 1865, the St. Patrick's Day flood. Its mate crossed the river again on the Antes Fort side of Long Island. Prior to this bridge, the Antes Ferry operated between 1817 and 1838. This photograph was taken by Jonathan Potter.

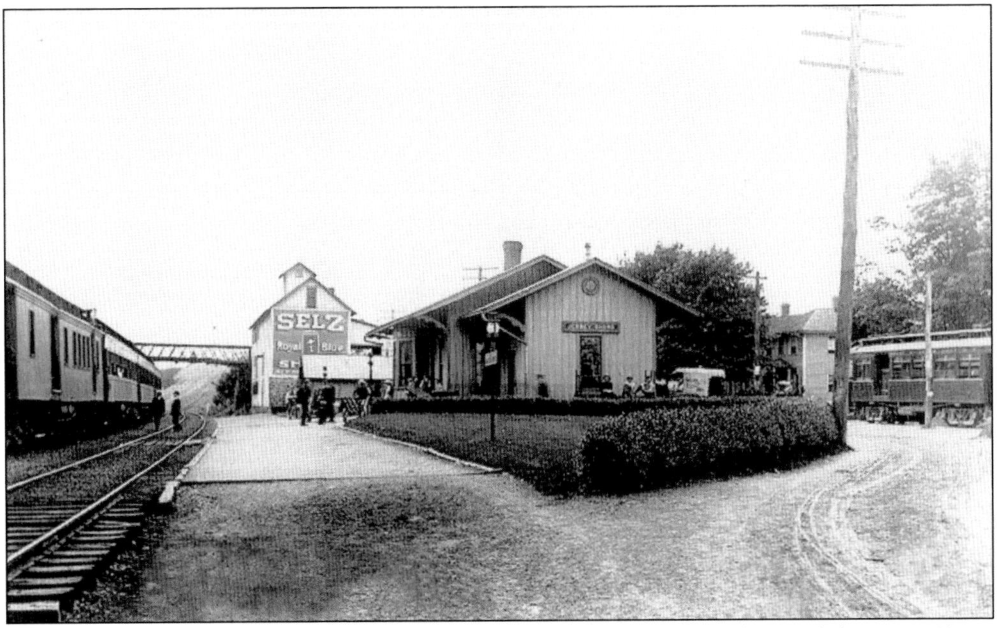

The Pennsylvania railroad station at Antes Fort was built about 1856 and named the Jersey Shore station. At that time the line was called the Philadelphia and Erie Railroad. The most expensive part of the line was excavated here and was known as the "Deep Cut." The company that finally completed the job made use of the first steam excavator ever used in this area. During the early 1900s, 12 passenger trains passed through here daily. This station was torn down in 1961.

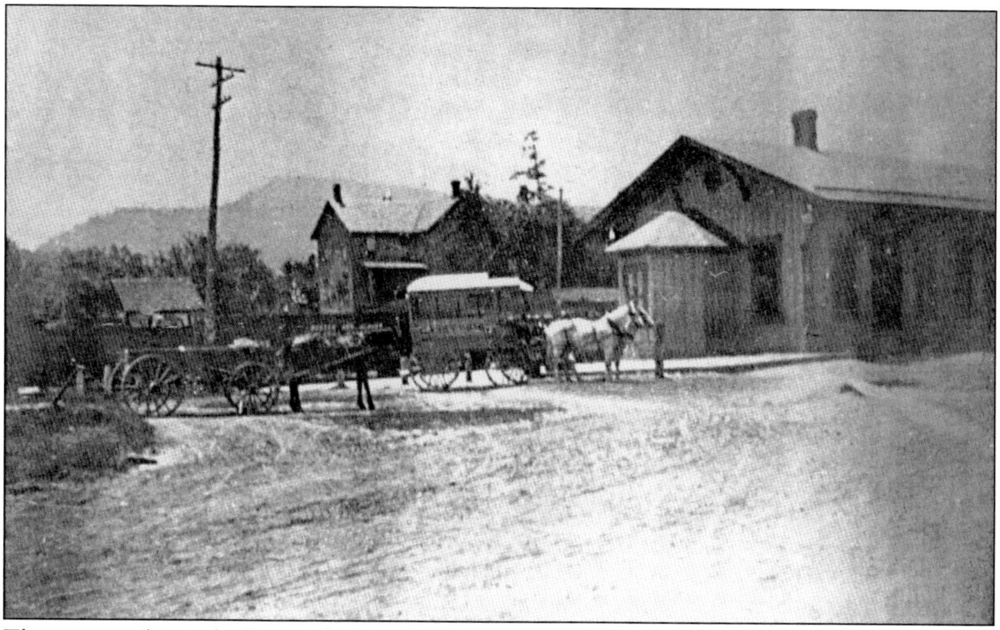

This picture shows the Jersey Shore stagecoach that was used to transport passengers, mail, and light freight between the railroad and Jersey Shore. Such a coach pulled by two white horses is shown in an 1873 engraving of the "Birches" near the island. The stage was replaced by trolley service in 1905, and when it stopped, about 1923, a bus, operated by Ernest Brown, carried about 20 passengers as well as the mail to and from town.

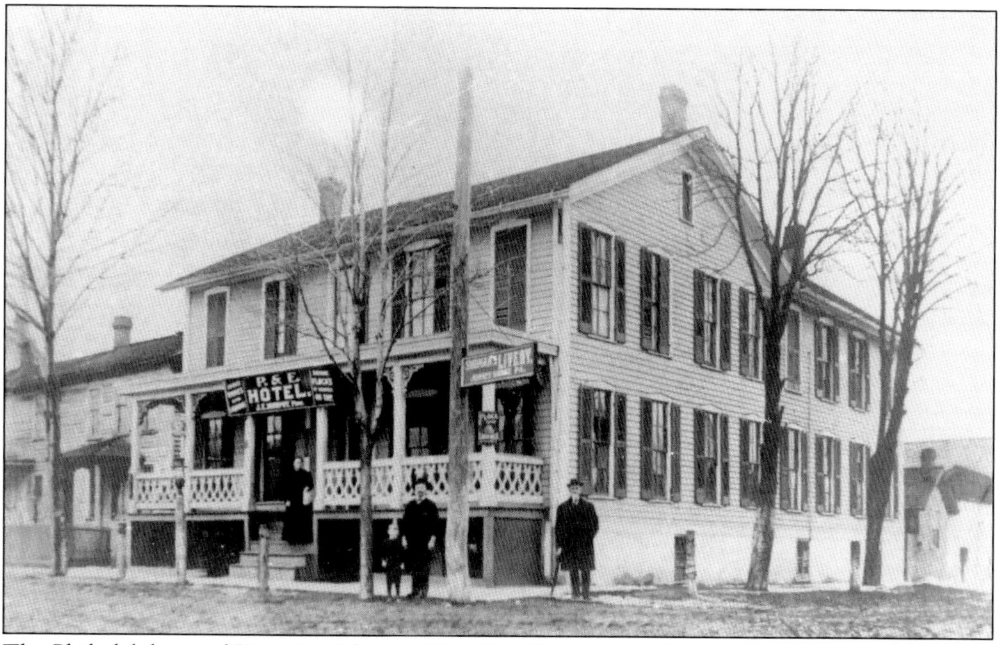

The Philadelphia and Erie Hotel (Antes Fort Hotel) was located across the main road from the train station. Here rooms could be rented, baths taken, hair cut, and dinners served. Drinks were available at the bar. Advertisements on the hotel include Flock's Beer and Shuman Livery. J. E. Murphy was the proprietor.

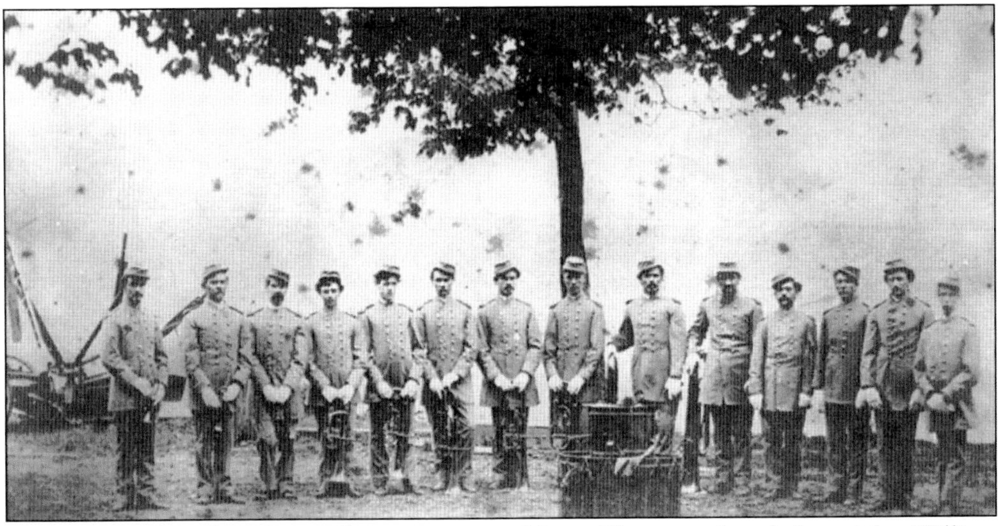

Civil War soldiers from Jersey Shore are pictured here. They are, from left to right, William Robinson, Grant Keyser, James Seeley, Charles Kline, John Kline, Bert Smith, William Leininger, Matt Schwer, William Schwer, Henry Crist, Bob Garverick, Tom Shortlidge, James Davidson, and W. Mullin. In June 1862, the council ordered a special tax be laid for the maintenance of families and volunteers fighting for the Union, $1.75 per week for wives and 50¢ for children per week plus a $10 bounty paid to each volunteer.

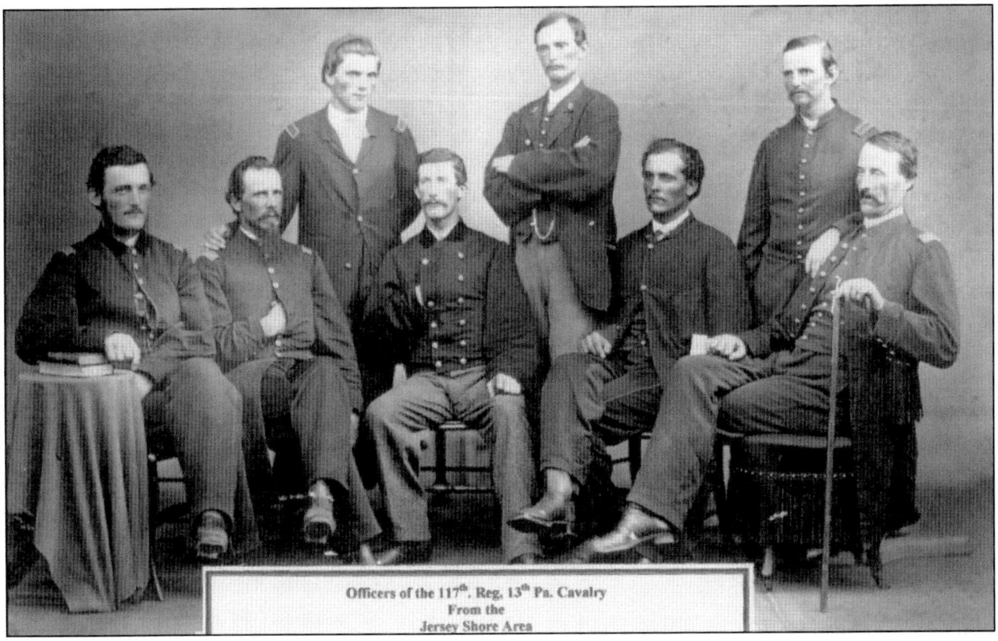

Officers of the 117th Regiment 13th Pennsylvania Cavalry, from the Jersey Shore area, pose in Philadelphia for this photograph after the war. From left to right they are Capt. James Bell, Company D; A. H. Glossonier, Company H; Lt. James M. Antes; Maj. George F. McCabe; Capt. Peter "Dock" Bricker, Company F; Lt. John R. Smith, Company G; Capt. Curtis H. Eldridge, Company B; and Capt. Robert Brown, Company G. The 13th Cavalry fought at the battles of Winchester, Culpepper, Rappahannock, Wilderness, Beaver Dam Station, Hawes Shop, Jones Bridge, and Malvern Hill.

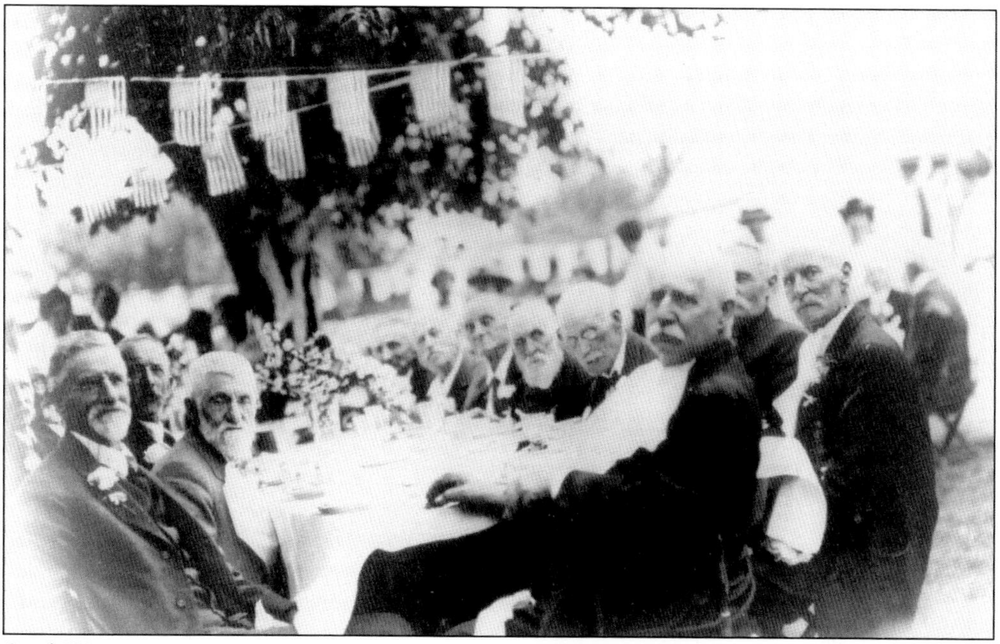

Civil War veterans were entertained at the home of Mrs. James Krom after each Decoration Day parade. The first Grand Army of the Republic (GAR) post was established in Jersey Shore on September 18, 1867, but disbanded on September 19, 1868. There were 47 members. The Major Keenan Post No. 349 was organized with 42 charter members on June 26, 1883. At its high point, 128 men were registered in the book.

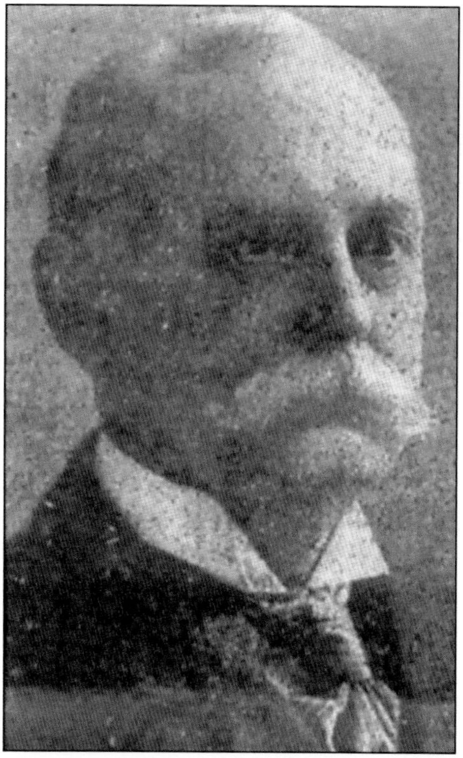

Peter Dock Bricker enlisted in the 13th Cavalry, 117th Regiment, at the beginning of the Civil War and was promoted to captain on August 11, 1864. He had a remarkable war record including capture by the enemy. He served time in both Libby and Andersonville prisons. He was admitted to the bar in 1866 and came to Jersey Shore in 1867, serving as burgess a number of times. He was always interested in the betterment of the town and was loved by its people.

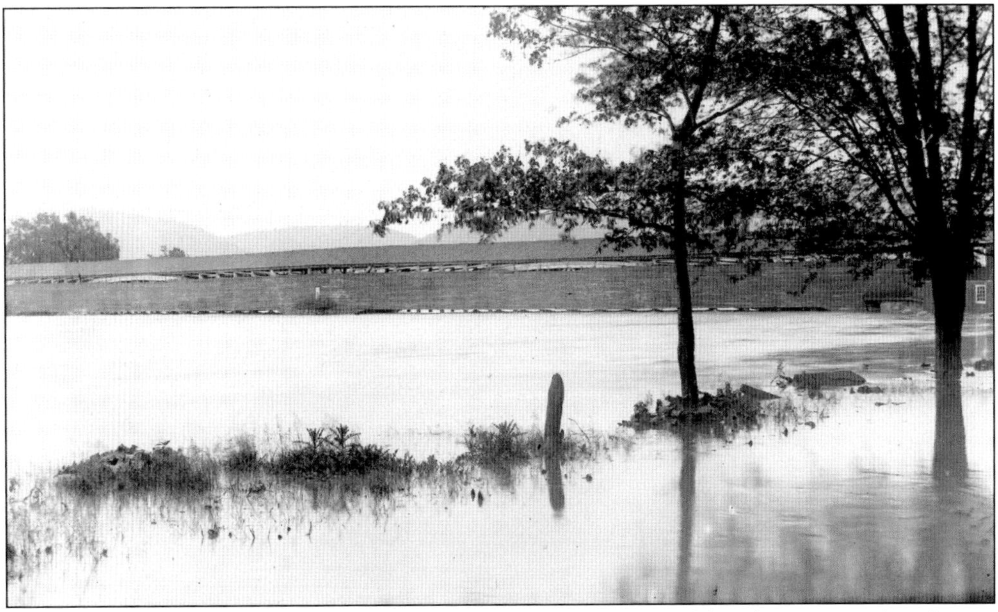

The second set of covered bridges was built by Aaron Kline and his three sons after the ice flood of March 1865 and lasted until the June flood of 1889. This photograph was taken by William H. Garman shortly before it washed out. Houses, barns, livestock, and millions of board feet of logs floated by. The Wolfe sawmill at Waterville was washed out and carried past Jersey Shore intact—an impressive sight.

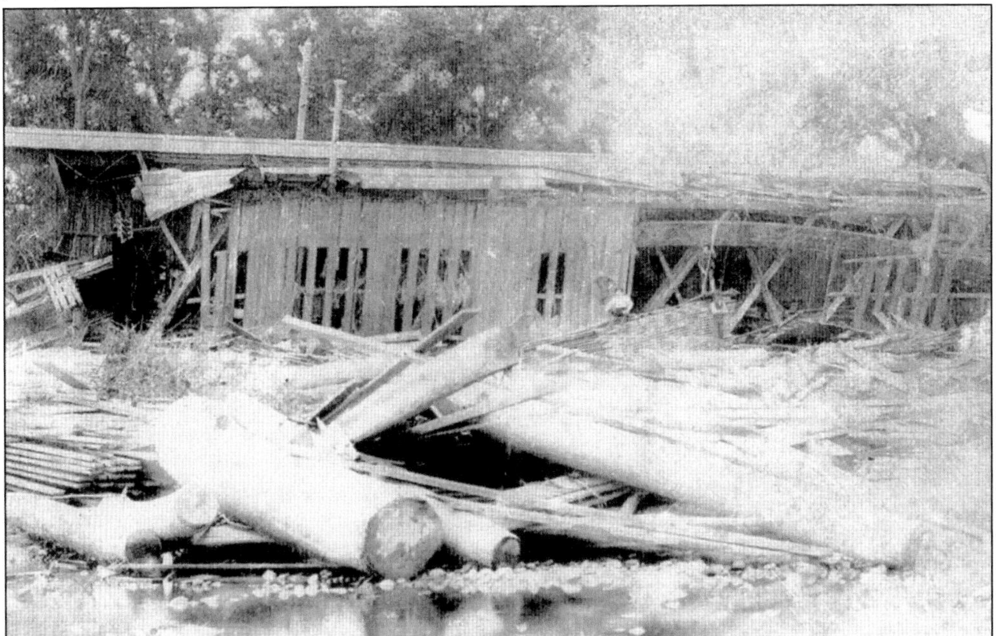

Here are the remains of one of the Jersey Shore covered bridges hung up on Ransom Island downstream from town. James Gohl of Salladasburg saw a whole house float by with smoke still coming out of the chimney. He also saw a team of horses swimming side by side. He called to them, and they turned toward him and swam to safety. The team belonged to Tom Blackwell.

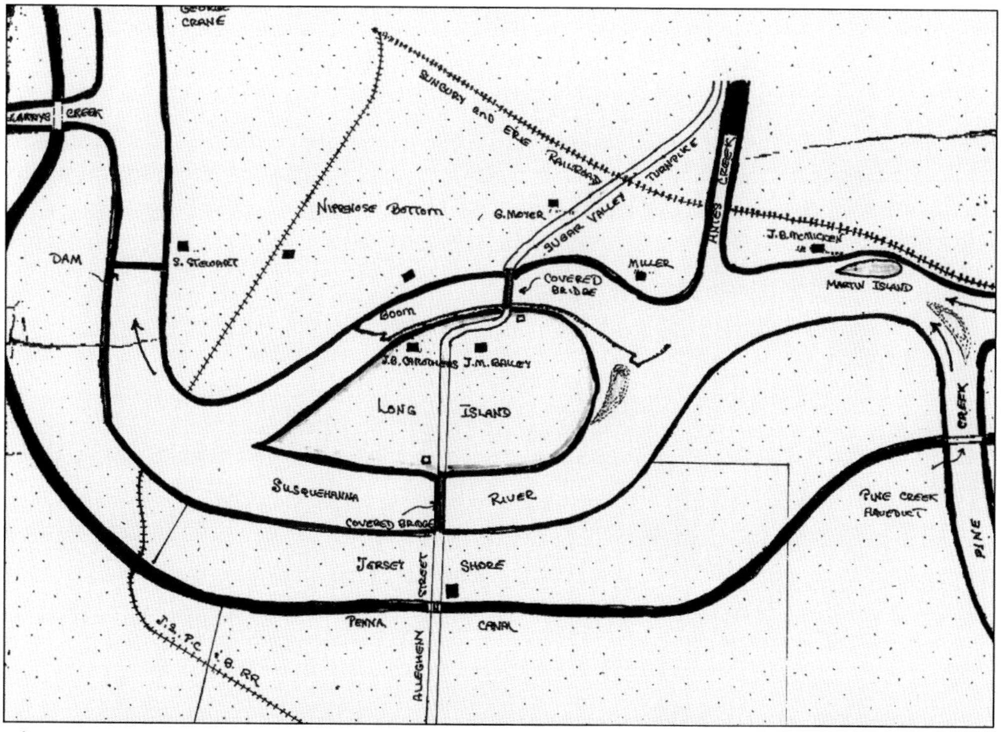

This is a Civil War–era map of the Jersey Shore area showing Long Island and the two covered bridges of the Sugar Valley, or Lewisburg Turnpike. Two railroad lines are shown, the Sunbury and Erie and the Jersey Shore and Pine Creek. Pine Creek and the canal aqueduct are shown to the west, and a dam is shown across the river at Nippenose Bottom, also a log boom on the far side of Long Island that was built in 1869.

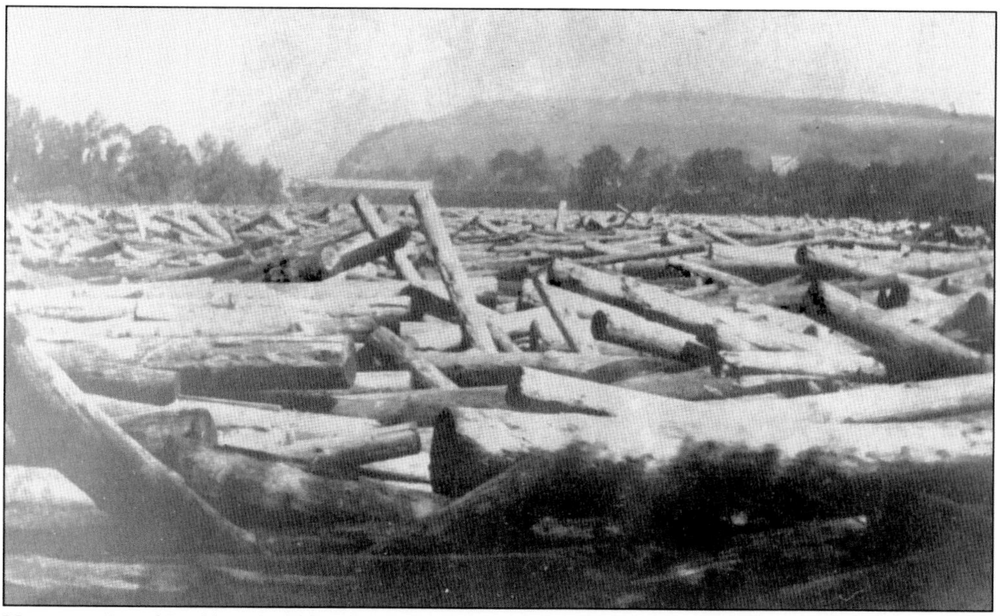

Here is a "catch" of logs held by the Jersey Shore boom located on the Antes Fort side of Long Island. One of the covered bridges is visible below the eastern end of Boat Mountain.

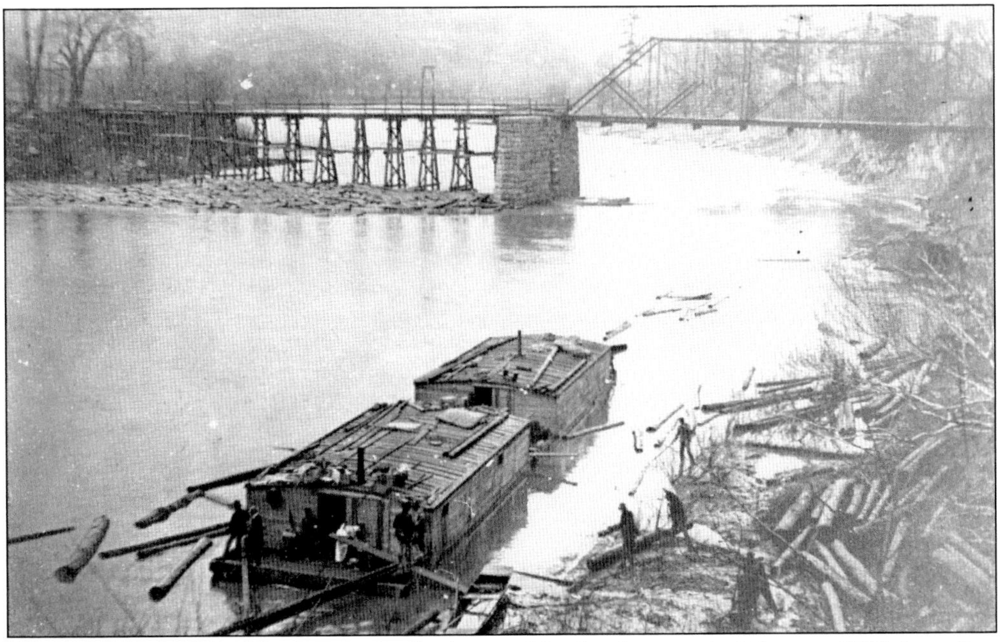

The second island steel bridge was badly damaged by flooding ice in February 1908. Logs line the riverbank, and two lumber arks are shown just upstream of the bridge. Other pictures show the same span, which fell in December 1907. Trolley service was disrupted, and people from Nippenose Valley could get to town by way of Pine Mountain and the Sour Ferry. There have now been five bridges across the river at this point.

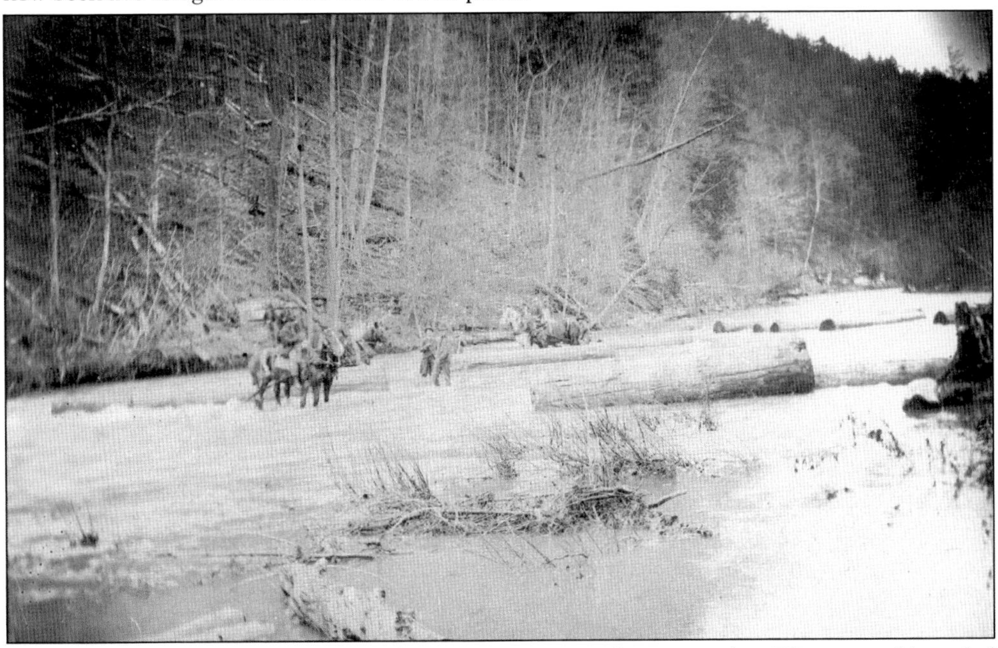

The Pine Creek area held the last of the state's vast store of virgin timber. The cut and branded logs would be floated downstream on high water to awaiting mills. Those close to Jersey Shore included Phelps Dodge, Trump Mill, and Woods and Childs. Timber for the construction of the First Methodist Church was floated down Pine Creek and the river to Jersey Shore.

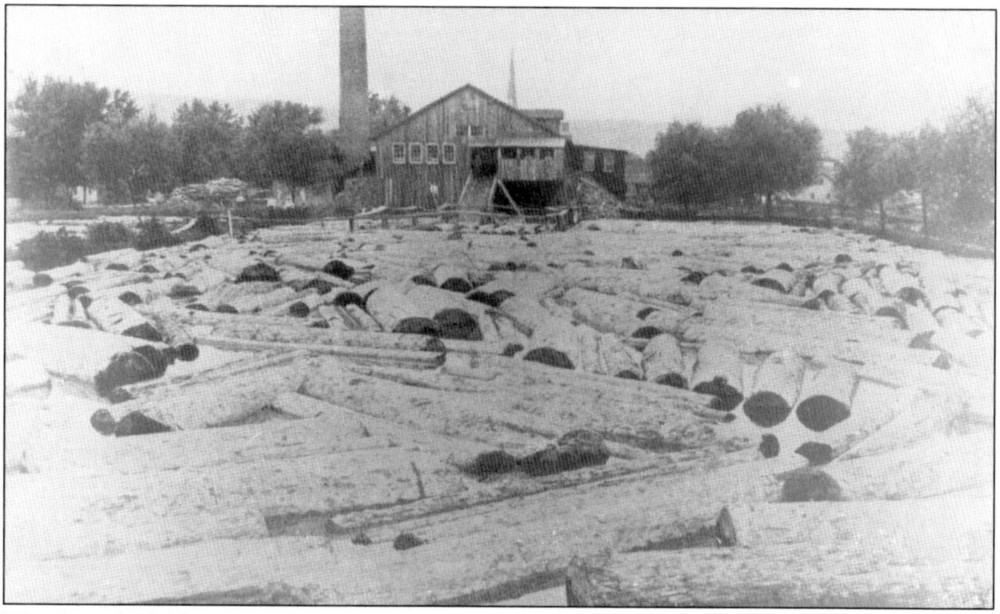

Woods and Childs Sawmill was located between Locust and Cemetery Streets in Jersey Shore. The logs shown are contained in the canal basin on the Broad Street side of the canal. Every log shown is a northern white pine two to three feet in diameter. This old mill was originally a distillery built in 1838 and was converted into a sawmill in 1858 for Delate and Chilley. The mill was finally purchased by Wood and Childs in 1870 and operated until the 1889 flood.

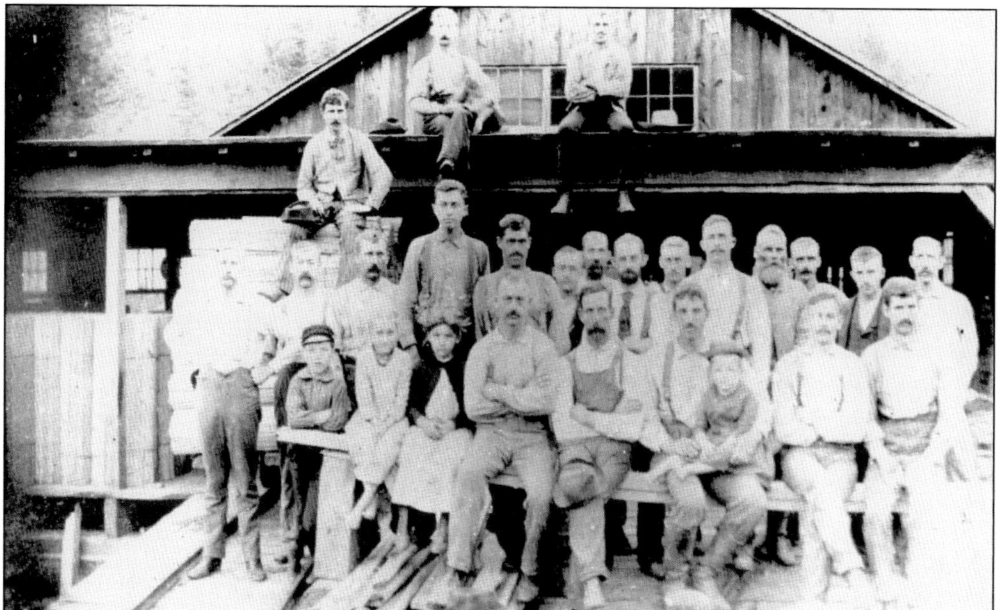

Woods and Childs lumber operation moved to a place called Utcenter, which was located about two miles downstream from Slate Run on Pine Creek. Many employees resided at the boardinghouse, and on Saturday night square dances were held with music provided by Art Callahan at the organ and Max Bradley and Bill Maffett on fiddle and accordion. The date on this photograph is 1892.

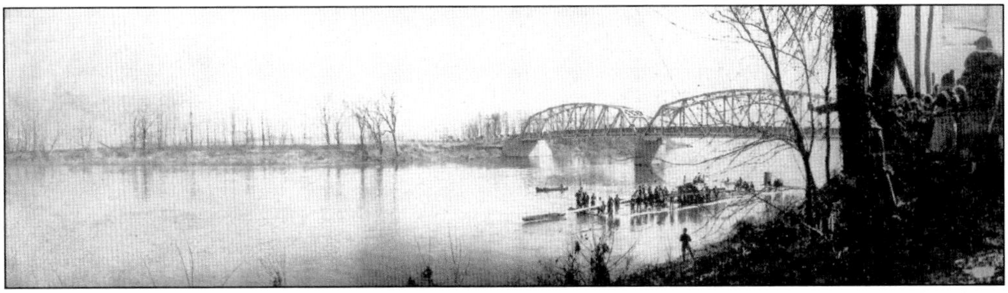

The last raft is pictured leaving Jersey Shore on Saturday, March 19, 1938. It was 112 feet long and 28 feet wide and was made of some 35,000 board feet of large white pines cut near the source of the West Branch of the Susquehanna. The raft tied up at Williamsport that night, and the next day, Sunday, seven lives were lost when the raft hit a pier of the railroad bridge at Muncy.

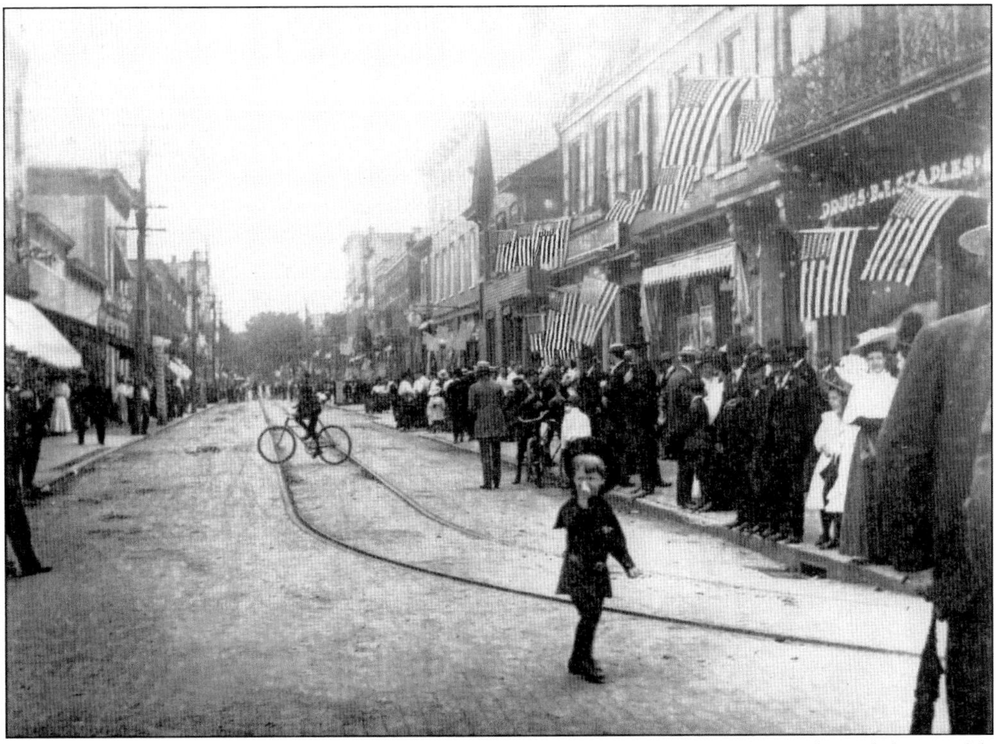

The old river town of Jersey Shore boasted many substantial dwellings that reflected the wealth of its prominent citizens. There were Federal bricks and Greek Revival designs and Victorian mansions, large hotels, an iron foundry, churches, stores, and businesses. The old wealth was tied to the river and the canal as well as the lumber industry.

Two

North Main Street

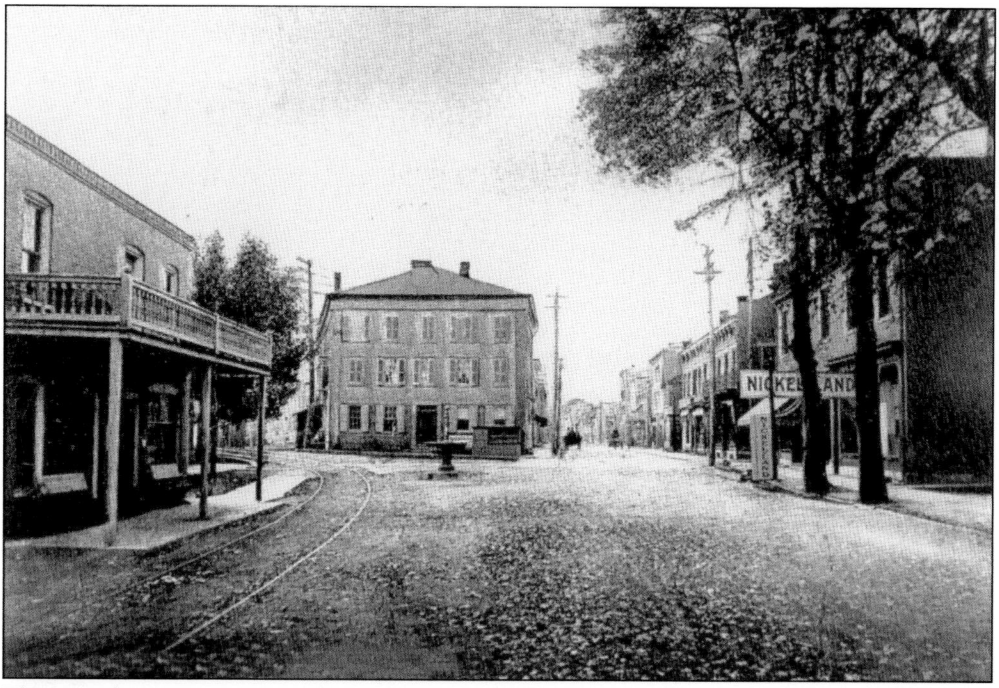

This was the main square at the bridge in downtown Jersey Shore around 1914. Charlie Letts' restaurant is on the left with the trolley rails of the Jersey Shore and Antes Fort Railroad in front. The three-story building was built about 1845 by George Crane for his son Robert and was known as "Crane's Arcade." The Hepburn building is to the right occupied by a business called Nickelland.

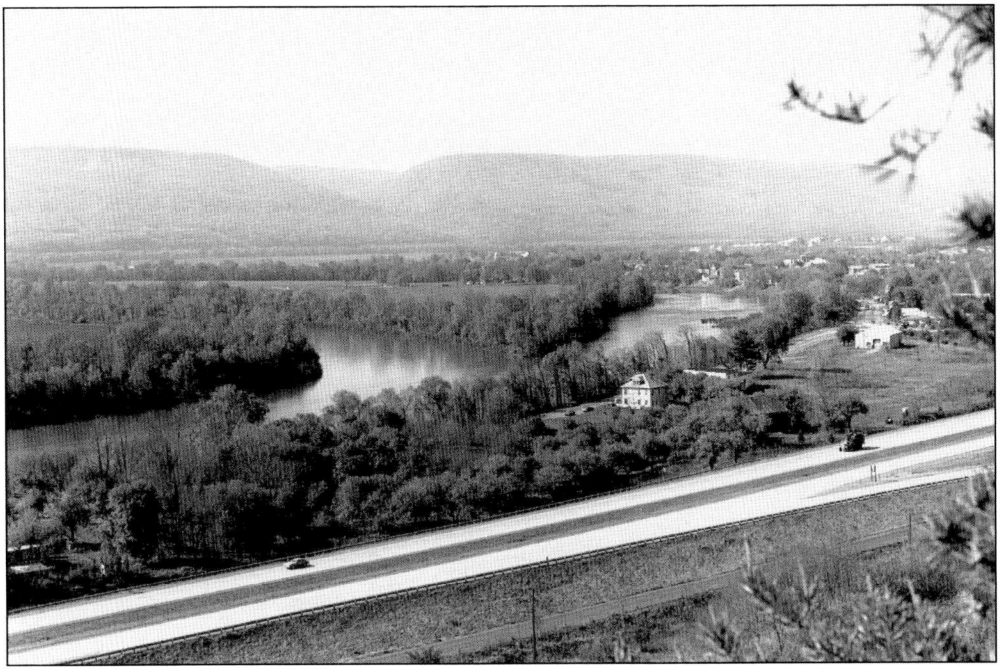

Long Island lies east of the town and was given this name by the first permanent inhabitants who were from New Jersey. The 150-acre island was deeded to Thomas Forster in 1785. He built a large stone house there in 1789. John Bailey bought it in 1915, and for years the place was called Bailey's Island.

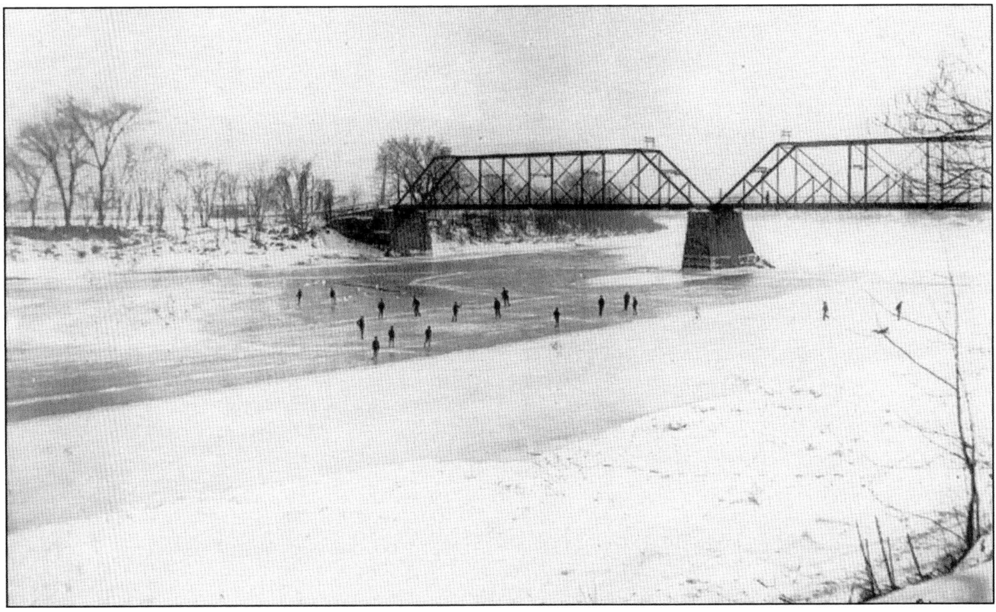

Under the right conditions, ice would freeze as smooth as glass and be perfect for skating. Later in winter, the annual ice harvest would begin with a frolic and horse race on the river. In 1851, the race was between Bill Hepburn and Willard Slonaker. The biggest users of ice included Charlie Hauser's brewery and Bill Schwer's Meat Market as well as Alex Zettle, who sold more ice cream in town than anyone else.

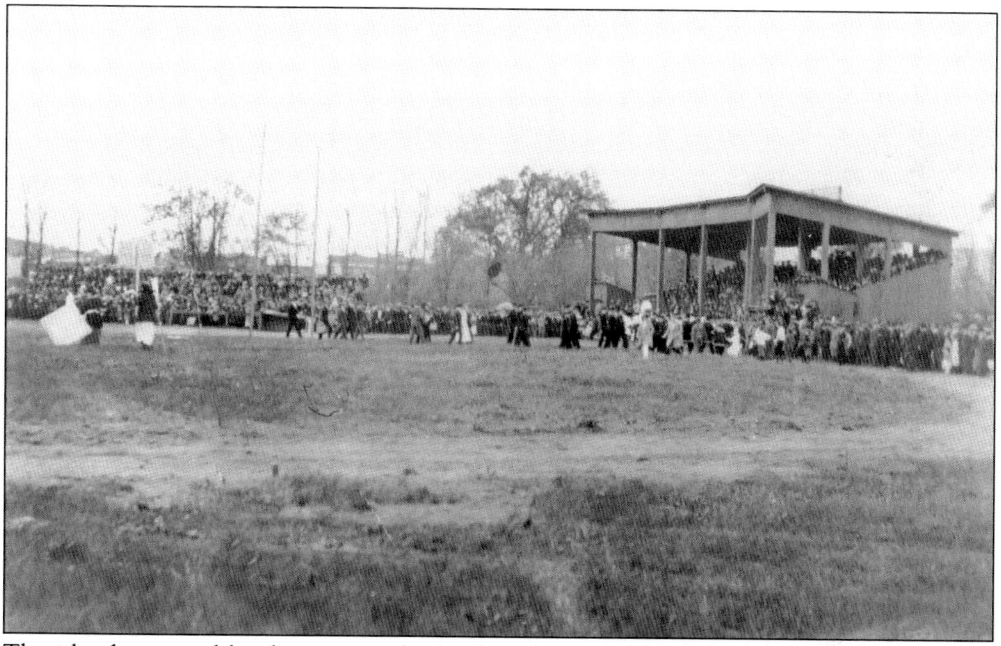

The island was used by the town and school as the site of football and baseball games. The band played, and the girls cheered. Here one sees full bleachers with a backdrop of buildings from across the river. Circus acts would arrive by train in Antes Fort, and after, a circus parade through downtown would set up here on the island. People are still finding old coins here with metal detectors.

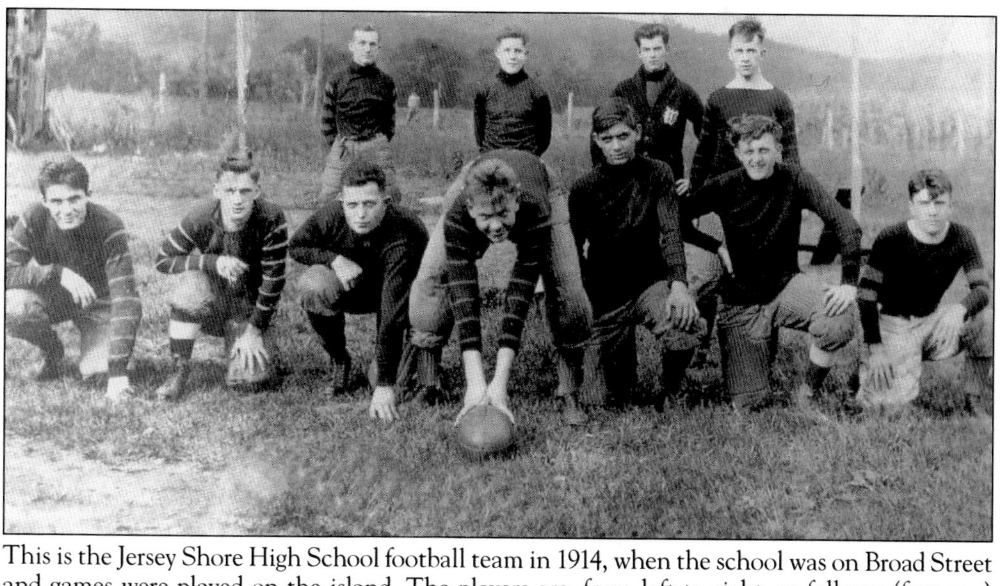

This is the Jersey Shore High School football team in 1914, when the school was on Broad Street and games were played on the island. The players are, from left to right, as follows: (first row) Fred Lesman, Bobby Dingler, Pat Jones, John Overdorf, Roy Whipple, Charlie Saft, and Joe Crist; (second row) Roscoe Wolfe, Paul Turbet, Charles Beltzer, and Boyd Tobias.

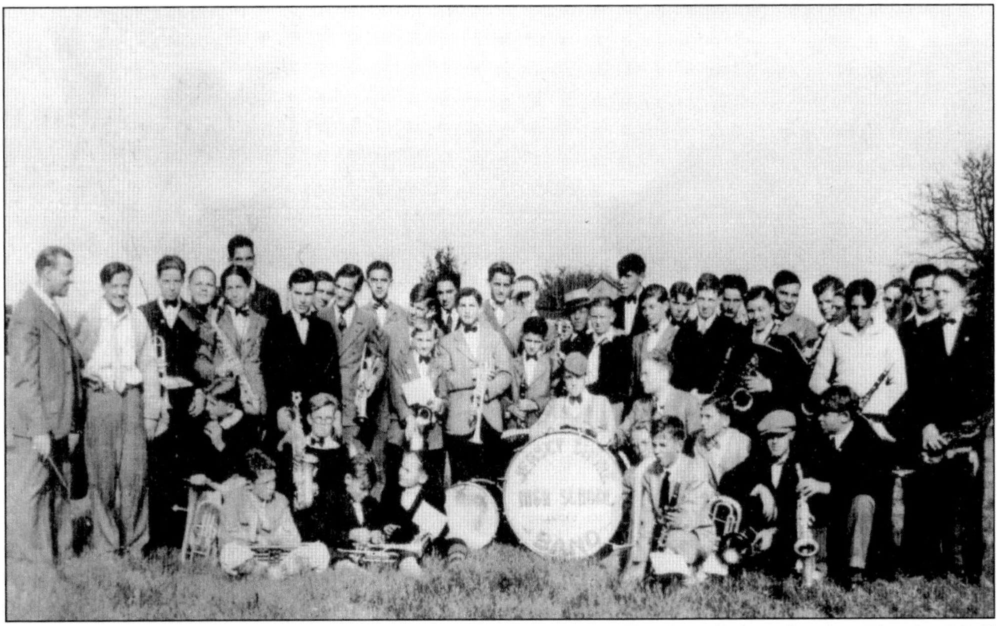

The first Jersey Shore High School Band is shown on the island with bandleader Charles Noll of South Williamsport. The band formed in 1925 when the new high school was built on Allegheny Street. It started with 12 members and grew to over 40 by 1929. The assistant director was Kermit Noll Sr.

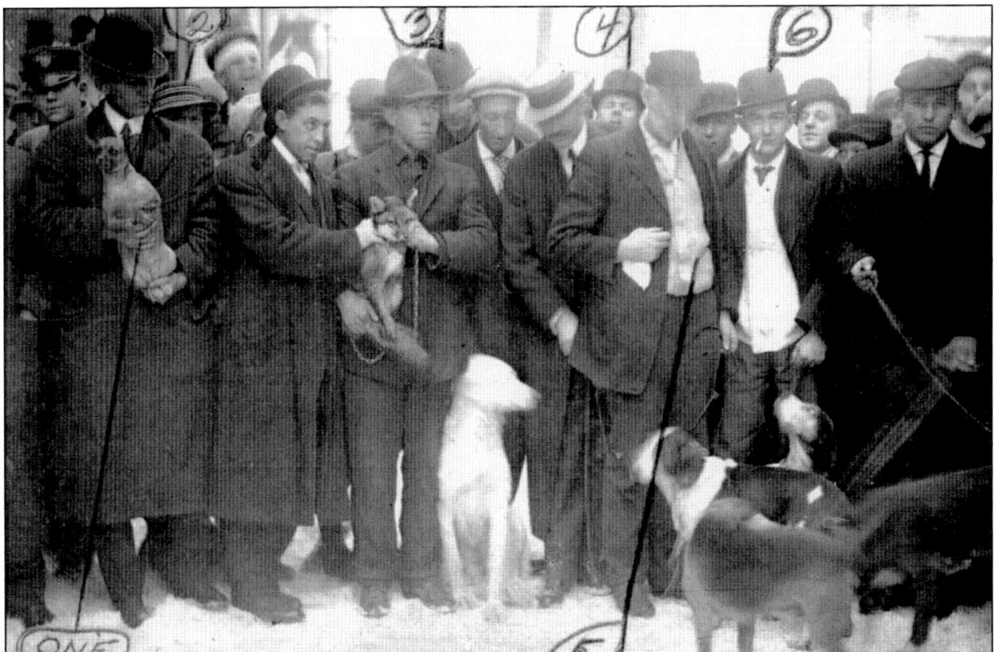

An old-fashioned fox chase is about to begin in front of the home of Moss Traveler. Identified are 1. "Doc" Seely and dog, 2. Chet McElroy (with striped hat band), 3. Harry Peck, 4. Tom Stenner (of Crowe and Stenner Hardware), 5. Sherm Brown, and 6. Joe Heinbach. "Upon release the fox headed for the island and was caught by I don't know who," said James G. Seely.

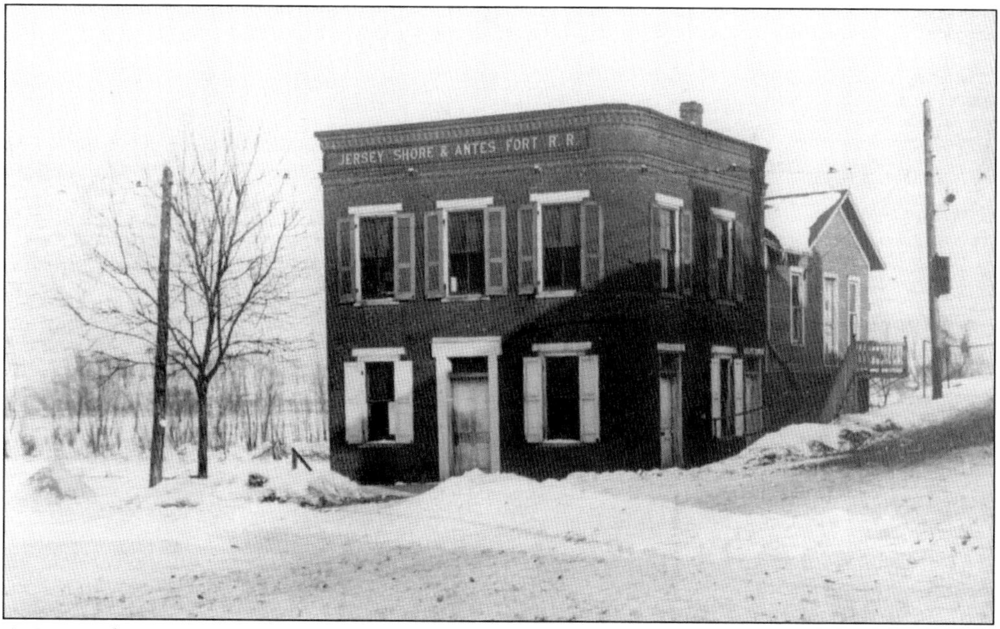

A *Jersey Shore News-Letter* of October 1854 indicates this building, which is attached to the tollhouse next to the toll bridge, is near completion. It was built by William Hepburn and, by 1902, belonged to the trolley company. Bridge tolls were as follows: one horse and a buggy was 15¢, two horses and a buggy or wagon was 25¢, three horses and a wagon was 35¢, four horses and a wagon was 40¢, a horse and a rider was 10¢, a horse without a rider was 5¢, a sheep or a swine was 2¢, and a cow was 5¢.

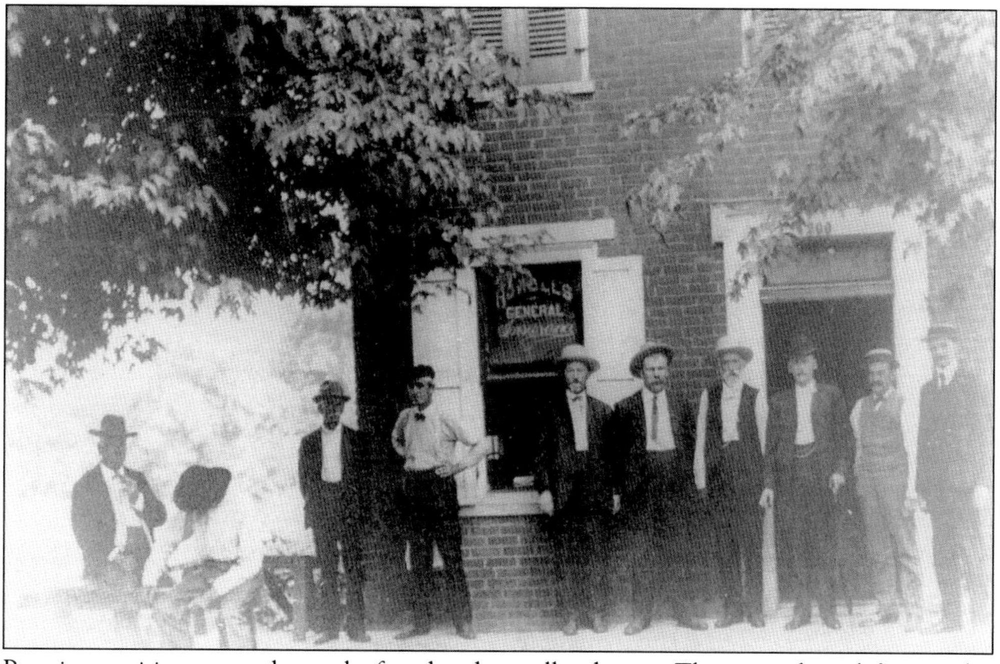

Prominent citizens are shown loafing by the trolley house. They are, from left to right, Capt. Frank Wilson, Rube Calehoof, Baird Dunn, William T. Ferrar, Dr. M. L. Mensch, Dr. S. E. Bickel, M. T. Howell, Dr. John Nevins, Frank Trump, and Robert M. Bubb.

TIME TABLE.

Jersey Shore & Antes Fort R. R.

For the Information and Government of Employes Only.

No. 19. **In Effect 7 A. M., Sunday, Nov. 1, 1908.**

	2	4	6	8	10	12	14	16
	A. M.	A. M.	A. M.	P. M.	P. M.	P. M.	P. M.	P. M.
JERSEY SHORE, Leave.	*7:10	*9:30	*11:10	‡12:15	*2:45	*6:05	*7:05	*10:05
ANTES FORT	7:18	9:38	11:18	12:23	2:53	6:13	7:13	10:13
NIPPONO, Ar.		9:46						

	1	3	5	7	9	11	13	15
	A. M.	A. M.	A. M.	P. M.	P. M.	P. M.	P. M.	P. M.
NIPPONO, Leave.		*9:50						
ANTES FORT,	*7:52	9:58	*11:46	‡12:25	*3:17	*6:31	*7:25	*10:31
JERSEY SHORE, Ar.	8:00	10:05	11:54	12:33	3:25	6:39	7:33	10:39

This trolley company was organized by Robert McCullough, C. B. McCullough, Hamilton Humes, James Calvert, M. T. Howell, and John Reilley. Its charter was granted on May 18, 1904. The service began on February 1, 1905, and closed approximately 20 years later. A detailed history of this operation, *A History of the Jersey Shore and Antes Fort Railway*, was produced by Gene Gordon in 1961.

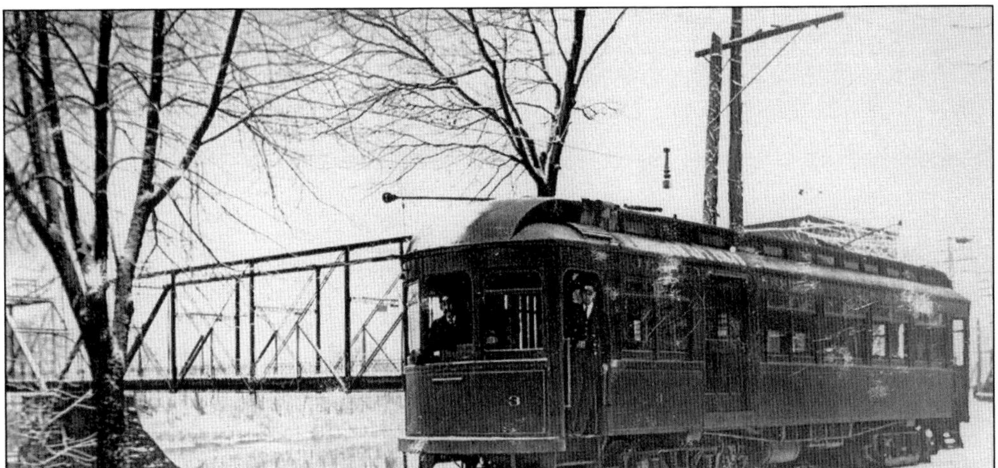

The Jersey Shore and Antes Fort Railway Company owned two such passenger cars and a baggage car. The trip to the Jersey Shore Railroad station at Antes Fort was about two and a half miles or 10 minutes. In order to carry mail and freight the company was chartered as a steam railway, and the contract to carry it was awarded to Ernest Brown. This car, built in 1905 by the Niles Car Company, is presently located at the Pennsylvania Trolley Museum in Washington, Pennsylvania.

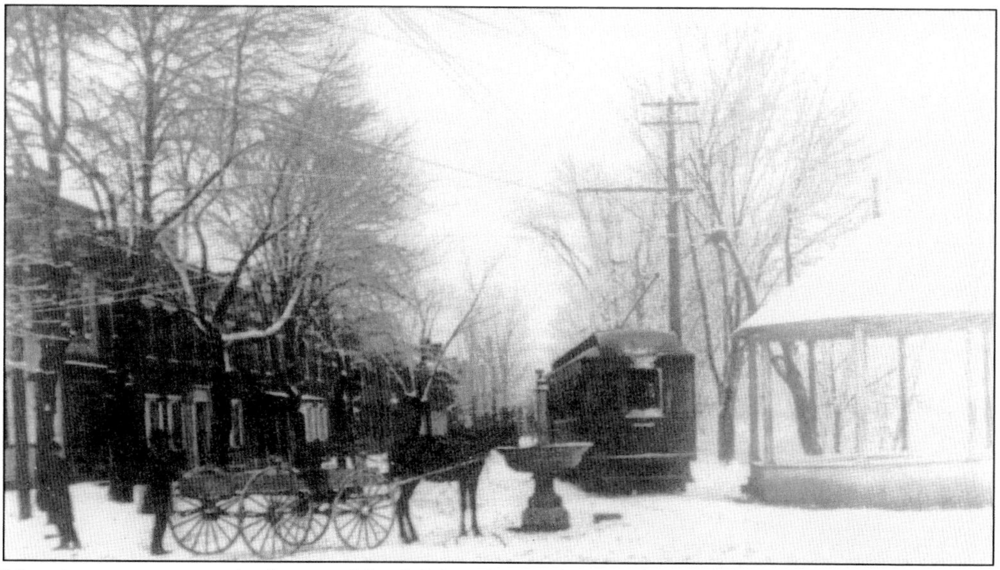

Here is a wintry scene looking up North Main Street from in front of the trolley house. A row of beautiful homes lines the west side of the street. On the riverside is the band shell that was built for the New York Central Band, which was organized by Henry Whipple in 1904. In the middle of the road is a fountain for horses, placed there by the local chapter of the Women's Christian Temperance Union (WCTU), which was organized on December 18, 1878.

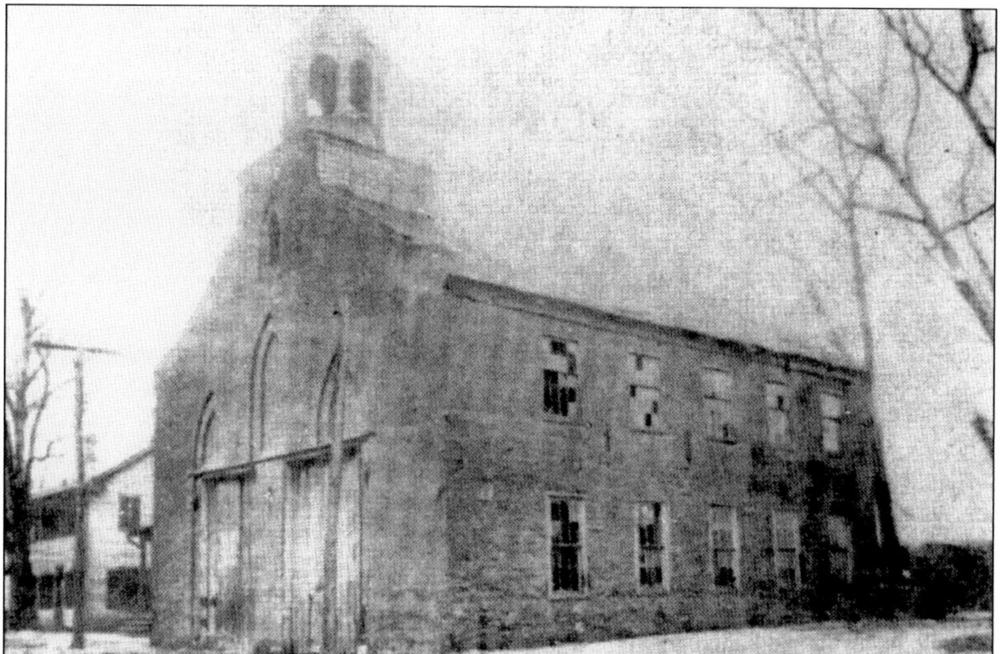

This brick building was constructed in 1832 as a church by the Baptists and Presbyterians. The Baptists left in 1844, and the Presbyterians left in 1850. It next became the West Branch High School, which lasted until approximately 1884. The trolley company bought the building in 1905, cut big doors in the front, and used it as a trolley barn. This building, which sat in the middle of Seminary Street, was torn down about 1930.

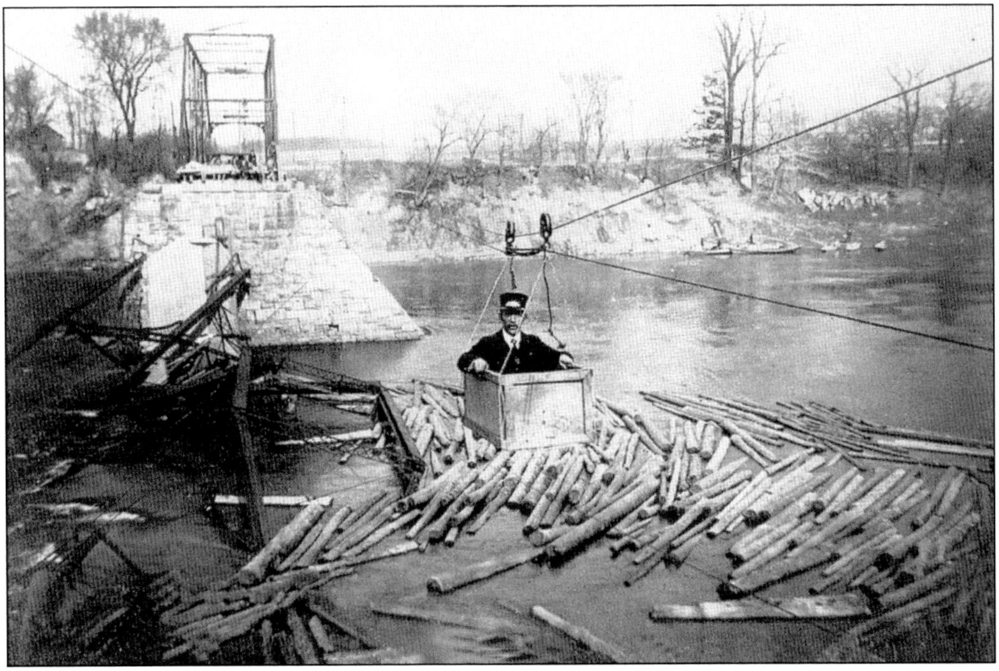

When the river bridge on the Antes Fort side went out due to high water and ice early in 1908, an aerial cable car was constructed to temporarily keep transportation and mail service open between Jersey Shore and Antes Fort. A temporary bridge over which the trolleys could run was built and used by the company until the new bridge was completed by late spring.

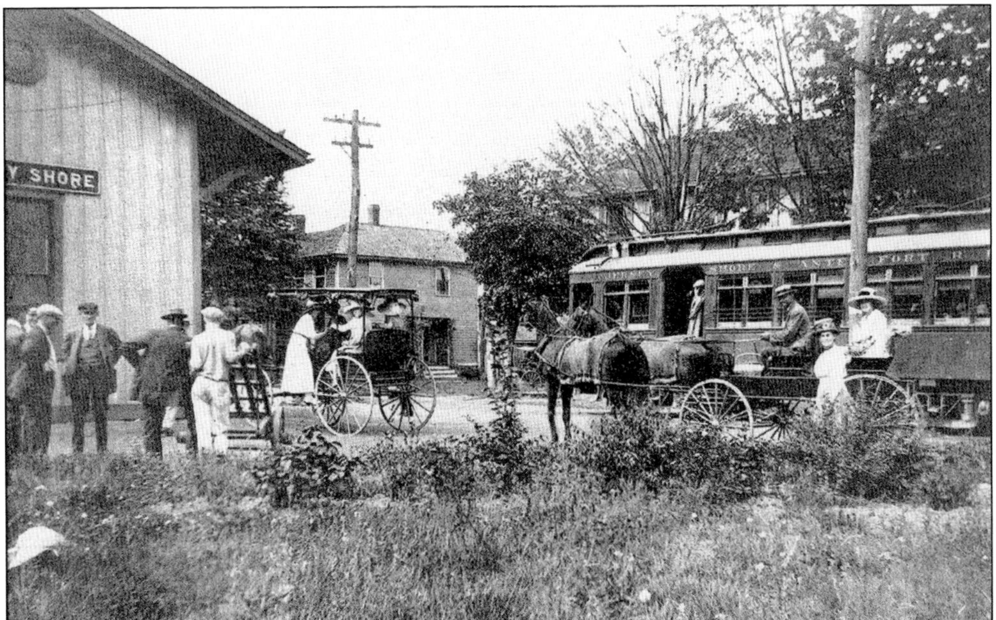

Trolley service replaced the stagecoach run between Jersey Shore and the Pennsylvania Railroad Station in Antes Fort. An advertisement in the *Jersey Shore Herald* of December 6, 1913, boasts, "8 cars are run daily making use of 20th century transportation methods by the use of electric power, solving the problem of local rapid transit."

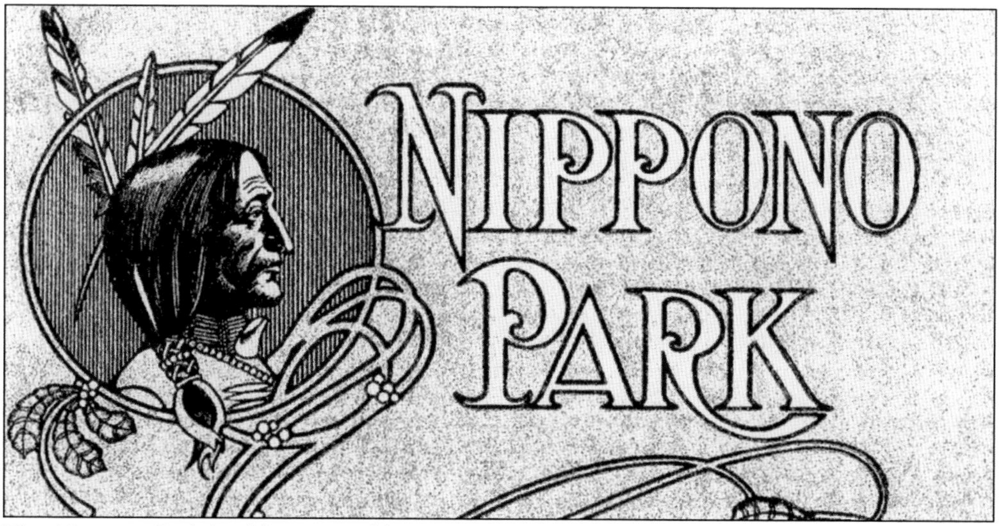

This Nippono Park booklet, printed by Grit Press, was published by the Jersey Shore and Antes Fort Railroad Company to promote the two-mile run from Antes Fort to this popular resort. The land had belonged to the Clancey brothers who developed it into a desirable picnic area by 1888, followed by other gradual improvements. The first trolley runs to the park began in May 1905, peaked in 1912, and lasted on a downhill slide until summer 1915.

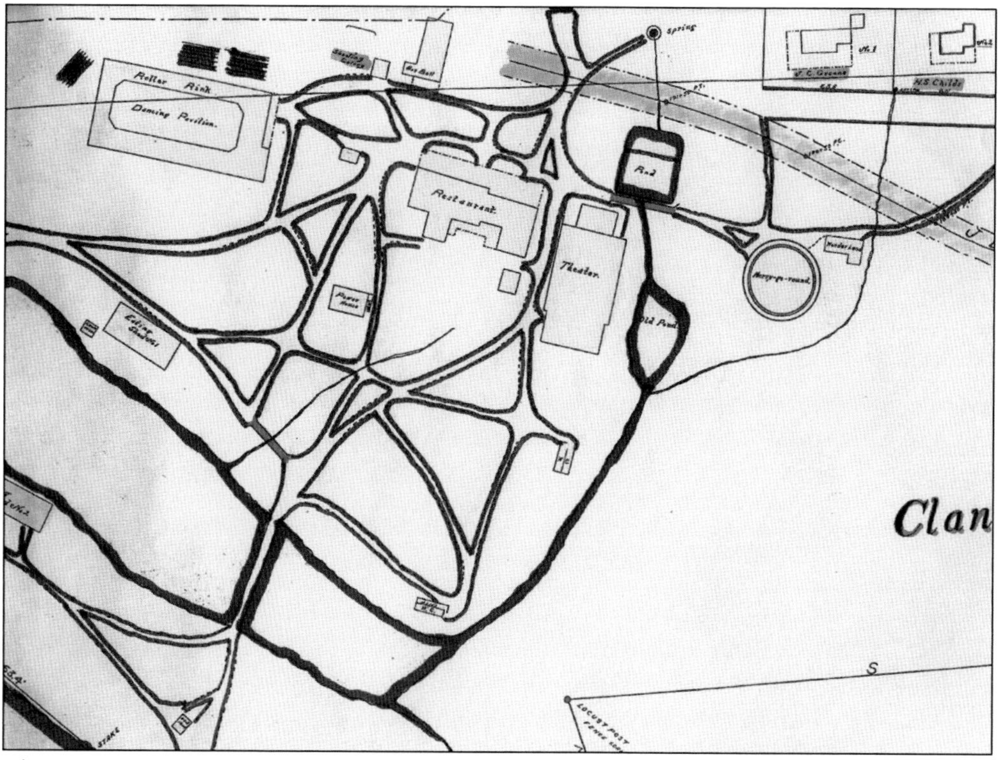

This is a section of a map of Nippono Park drawn by C. B. McCullough on October 12, 1908. Not shown on this map section are some 80 cabin lots that extend westward from the park on both sides of the railroad and trolley line. Sixteen lots show cabin designs on them. The names include Sallada, Childs, Myers, Dorey, Seeley, McCullough, Shemp, and Gamble.

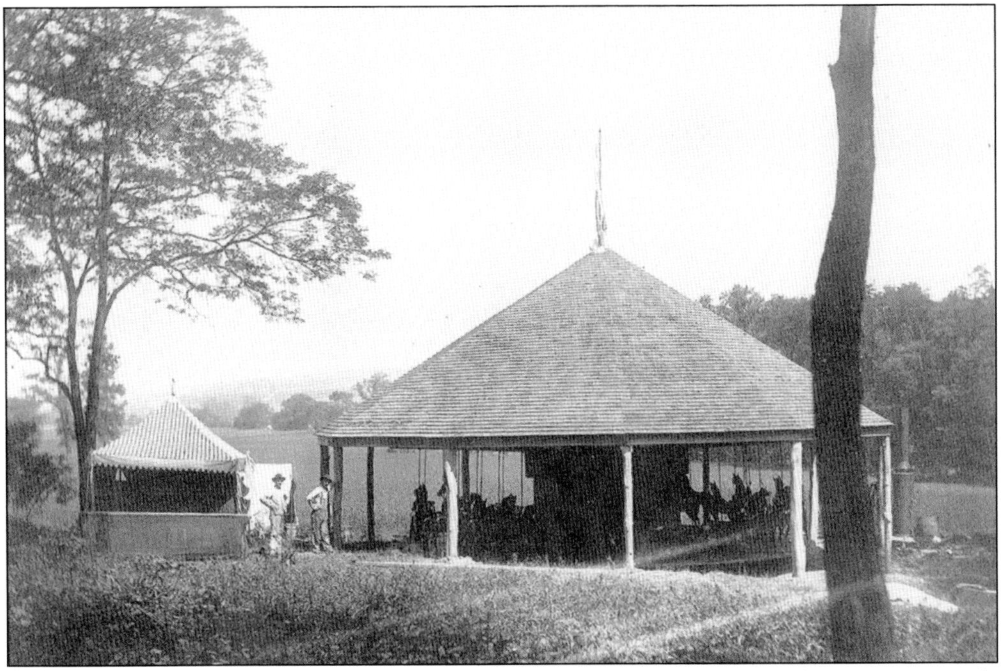

Here is a coal-fired, steam-operated merry-go-round and a concession stand at Nippono Park. The ride cost 5¢. This park along the West Branch of the Susquehanna could be reached by horse and carriage, trolley, the Pennsylvania Railroad, and boat. A post office was established here in 1892. It was one of the best family-oriented parks along this section of the river.

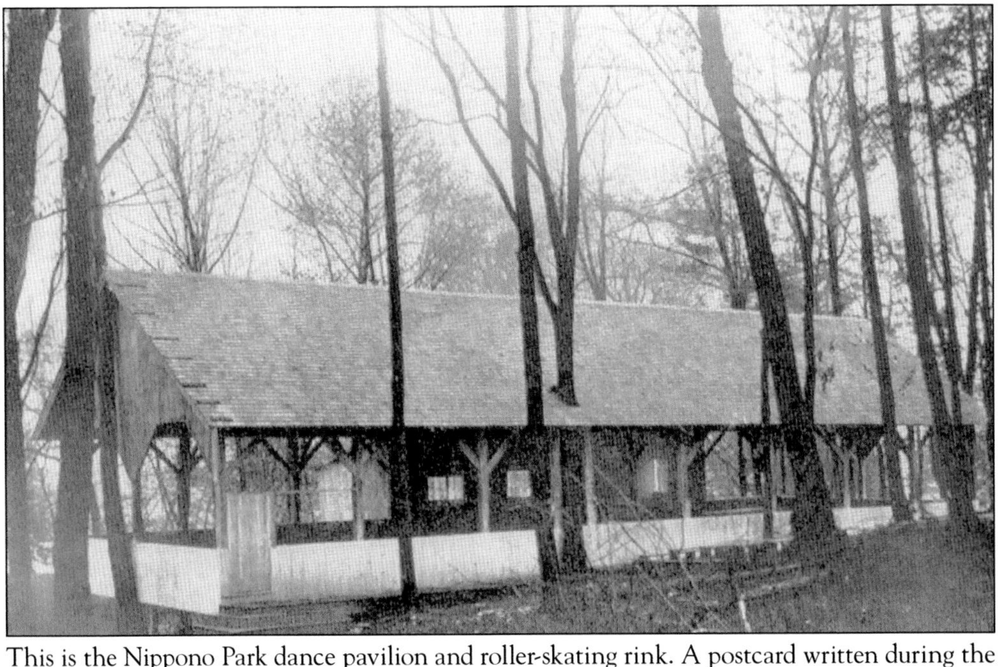

This is the Nippono Park dance pavilion and roller-skating rink. A postcard written during the summer of 1909 reads, "Went to Jersey Shore this afternoon and took a ride in an automobile for 1 hour and 10 minutes—we went about 18 miles. It was simply great! I went to the skating rink at Nippono Park last night and they even showed free moving pictures."

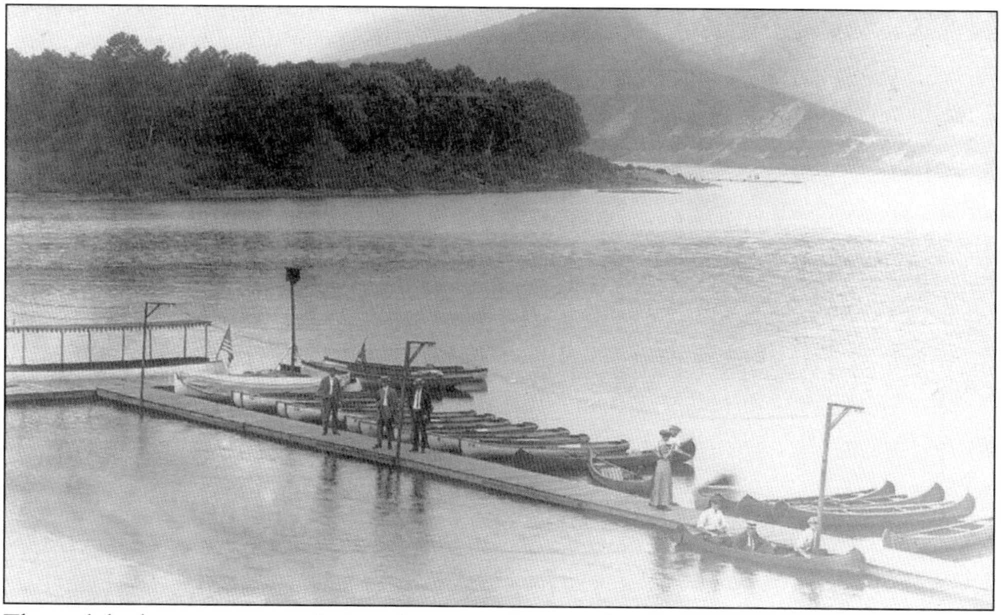

The park had great accommodations for private boats and canoes, with ample floats and docks extending out into the river as well as a fine sandy swimming beach and bathhouse opposite Crane's Island. The fishing was not bad either.

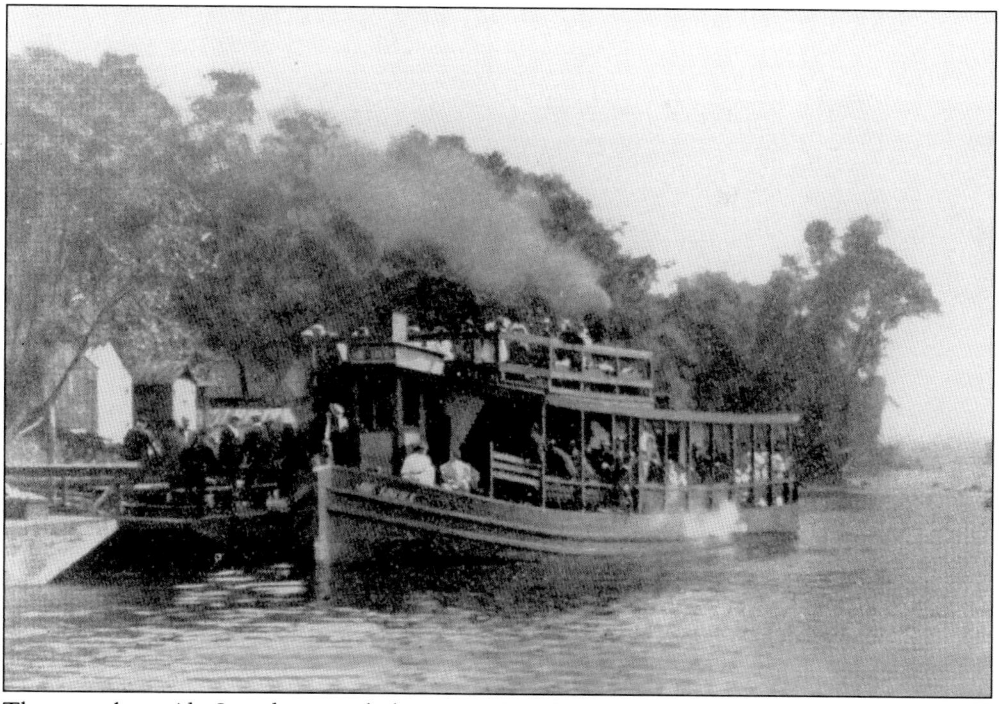

The steamboat *Abe Lincoln* carried pleasure-seekers between Williamsport and Nippono Park. The one-hour trip must have been very exciting. For many years, some river towns seemed to turn their backs on the West Branch. But today the river is cleaned up and provides wonderful recreation to tourists as well as locals. Pine Creek and the river are potential assets to places like Jersey Shore.

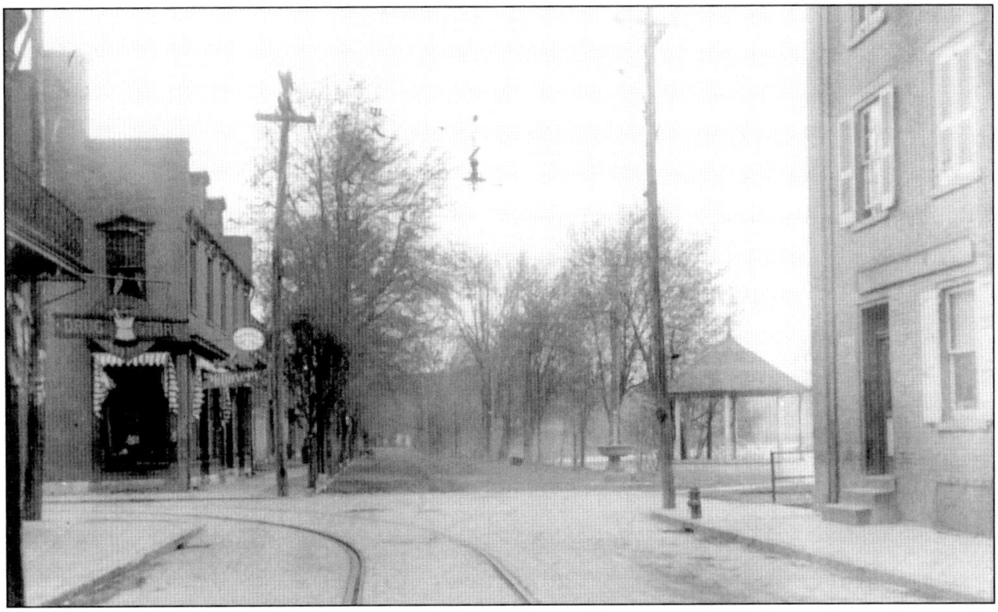

The corner of Main and Allegheny Streets (looking north) around 1904 shows the trolley tracks for the Jersey Shore Electric Street Railway Company, but not for the Jersey Shore and Antes Fort Company. Although operated by many of the same people, the two lines did not connect. The track headed up Allegheny Street and extended out to South Avis and the large New York Central Railroad Shops. Dr. Baer's drugstore is shown on the far left corner in what was called the Hepburn building at that time.

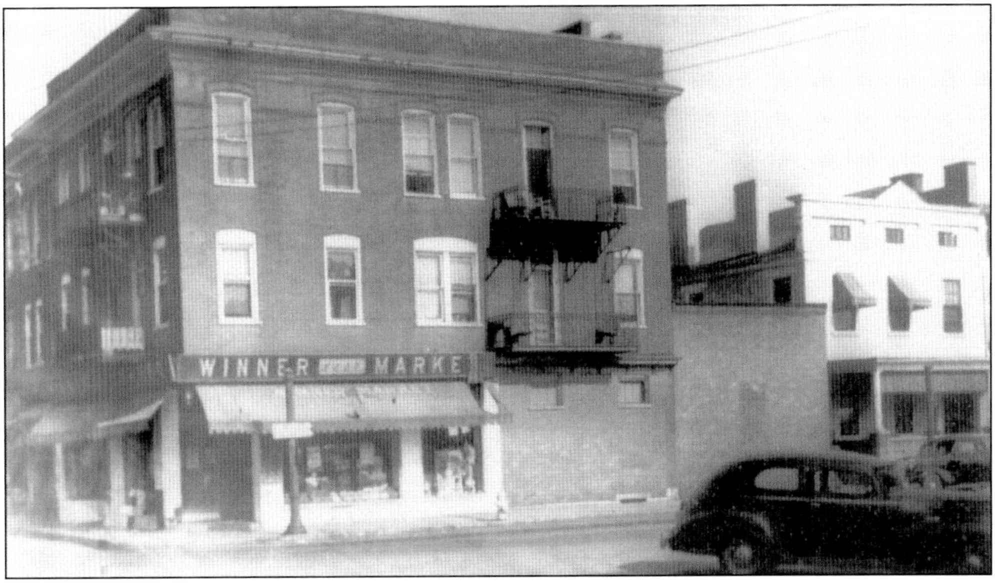

In heading up North Main Street, the Hepburn building, seen in the last picture, has been replaced with another called the Mamolen building, which at this time (1930) was occupied by Winner Market. John Brownlee managed this market for 11 years. A business called Nickelland was here before, and J. J. Newberry Company occupied the Allegheny Street side. The Robert Crane house is seen to the right. He ran a store in the Crane Arcade and was burgess during 1848–1849.

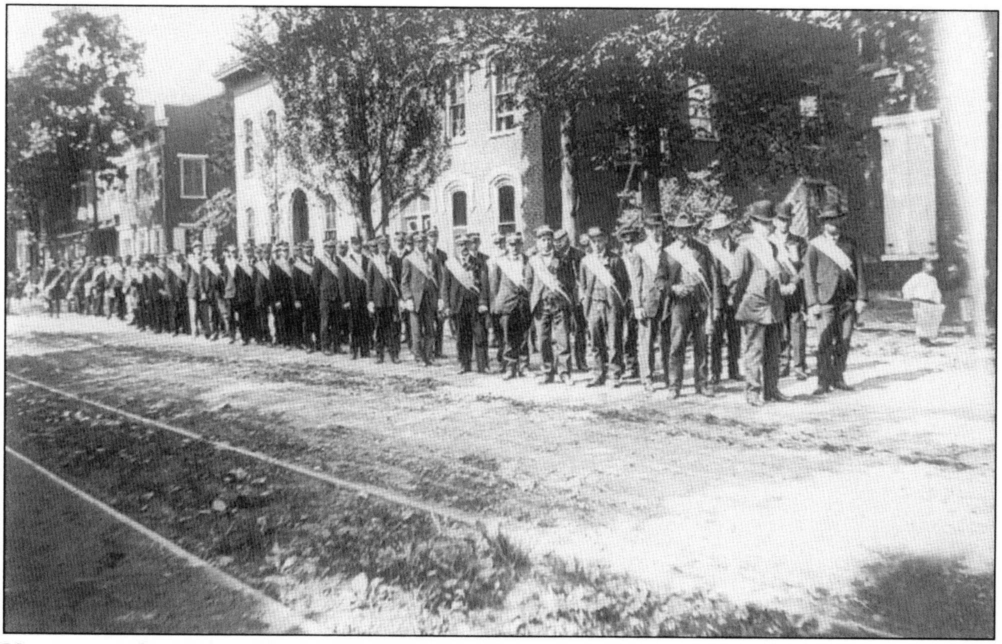

Here, in readiness for a Decoration Day parade, stand members of the Jersey Shore Patriotic Order of the Sons of America (POSofA). This organization took charge of patriotic events as the old members of the GAR died out. They are lined up in front of the former Alexander Brown home, which had been sold to the Fraternal Order of the Eagles.

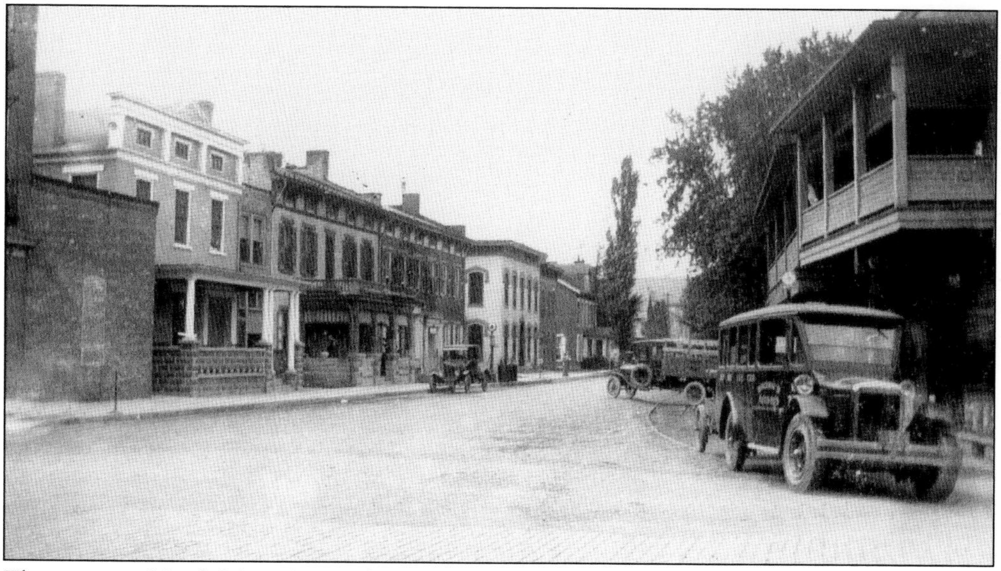

This view up North Main Street shows the yellow brick paving that was laid in 1906 by John Britz Company on Main and Allegheny Streets. The bricks were made by the Reese Hammond Fire Brick Company and were laid on a six-inch base of concrete. The bill was $7,000. The Robert Crane house is to the left, followed by the James Williamson home, John Sebring store and home, the Eagles Club, Kelchners, Frank Barrett, and Frank Painter. Elder's restaurant is on the right with Brown's Auto Bus in front.

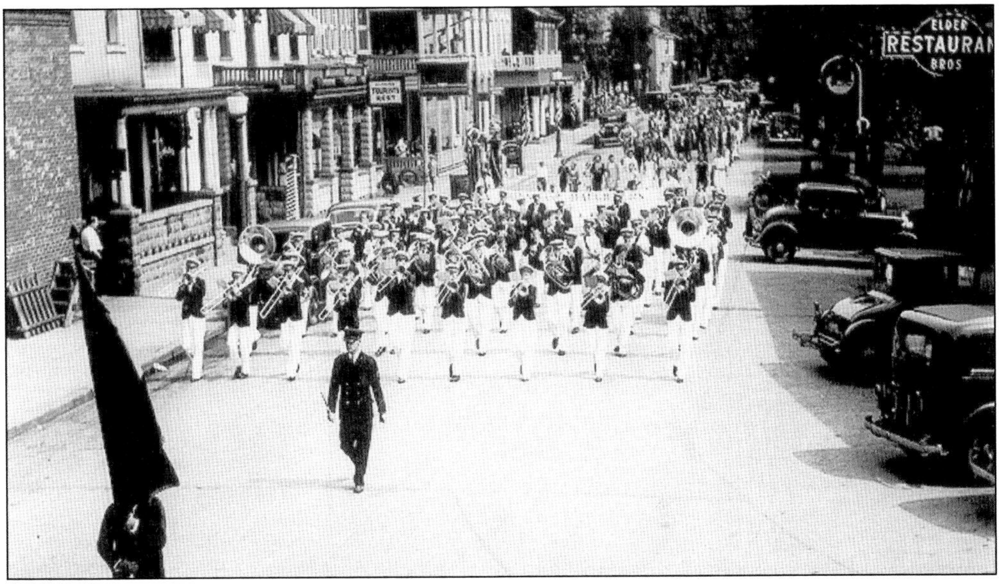

The Jersey Shore High School Band, under the direction of Frank L. Schoendorfer, is marching up North Main Street in the 1930s. This was a 75-piece band with nine trombones across the front. The restaurant to the right was started by Charles Letts in 1908. It was sold to Charles, Henry, and Edward Elder in 1919 and then to Richard Beach in 1956, who ran it until "redevelopment" took the building in 1976. A wonderful view of the river could be seen out the restaurant windows!

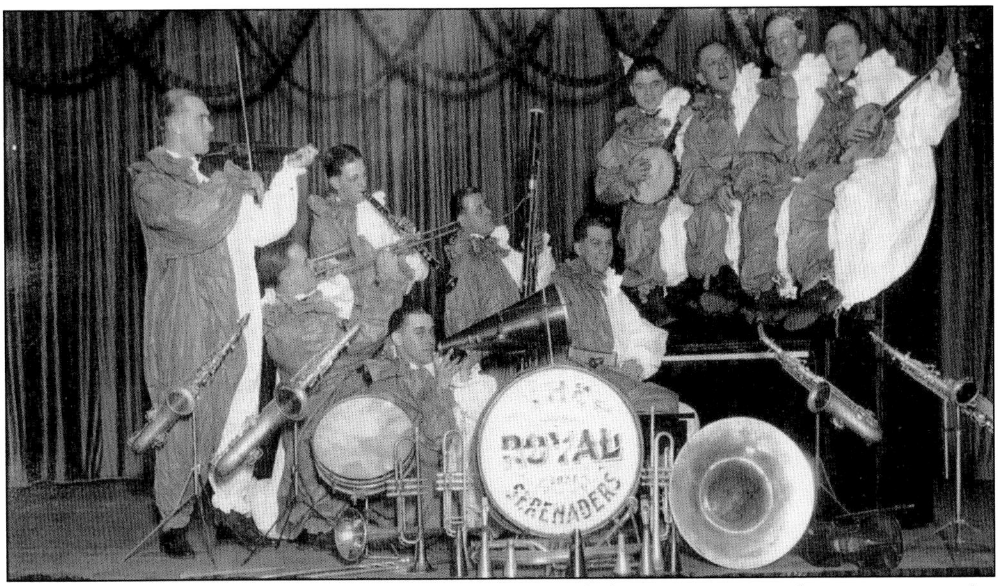

The Royal Serenaders dance band formed in 1924, and this picture was taken onstage at the Eagles Club. Weekend dances drew large crowds with plenty to drink—until Prohibition. The young man, second from left, playing the slide trumpet, was Frank L. Schoendorfer, Jersey Shore High School Band director for 35 years and the son of Frank Schoendorfer, leader of the famed New York Central Railroad shops at Avis. This orchestra was followed by another called the Pied Pipers. Its members included Frank Schoendorfer, Lou Piper, Bob Mencer, Charlie Vairo, and Lester Hale.

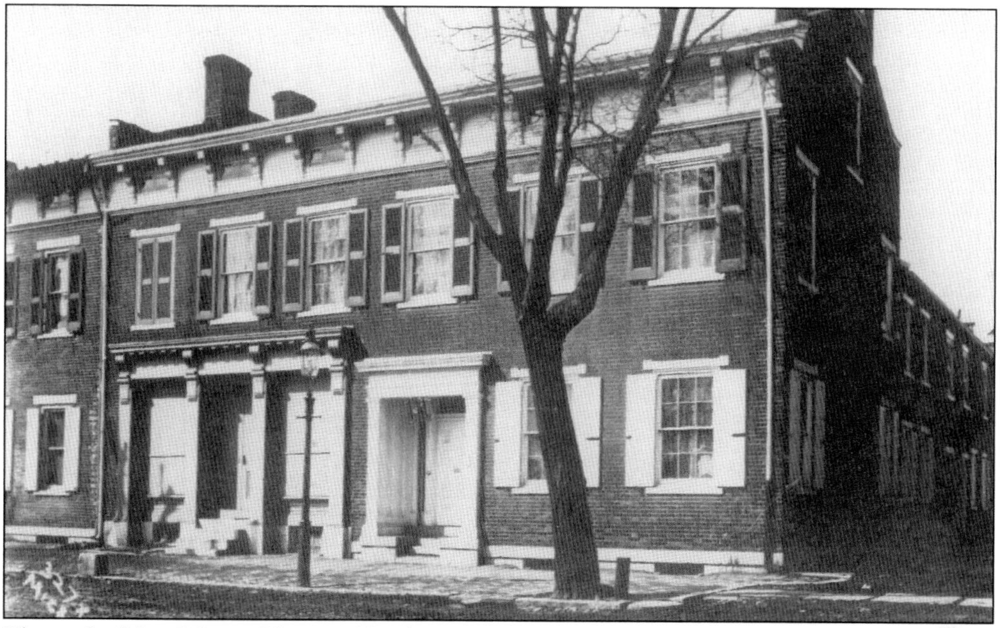

This is the John Sebring Place on North Main Street. John was one of Jersey Shore's first men of substance. His home had a storefront on the left side out of which he sold dry goods, groceries, boots, crockery, and glassware. He was also president of the Jersey Shore Bridge Company, which owned the covered toll bridges. There are large ovens in the rear of this building, likely used to cook meals for canal men as the canal ran behind the building.

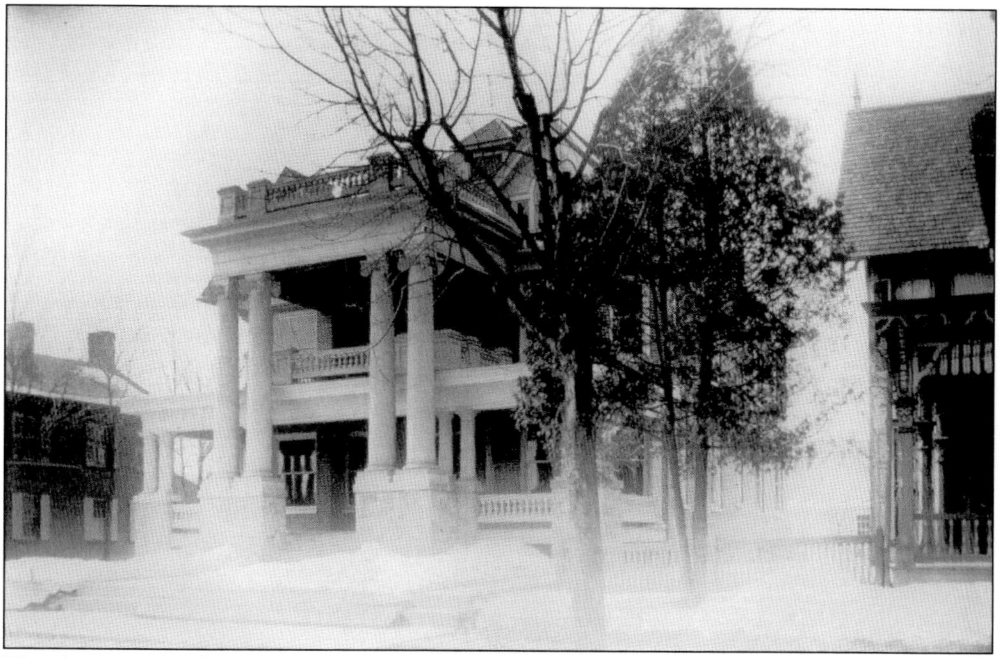

This house started out as the home of William Childs but served as a private educational institution connected with Dr. Sanford's private hospital where "defective" children were received for care, treatment, and education. It was known as the Keystone Sanatorium. The Elks Club purchased it in November 1912 and the BPOE Lodge No. 1057 is still located here.

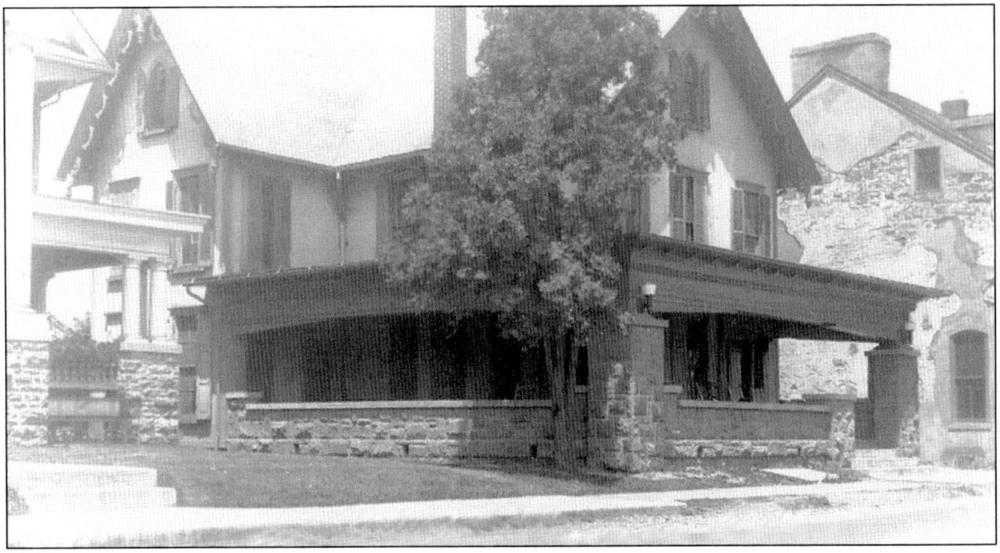

This was originally the home of James Gamble Jr. It was built between the home of William Childs and the Globe Hotel. It was purchased by the Loyal Order of Moose in 1943 and used until around 1996 when it was demolished and a new structure was built. This organization was founded in 1888, and the Jersey Shore Lodge was established on April 24, 1910. The first meetings were held in the W. T. Ferrar building on Allegheny Street, and O. B. Robbins was the first governor.

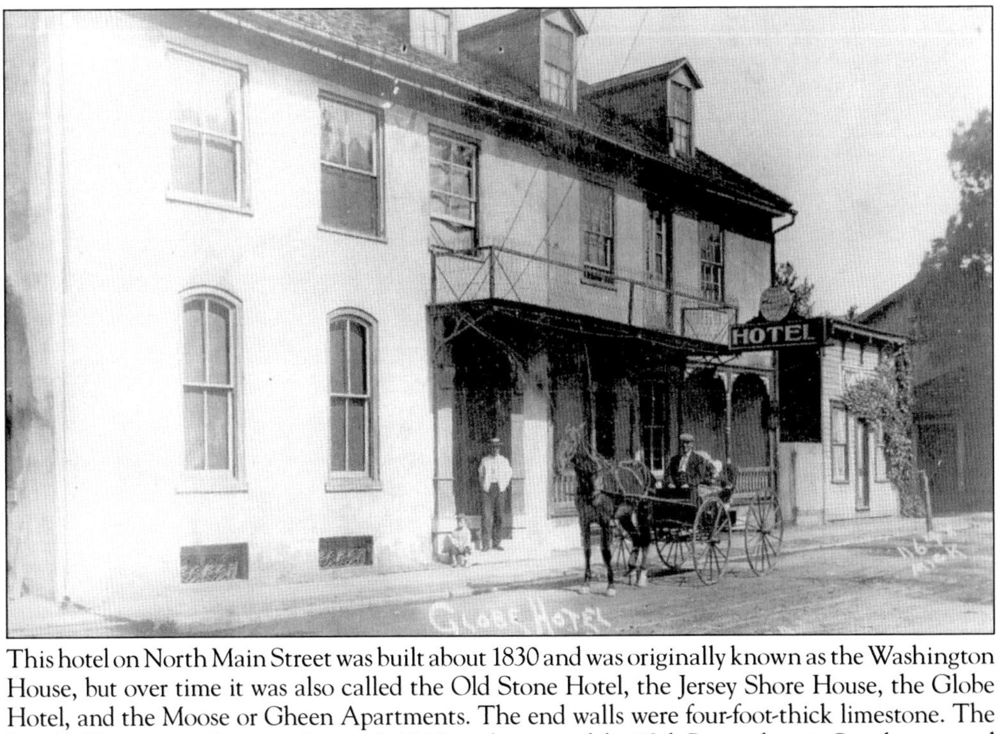

This hotel on North Main Street was built about 1830 and was originally known as the Washington House, but over time it was also called the Old Stone Hotel, the Jersey Shore House, the Globe Hotel, and the Moose or Gheen Apartments. The end walls were four-foot-thick limestone. The hotel lobby was very busy on August 1, 1865, as the men of the 13th Pennsylvania Cavalry stopped in, signed the book, and had a drink. What tales these walls could tell.

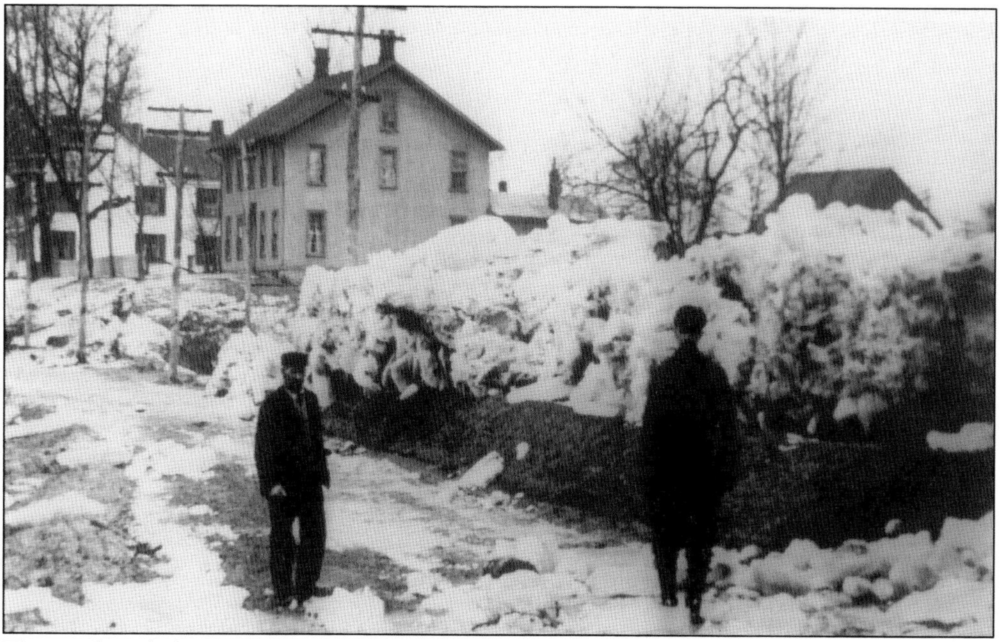

The north end of Main Street used to end in two sizable homes as this picture taken on January 15, 1910, shows. The next to last house in this picture was the old Baily/Allen/Kohr home built around 1850. Bill Kohr lived here for 98 years, and over time the place served as the post office and meeting place for the Masons. In 1876, the last house was owned by the Maffett family, followed by Louis Hirsch and Ed Bassett.

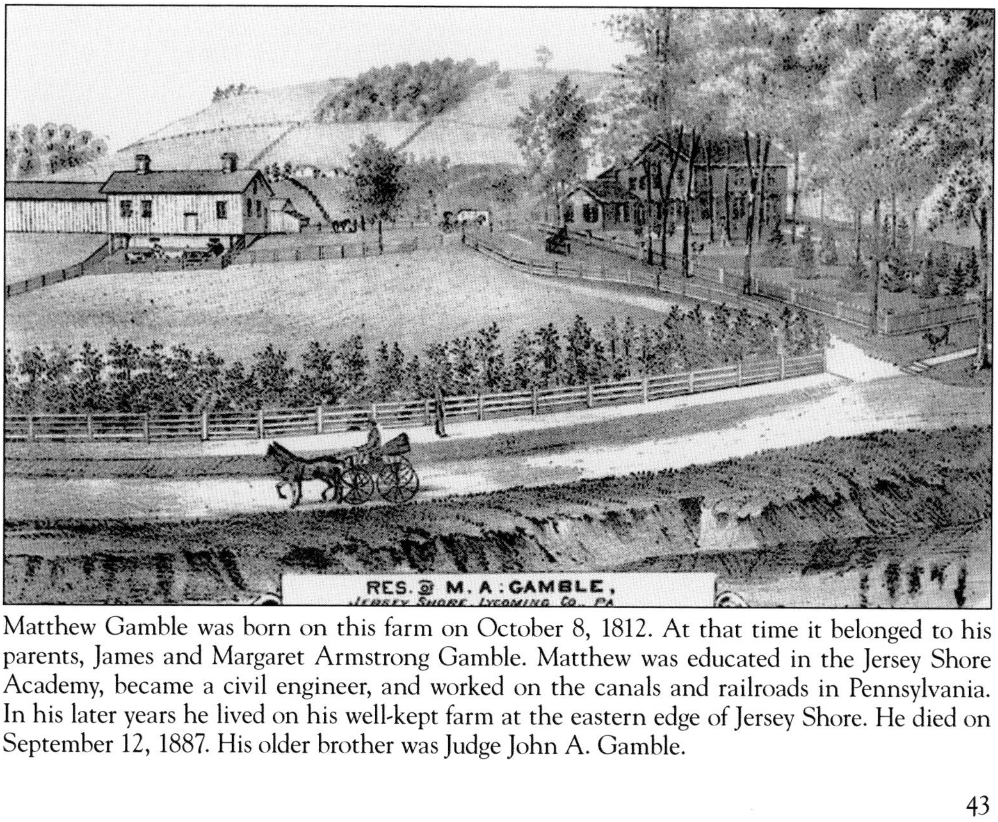

Matthew Gamble was born on this farm on October 8, 1812. At that time it belonged to his parents, James and Margaret Armstrong Gamble. Matthew was educated in the Jersey Shore Academy, became a civil engineer, and worked on the canals and railroads in Pennsylvania. In his later years he lived on his well-kept farm at the eastern edge of Jersey Shore. He died on September 12, 1887. His older brother was Judge John A. Gamble.

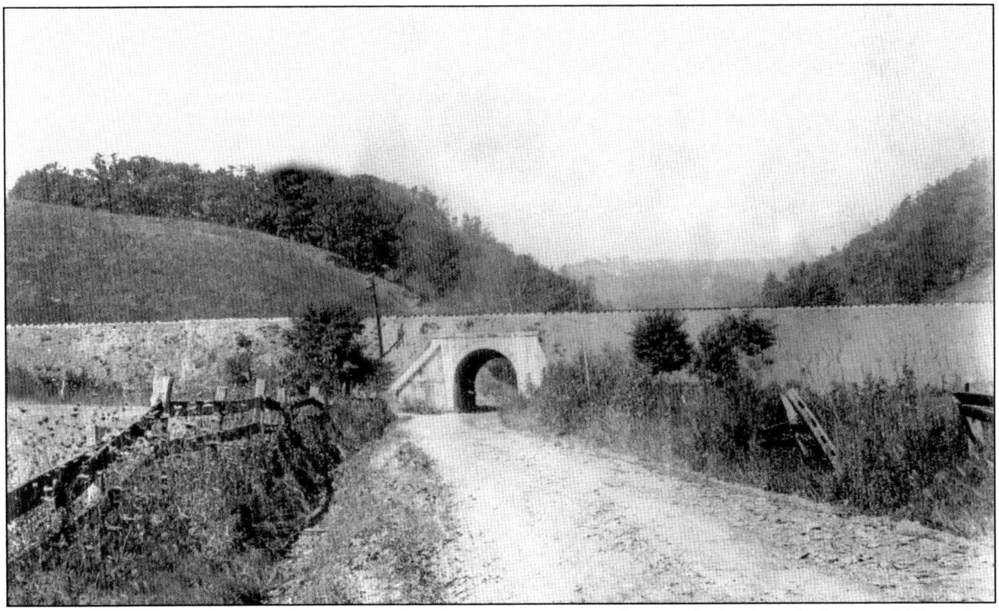

This stone railroad underpass was constructed by the Beach Creek Railroad about 1883 as the line went through Jersey Shore. It is located just east of the town at Nice's Hollow and was named for George P. Nice, an early businessman and prominent citizen of Jersey Shore. The next hollow to the west is Denniston, and to the east is Cement. It is interesting that such breaks in the mountains on the south side of the river are called gaps.

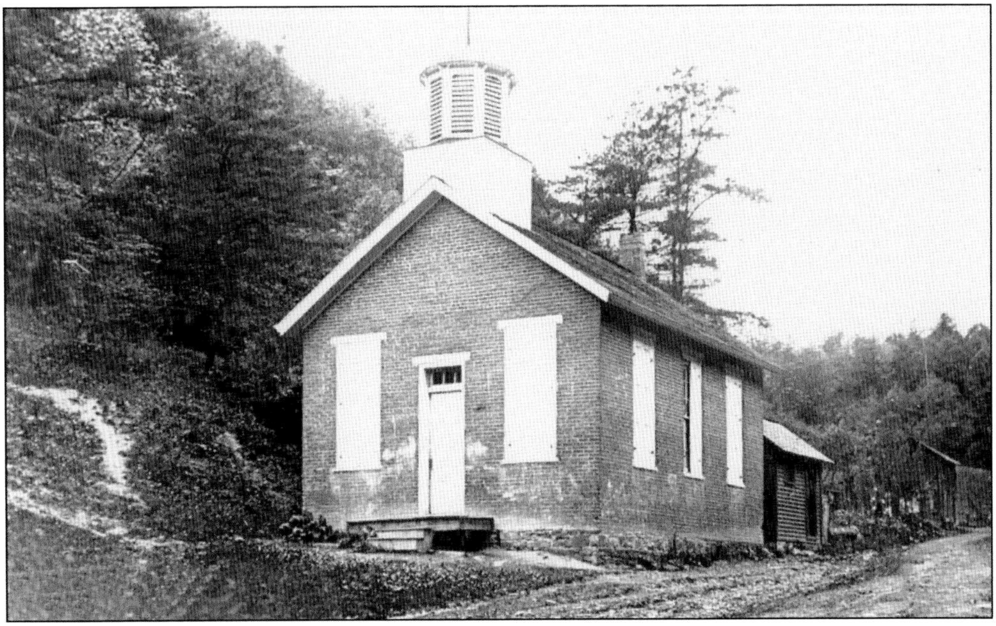

Nice's Hollow School lies just east of Jersey Shore on a one-half-acre lot that was purchased from J. P. Martin on June 8, 1878. The building was to measure 30 feet by 22 feet with walls 13 inches thick. The roof was to be of iron and the inside walls wainscoted up four feet. There were three windows per side, two in the front and all fitted up with four-foot shutters. A. P. Cohick built the cupola in 1884 at a cost of $24.88.

Three

SOUTH MAIN STREET

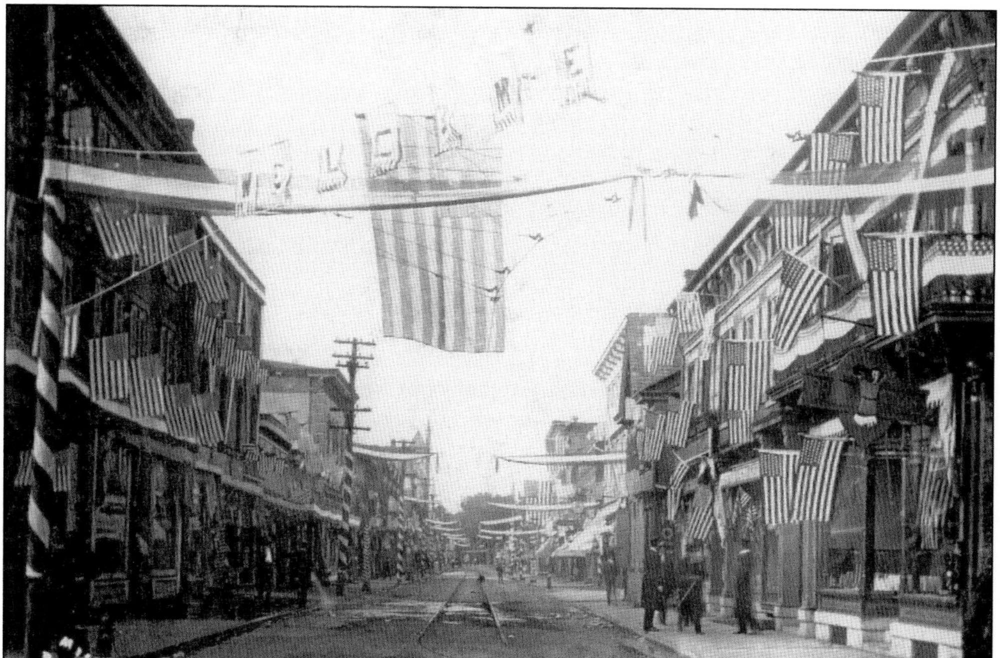

This is a view of South Main Street taken in the early morning on July 4, 1907. The New York Central shops at Avis brought significant new money to the town, and as the population rose the shopping district of the town flourished. A new borough hall had recently been constructed, and the water system had been updated; telephones were becoming more common, and electricity, which was turned on July 25, 1898, was lighting up the town with the purchase of 33 carbon-arc lights in 1901.

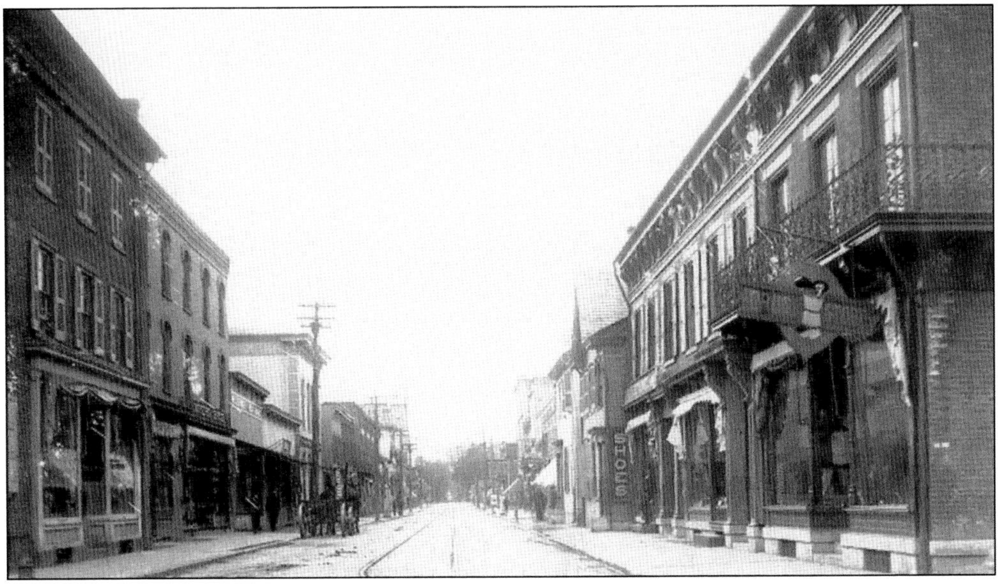

This photograph shows the first block business district of South Main Street about 1905. The large George Tomb building (built in 1855) is on the right side housing Staple's, and later Stephenson's Drug Store and the Albert Pott shoe store. Next was the Frank Gray residence where the Pickering Hotel would be soon built. To the left is the Crane Arcade (built in 1845) followed by Wilson Hardware, McLaughlin News Agency and Western Union, Schwer Meats, Betts Barber Shop, Zettle Bakery, and J. S. Banking Company.

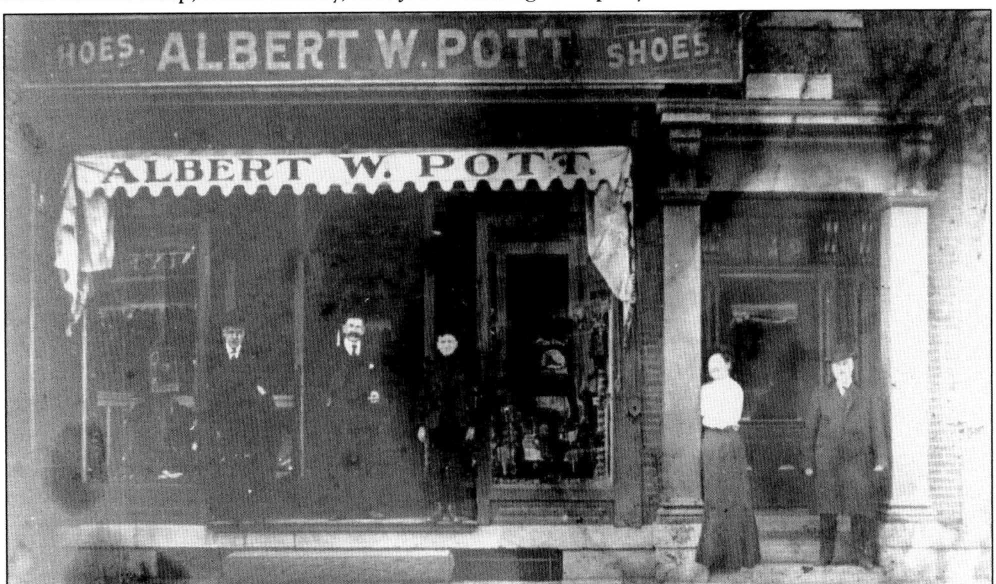

The Pott Shoe business, established in 1847, was the oldest established business in town. It was located on South Main Street opposite the Baptist church. When Charles Pott was named postmaster on December 21, 1887, he moved the office to this site, in the Tomb building at 131 South Main Street. The dividing line between North and South Main Streets was Thompson Street, but it has been Main and Allegheny Streets since 1912. After Charles, the business was run by James D. Pott. At his death in 1891 the business was taken over by his son Albert W. Pott.

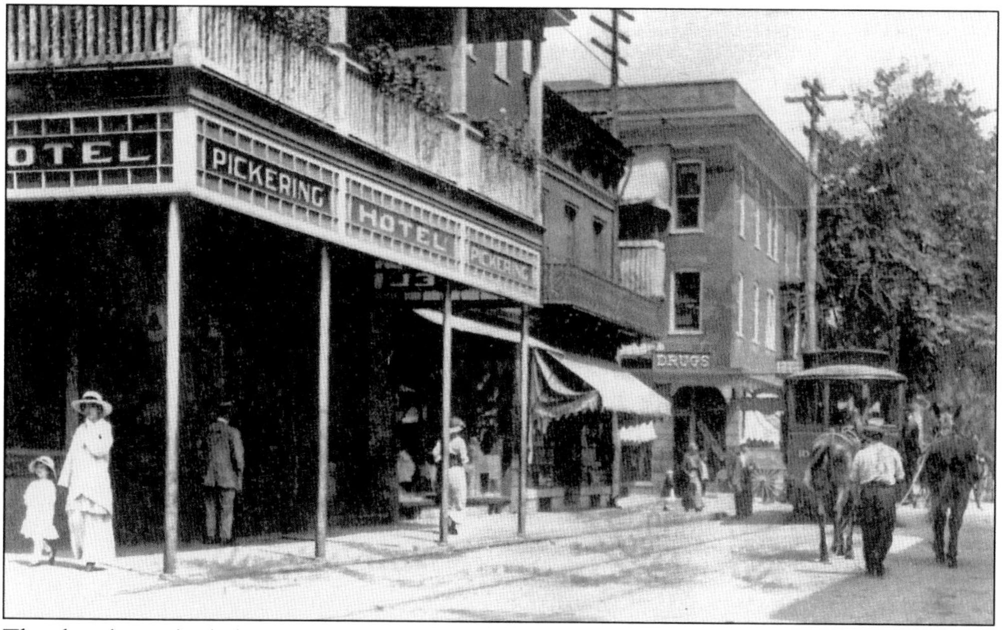

This hotel was built by Joseph Pickering in 1909. Joseph was from England and became a naturalized citizen in Clearfield on May 10, 1886. Other owners include Earl Bingman, Maynard Aungst of English Center, and Paul Sullivan, who ran the business for 22 years. After Pickering, it was called the Jersey Shore Hotel. It had 26 rooms plus a bar, lobby, spacious dining room, kitchen, bridal suite, and large apartment. The apartment was occupied by the management.

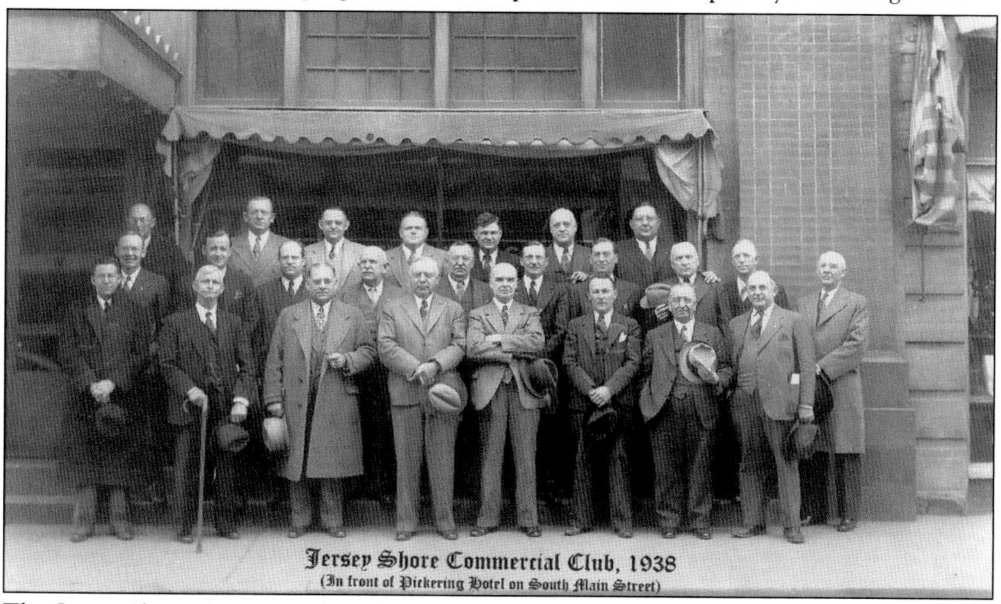

The Jersey Shore Commercial Club is pictured standing in front of the Hotel Pickering in 1938. The club members are as follows: (first row) William Rorabaugh, Kurt Cloud, Ned Crane, Dr. Hays, John McMillan, Mort Parker, Art Woomer, and Dr. Derk; (second row) Duke Wellington, Dr. Lauler, Clyde Carpenter, F. L. Person, T. A. Sallada, Roscoe Wolfe, Ben Jaffe, John Levegood, Guy Rorabaugh, and Charles Potter; (third row) Bill Camerer, Harry Mencer, Harry Smith, Dr. Sanford, Mr. Tate, Dr. Goodman, and Travette Bubb.

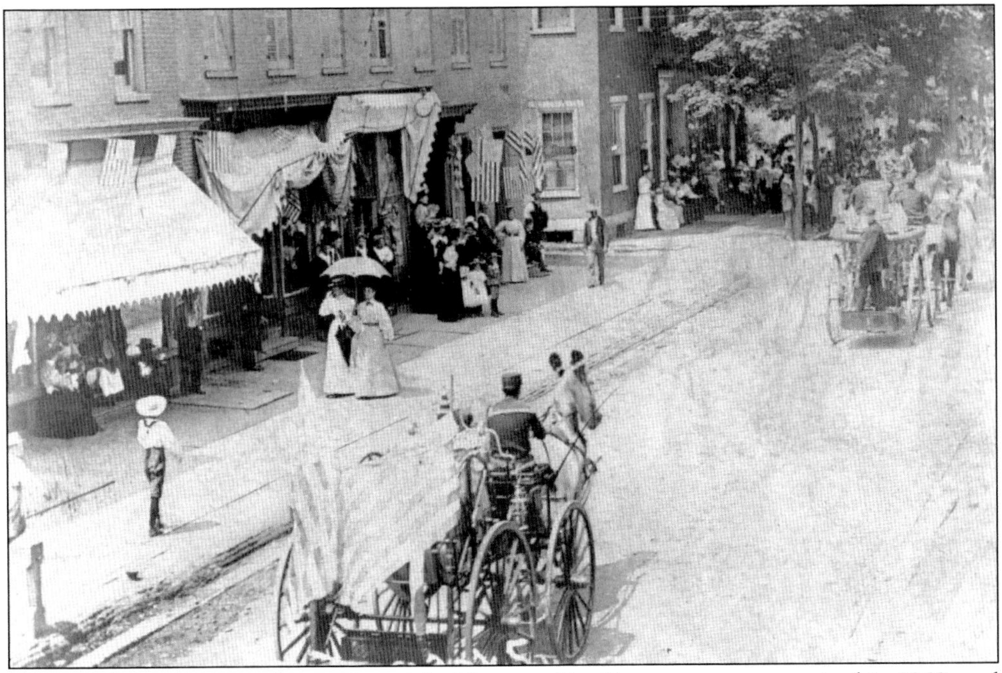

The first fire company in Jersey Shore, the Neptune Fire Company, was organized in 1860, and the citizens approved a special fire tax that allowed borough council to buy a new engine, leather hose, and hose carriage. Since someone burned down the old firehouse in April 1858, a new one was built by William Gates at the very end of Smith Street. Council met here for the first time on March 3, 1862.

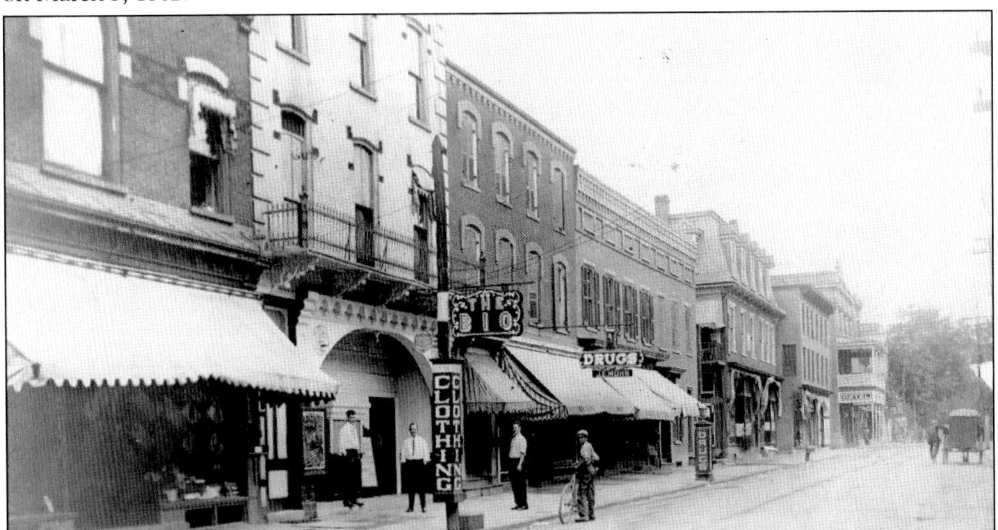

This picture shows the buildings along the west side of South Main Street constructed since the Franklin Hotel fire of 1871. The buildings are, from left to right, 1. the D. A. Bingman Clothing Store, the American Union Telephone Company, GAR headquarters, and Western Auto; 2. Dorey's Pool Room and Bio Theatre; 3. Mohn's Drug Store; 4. Leinbach's Drug Store, George Snyder Jeweler, Joseph Kelasner Jewelry, and D. Miles Barner; 5. the Franklin Hotel where the stagecoach used to stop in town.

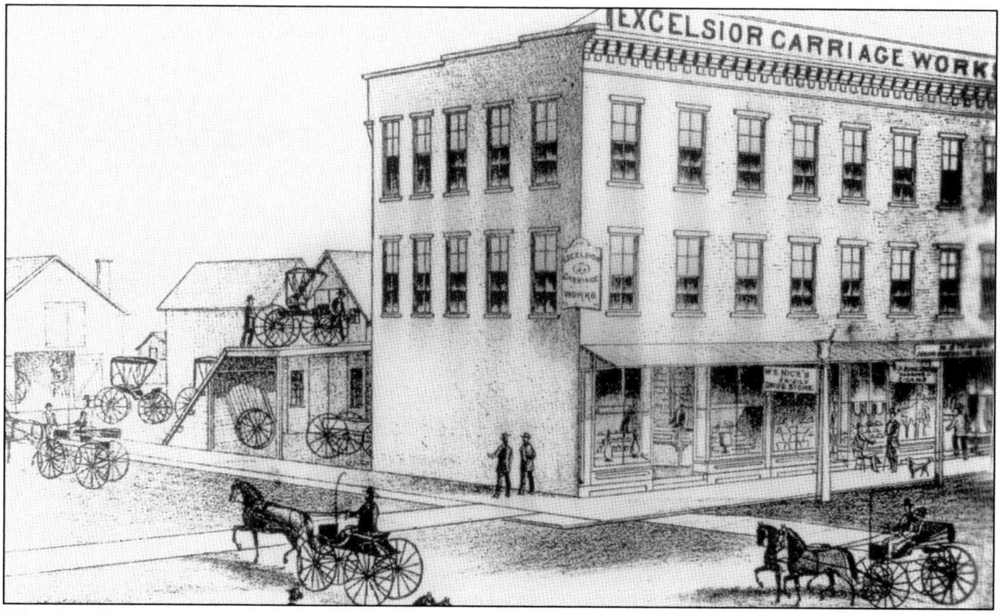

The Excelsior Carriage Works was located on the corner of South Main and Smith Streets. The original wooden building housed the carriage shop on the second floor. James Nice established the business in 1830. The Nice home was located where the Methodist parsonage was later built. This three-story building was constructed in 1880, and the storefront housed a barbershop, tin shop, cigar store, and Stamm's Hair Dressing Saloon. Nice's Corner was a popular loafing spot for young men.

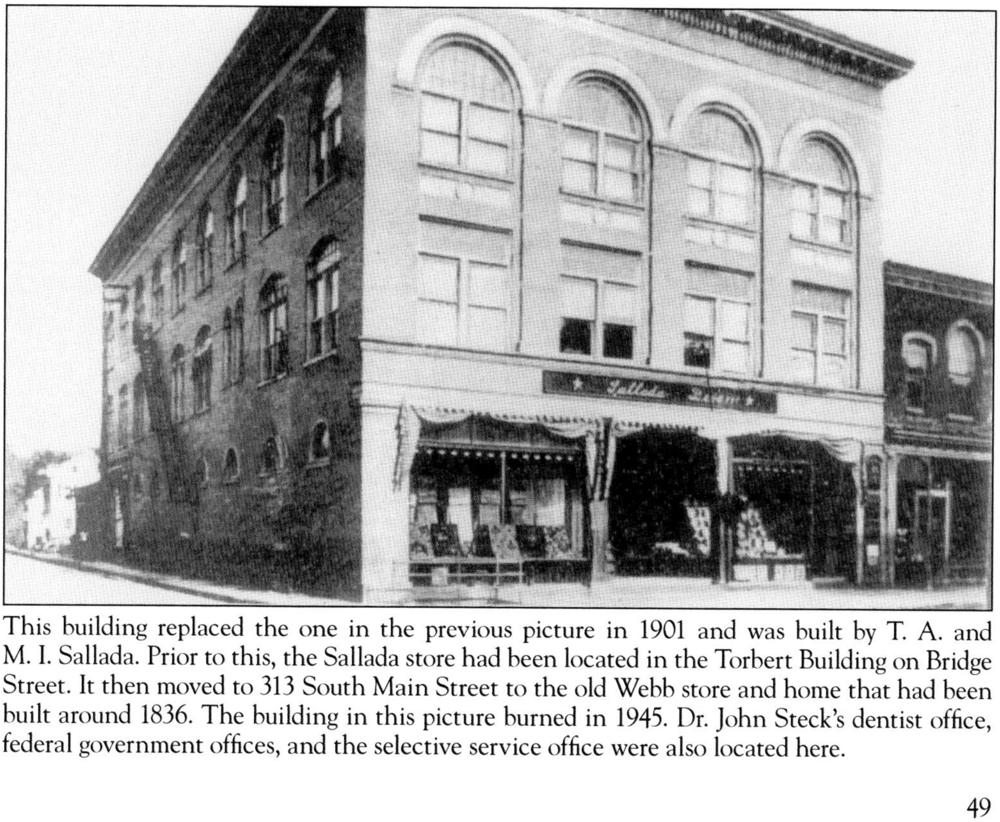

This building replaced the one in the previous picture in 1901 and was built by T. A. and M. I. Sallada. Prior to this, the Sallada store had been located in the Torbert Building on Bridge Street. It then moved to 313 South Main Street to the old Webb store and home that had been built around 1836. The building in this picture burned in 1945. Dr. John Steck's dentist office, federal government offices, and the selective service office were also located here.

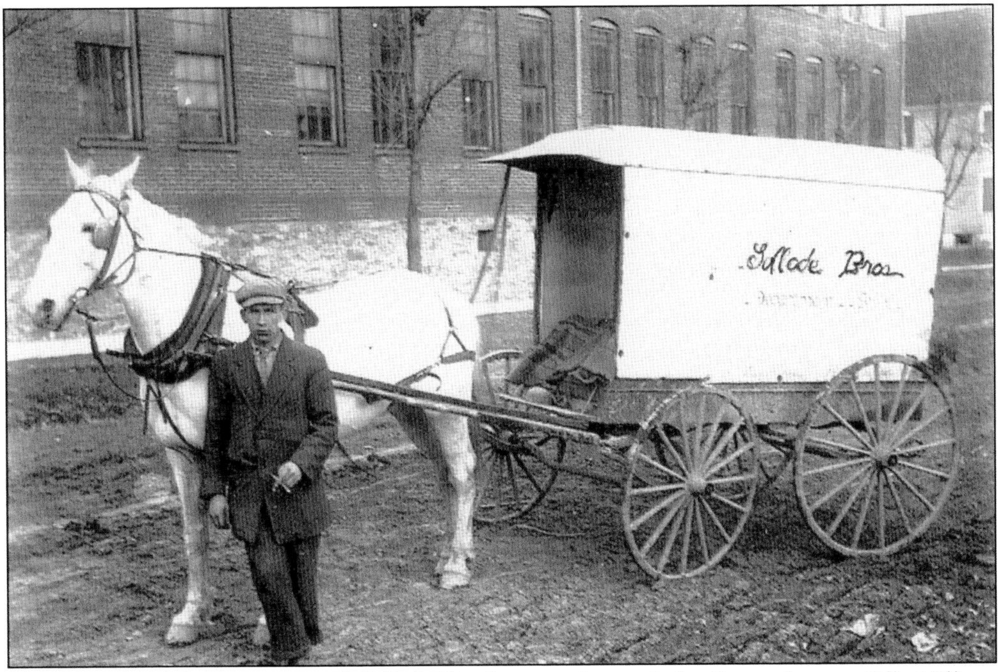

This was the delivery wagon of Sallada Brothers in front of the Susquehanna Silk Mill on Washington Avenue.

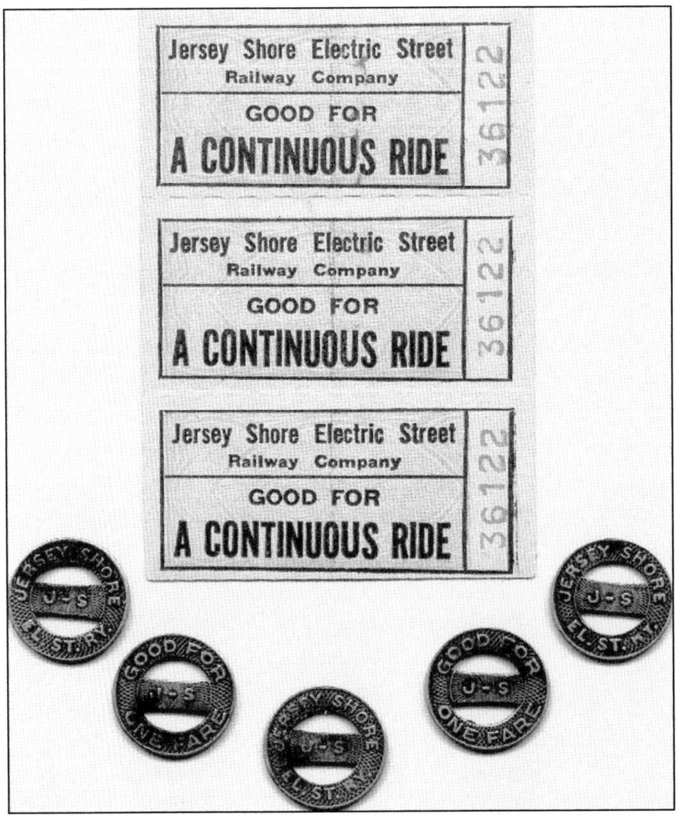

The trolley line of the Jersey Shore Electric Street Railway Company was built in response to the coming of the New York Central locomotive and machine shops to Avis, which was announced in 1901. Jersey Shore was afraid that the displacement of the Beech Creek yard, located in uptown Jersey Shore, would shift the center of population more toward Avis. To thwart this event this trolley system was built and began operation in 1903, thus providing workers with a convenient commute to work.

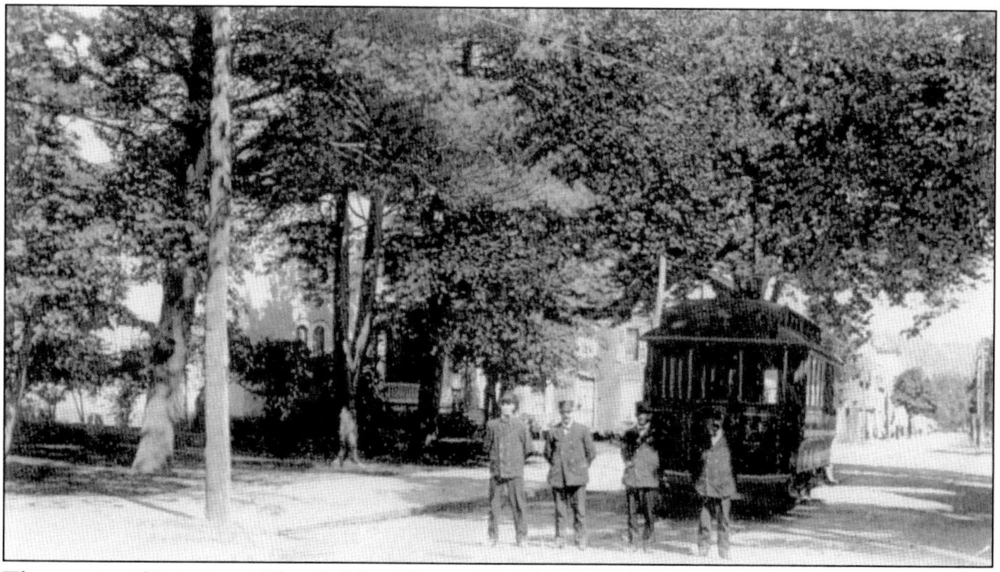

The corner of Locust and South Main Streets was the end of the line in Jersey Shore, where the contact arm connecting to the overhead electric cable would be reversed and the backs of the seats flipped over making the trolley ready for the return trip. The company office was located in the new Sallada building. This company was promoted by such men as Hamilton Humes, Robert McCullough, J. Henry Cochran, and H. C. McCormick.

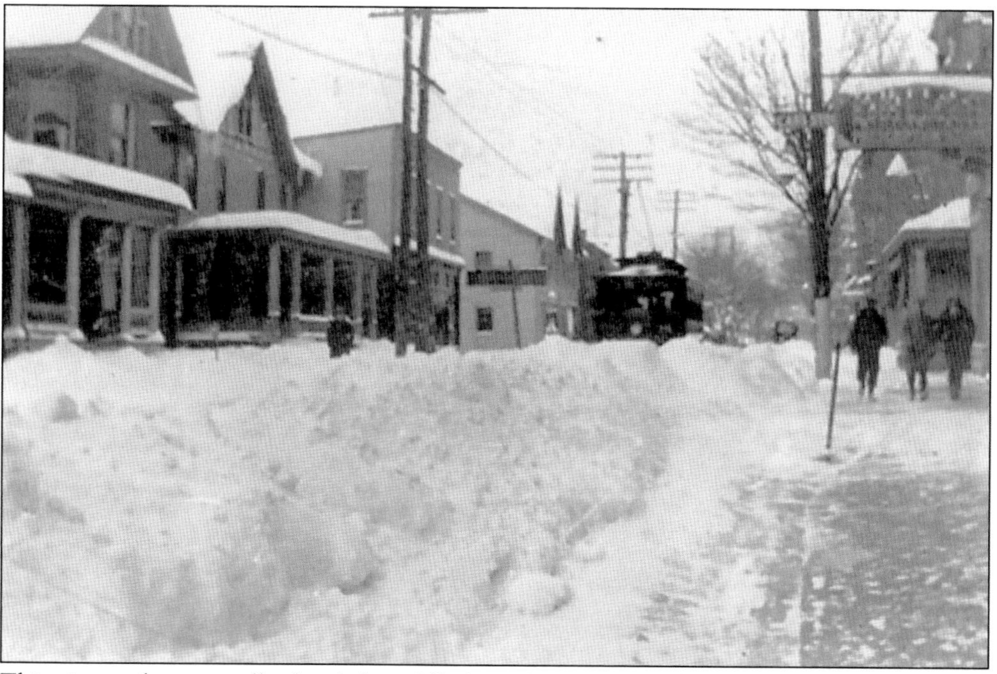

This picture shows a trolley headed up Allegheny Street at Canal Street. There is a sign to the right that says "car stop." The homes to the left were later owned by Dr. Ford Barner and Edward Toner. The square building on the corner was once the Jersey Shore Cycle Company owned by John Irvin. It became the sporting goods store of B. F. Burtnett in 1898. He also handled guns (black and smokeless powder) and gun repair.

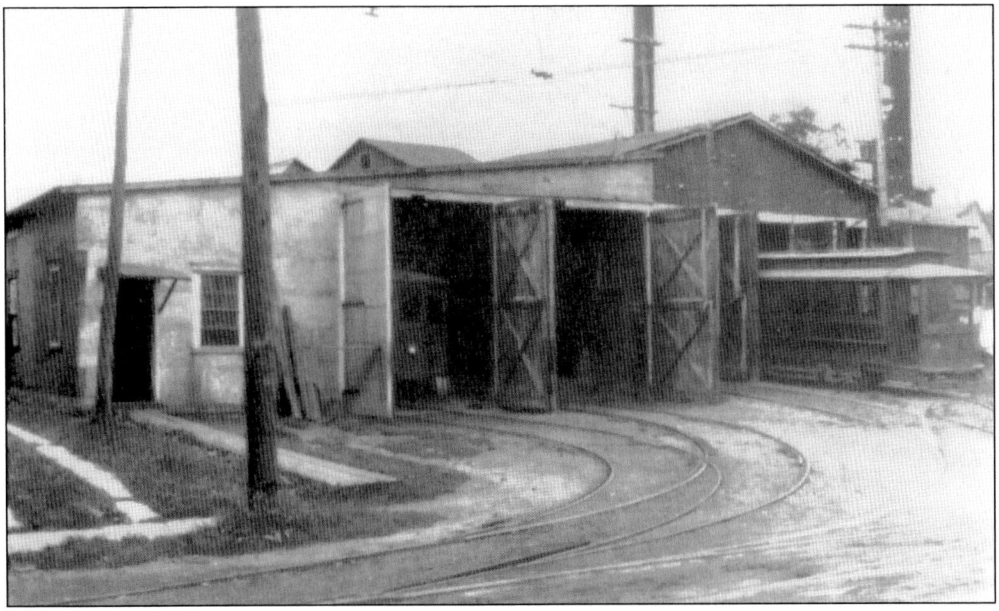

The 70-by-30-foot trolley car barn for this company was on Depot Street just west of the New York Central Railroad YMCA that was built along Allegheny Street in 1909. This was an L-shaped complex that included an office, car repair shop, blacksmith shop, and an engine generator shop. The company owned 18 cars over the years, but the majority of the cars were used to transport men to the Avis shops and would sit there until the close of the shift.

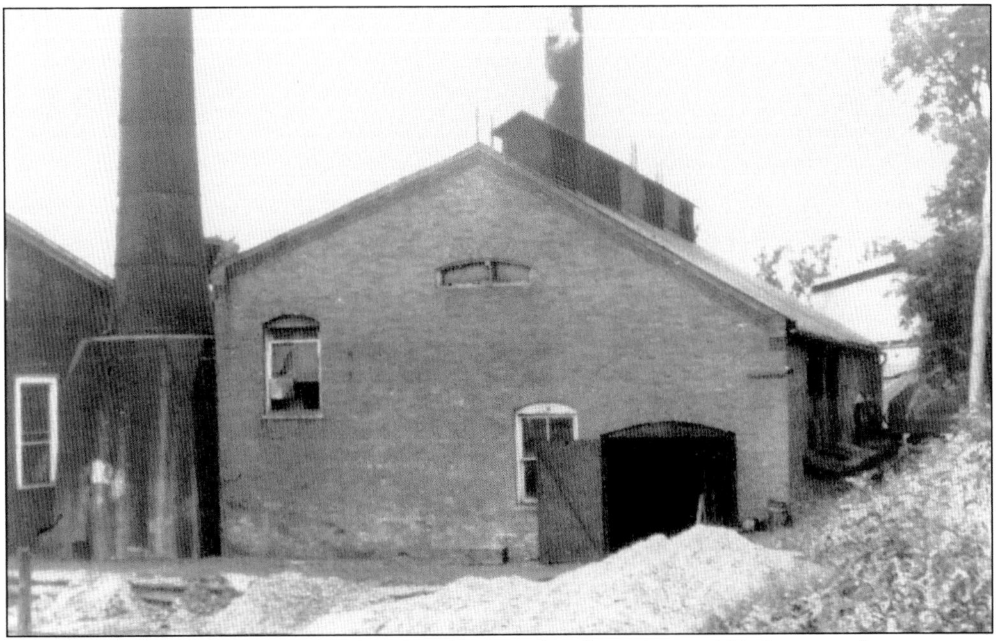

This is a Pennsylvania Power and Light photograph taken about 1924 showing the generator house of the Jersey Shore Electric Company when it was acquired by Pennsylvania Power and Light. The first electricity, used to turn on lights and run the trolleys, was provided by the Jersey Shore Electric Company, which built a small generator house on a 50-by-150-foot parcel deeded to them by the borough in September 1897. A. H. Squires was president of the light company.

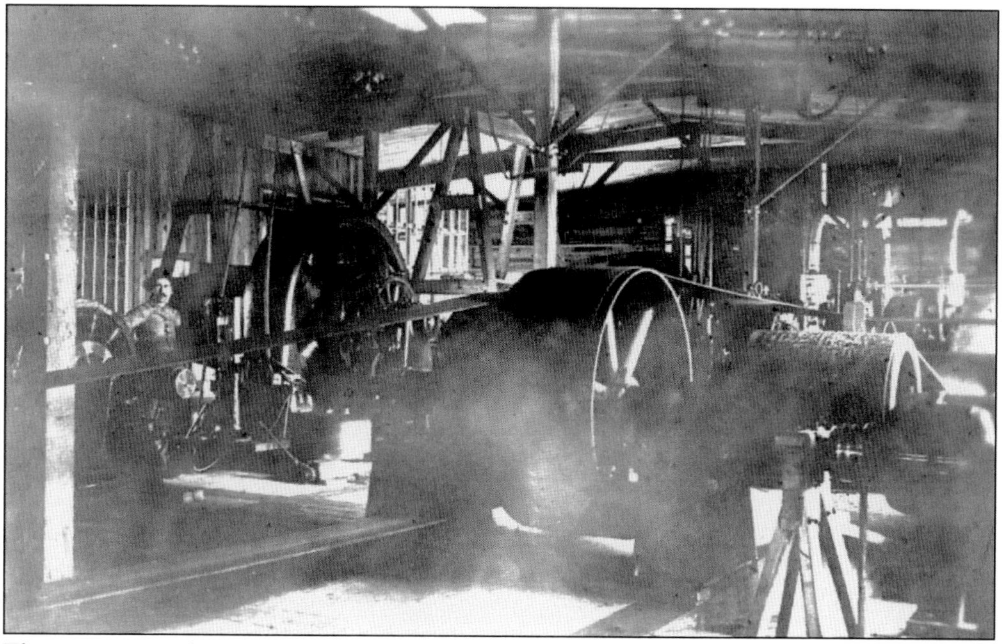

This is a picture showing the interior of the Jersey Shore Electric Company's powerhouse. The energy to make the DC power came from coal, which fired a steam boiler, which turned the generators. The new powerhouse, built in 1912, was much larger than the first and not only powered trolley operation but lit the streets of Jersey Shore and the surrounding area. The first electric lights were turned on June 25, 1898, with flags and banners waving and music provided by the Citizens Band.

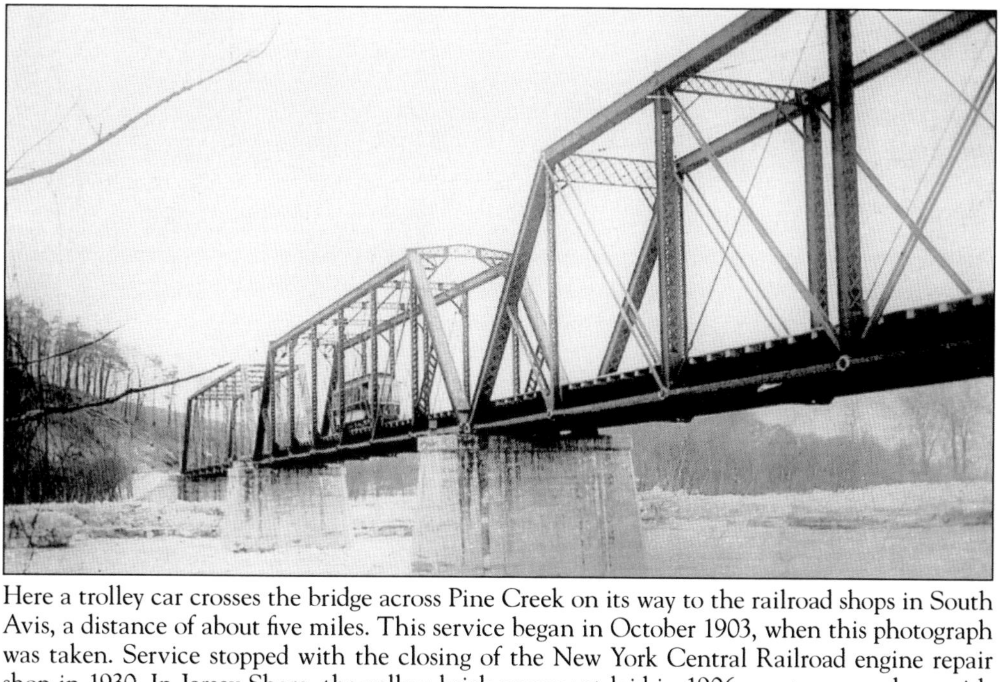

Here a trolley car crosses the bridge across Pine Creek on its way to the railroad shops in South Avis, a distance of about five miles. This service began in October 1903, when this photograph was taken. Service stopped with the closing of the New York Central Railroad engine repair shop in 1930. In Jersey Shore, the yellow brick pavement laid in 1906 was torn up, along with the trolley rails, and the streets repaved with concrete.

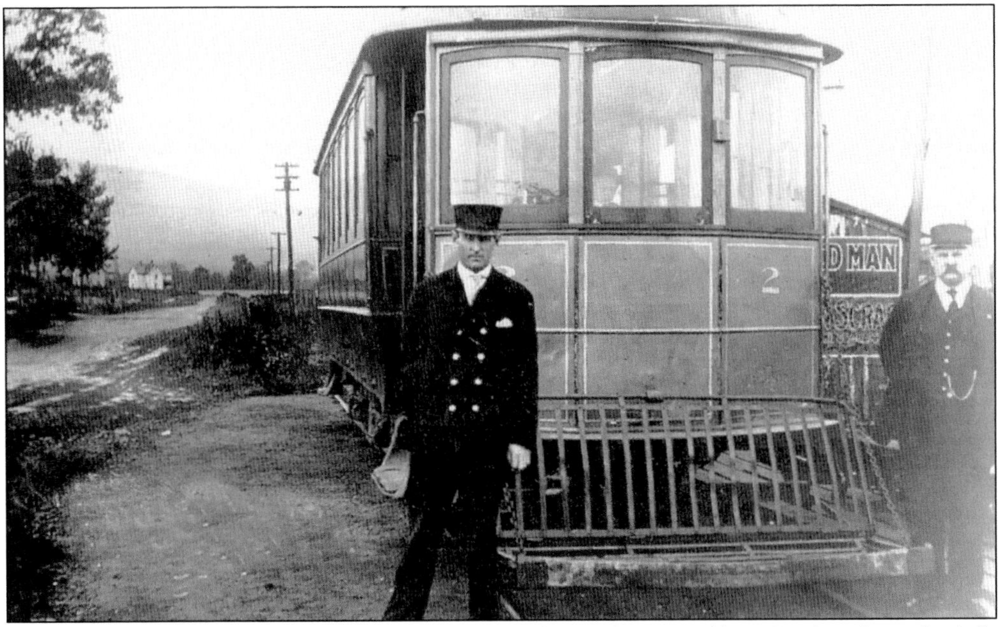

Trolley No. 2 sits at the terminal in south Avis with conductor William Limbaugh to the left. Land speculators and developers shaped the growth of the town in response to the coming of the New York Central shops. J. Henry Cochran formed the Cochran Land Company in 1902 and named the town Avis, after the first name of his wife and daughter. Two other land companies were Oak Grove and Harris Land. The first Fourth of July celebration was held at Avis Park with music provided by the Repaz Band and John Hazel.

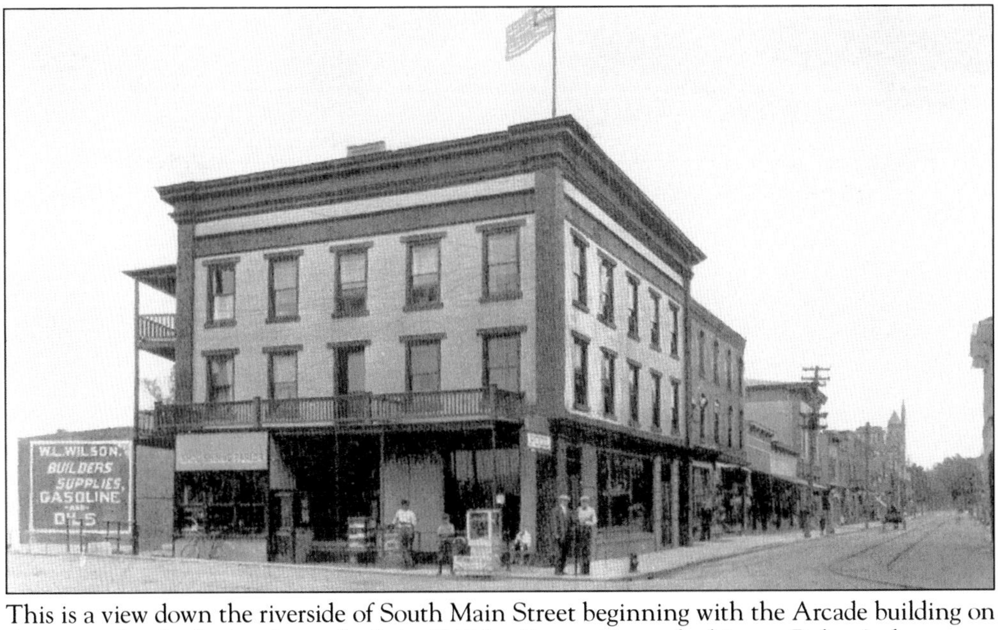

This is a view down the riverside of South Main Street beginning with the Arcade building on the square by the bridge. It was built in 1845 by George Crane for his son Robert's shoe store. L. L. Stearns started his business here in 1850, and Jacob and George Bubb purchased the building in 1854. The flag on top the building is for the post office, which was located here between 1911 and 1927.

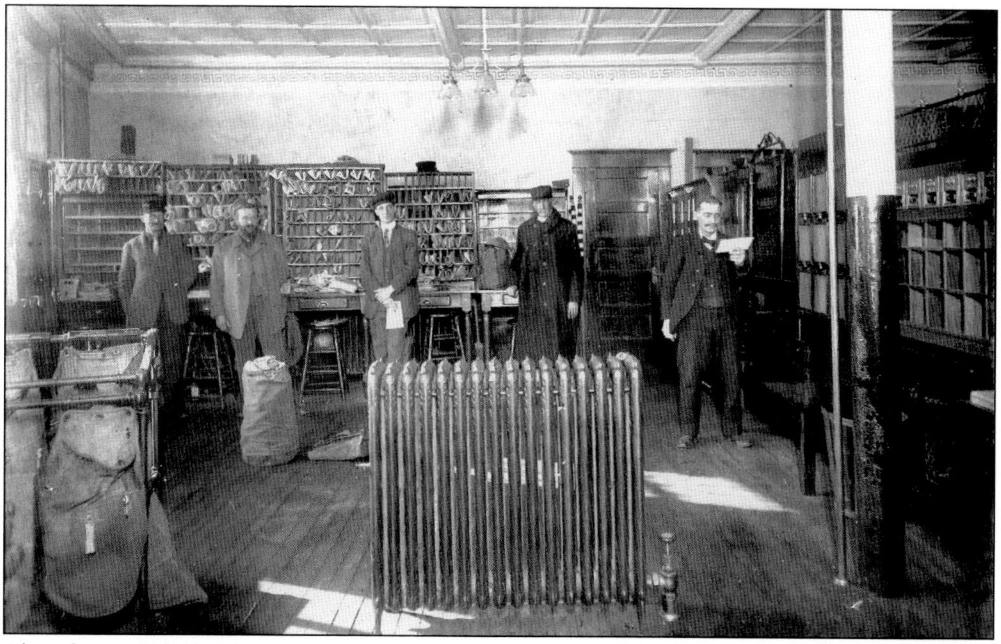

This photograph shows the interior of the sorting room when the post office was located in the Arcade building. Rural free delivery carriers shown, from left to right, are George C. Marshall, RD 1; Sam Fillman, RD 2; Reid Dorset, RD 3; J. Frank Huling, RD 5; and Harry Bodine, RD 4. Rural free delivery began in 1903.

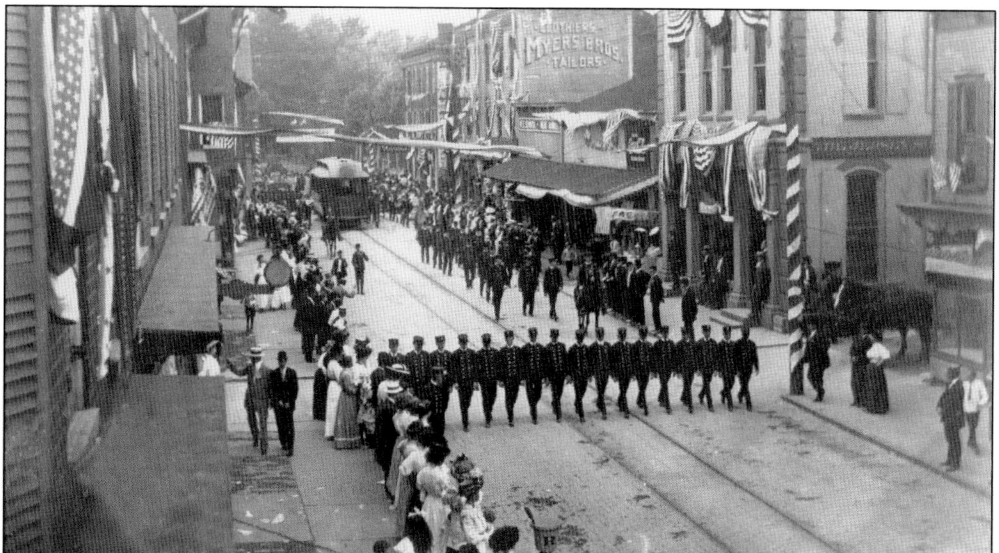

Back in August 1903, people would dress up for special occasions such as this fireman's carnival parade. Businesses from the square up included the Arcade; City Restaurant; Sam Molson's barbershop; Wilson's Hardware, Tin and Stove Shop; Myers Brothers Clothing; Schwer's Meats; McLaughlin News Agency and Western Union; Henry Betts Barber Shop; Alexander Zettle's Bakery and Ice Cream Store; and the Jersey Shore Trust Company. This photograph was taken from Leinbach's Pharmacy with Kelasner's Jewelry Store next advertised by the "pocket watch" sign.

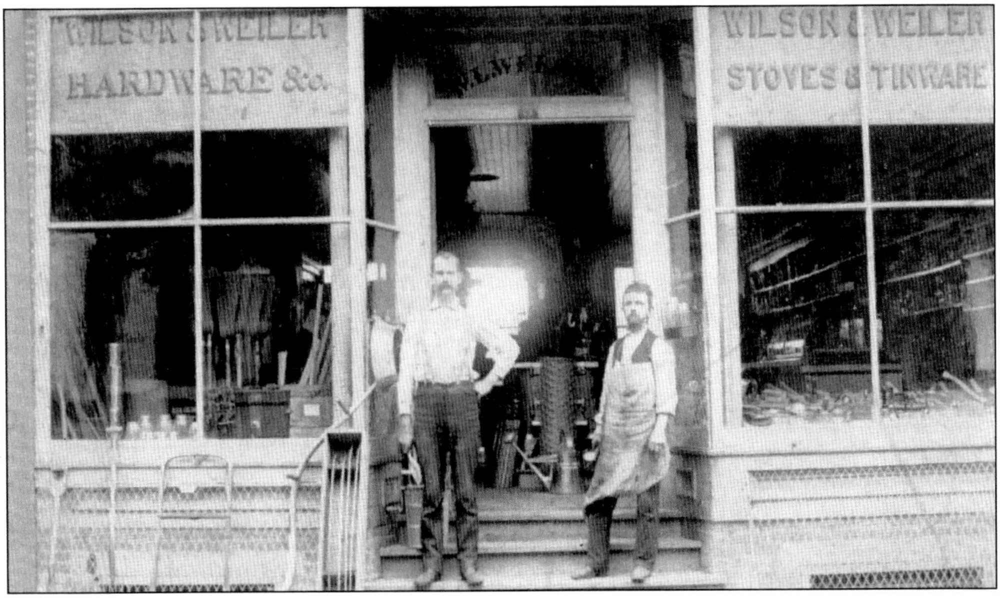

William R. Wilson came to Jersey Shore around 1855 and purchased the Shoup and Norton Tin Shop adjoining the Arcade. The William R. Wilson Company was founded in 1861 as a hardware and tinning business. The name was changed to William N. Wilson Company when William R. died in 1877. In 1879, it was purchased again by W. L. Wilson, who took George Weiler (right) into partnership. This arrangement lasted for 12 years, until 1881, when Weiler died.

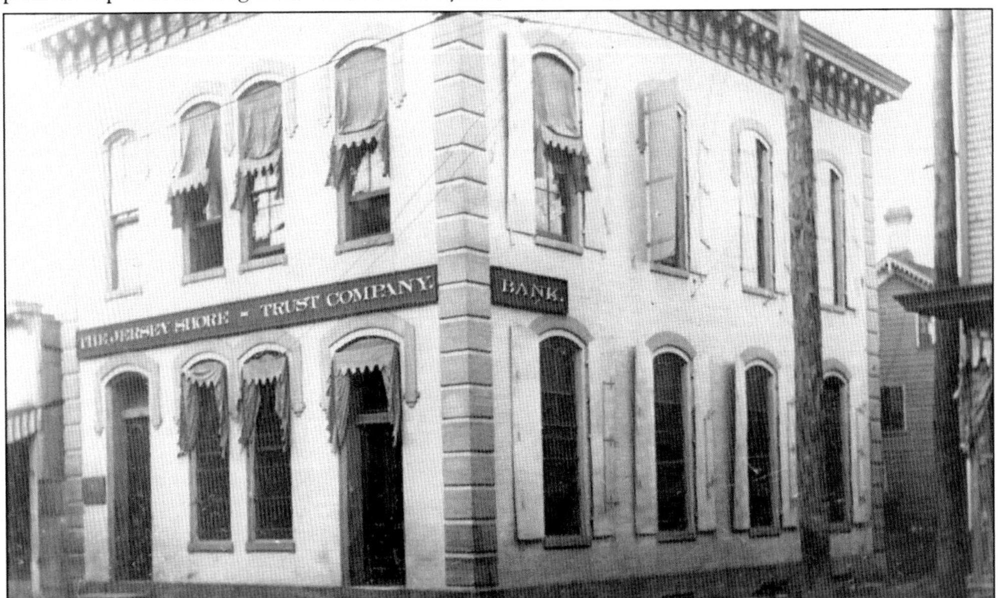

The Jersey Shore Trust Company was founded in 1869 by the private banking firm of Gamble, Humes, and White. From 1879 to 1906, it operated under the name of the Jersey Shore Banking Company and incorporated into a state bank in 1886. In 1906, the name changed again to the Jersey Shore Trust. *Jersey Shore Herald* wrote on December 14, 1870, "This was the former site of the Jersey Shore National Bank that was chartered here in 1857, bought up by George Sanderson and moved to Williamsport in 1871."

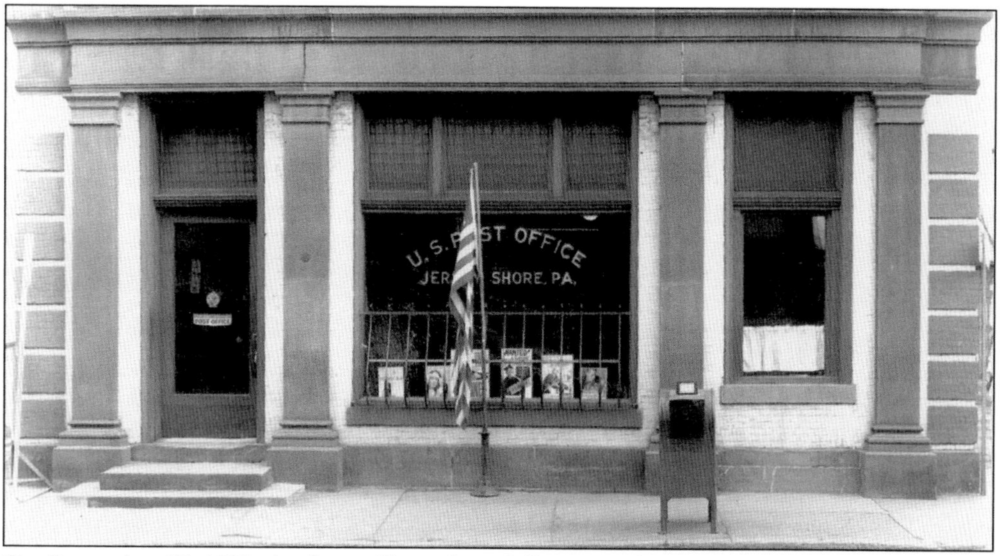

On September 27, 1927, the Jersey Shore Post Office moved to the old Trust Company Bank from the Arcade building and remained there until April 1, 1960, when it moved to its present site on Allegheny Street. The first Jersey Shore, or Waynesburg Post Office, opened on April 1, 1805, in Thomas McClintock's stone tavern at the corner of North Main and Seminary Streets. Thomas was the first postmaster.

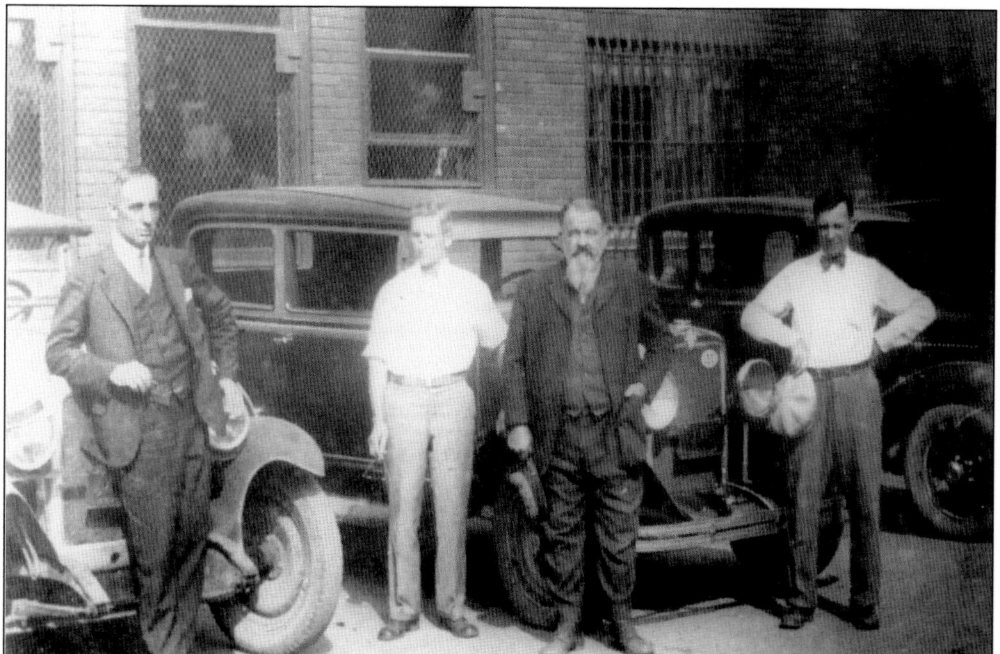

Here are the rural mail carriers at the rear of this post office on August 30, 1930. The mode of transportation is no longer horse and wagon. From left to right are Reid Dorsett, Frank Forcey, Sam Fillman, and John Slaugenwhite. This was Fillman's retirement day. He and Richard Davidson were the first rural free delivery carriers starting back in 1903.

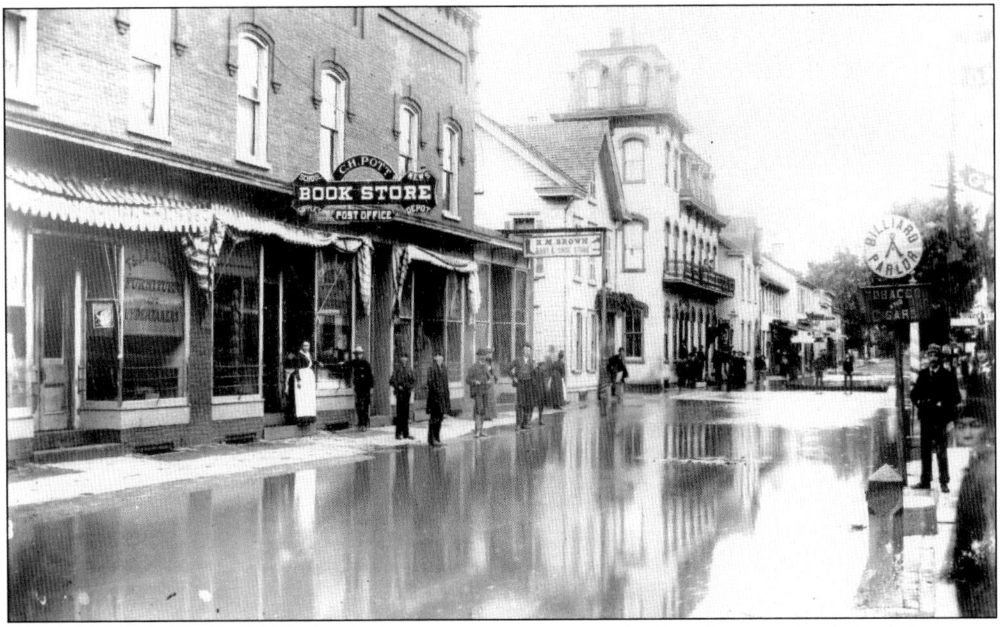

In more recent times, Thornton's Hardware store was in the building to the left. A hundred years ago it was John Calvert's Furniture and Undertaking Business, which was replaced by J. G. Levegood; Charles Potts Book Store, News Office and Post Office; then Robert Brown's Boot and Shoe Store, the Calvert home, and the Gamble Hotel at the corner of Smith Street. The POSofA had its headquarters on the second floor of the first building to the left.

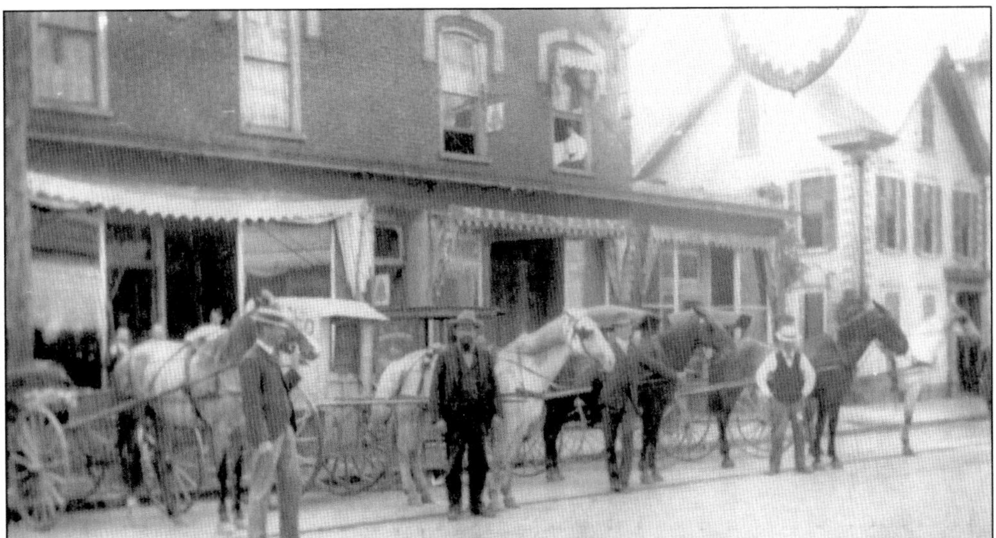

The Jersey Shore Post Office was located in the Calvert Building prior to 1911. This picture, taken in 1904, shows the rural free delivery carriers. From left to right they are George Marshall; Sam Fillman (RD 2, Tombs and Nichol's Run); Reid Dorsett (west of Pine Creek); and Harry Bodine (Nippenose Valley). Partially showing to the far right is J. Frank Huling (old River Road to South Avis). The limit for a horse was about 25 miles a day. Standing in the doorway were Warren Masters (postmaster), Harry Masters, and Anna Strayer.

Four

DOWNTOWN

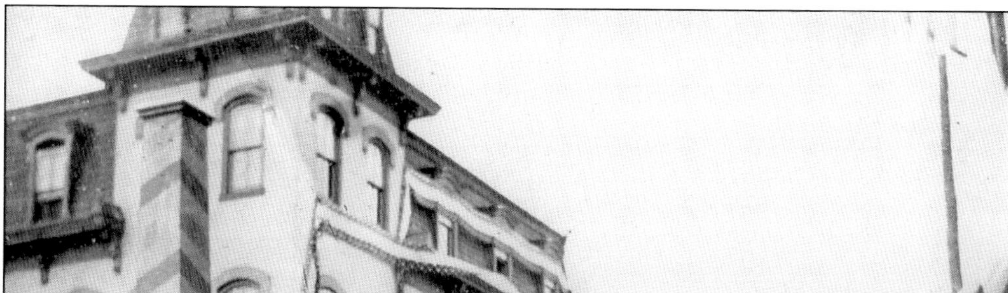

The new Gamble Hotel was ready to open on April 1, 1877. It was built by Joseph Gaus and run by his younger brother Andrew. Being close to the river made it popular with raftsmen who came in to eat and drink but would return to their arks for sleeping. In 1913, the hotel was under the proprietorship of the Jaffe brothers. Rates were $1.50 to $2.50 a day with rooms heated by steam and complete with electric lights, bells, and private baths.

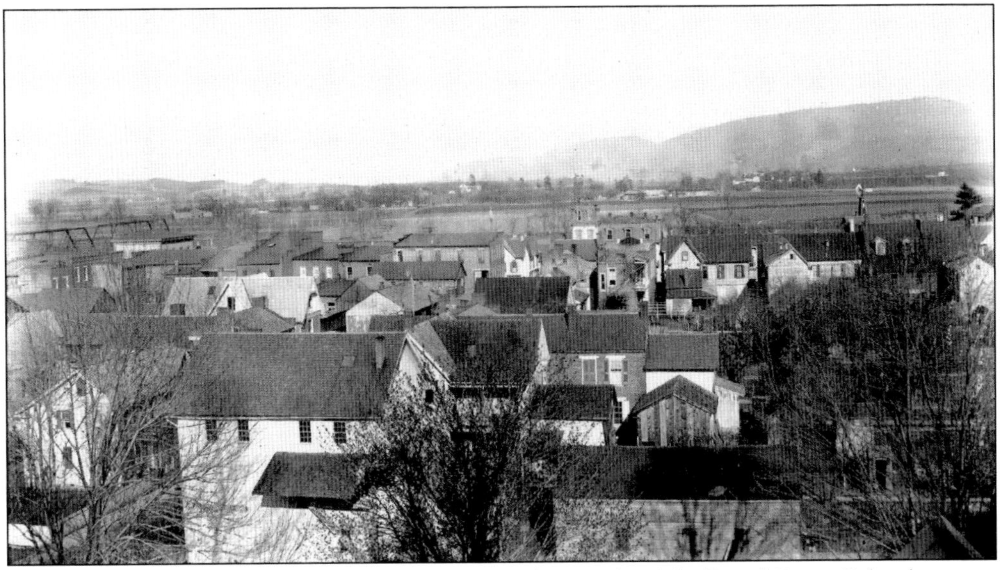

This is an easterly view of downtown as seen from the cupola of the Broad Street School prior to the 1917 fire. The canal was right below, and the white building to the left was a large granary. At the end of Smith Street is the Moss House and Gamble Hotel. The two bridges and Long Island are in the background as well as large homes and barns on the Antes Fort side. Note the water-pumping windmill to the right.

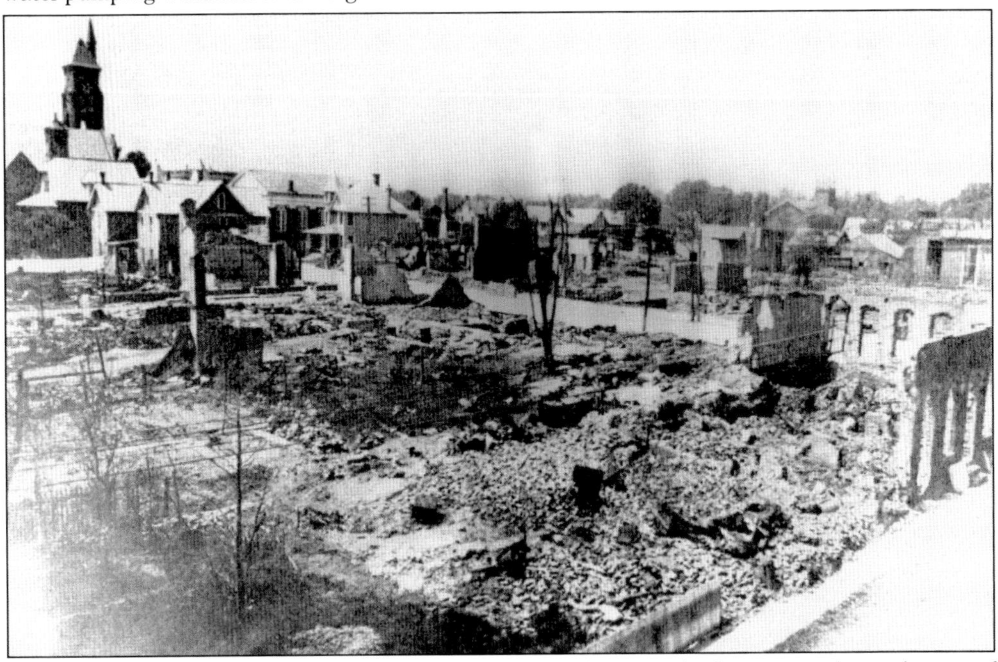

On Sunday morning December 9, 1917, the worst fire the town had ever seen burned most of the second block of South Main Street during a blizzard with temperatures near zero. Some 15 business buildings and houses and five barns burned before the fire was under control. The fire caused 32 families to lose their homes. This picture shows the remains of the Gamble Hotel from the rear at Smith Street. Lights and phones were out, leather fire hoses frozen, with hundreds of spectators and fire thieves at work.

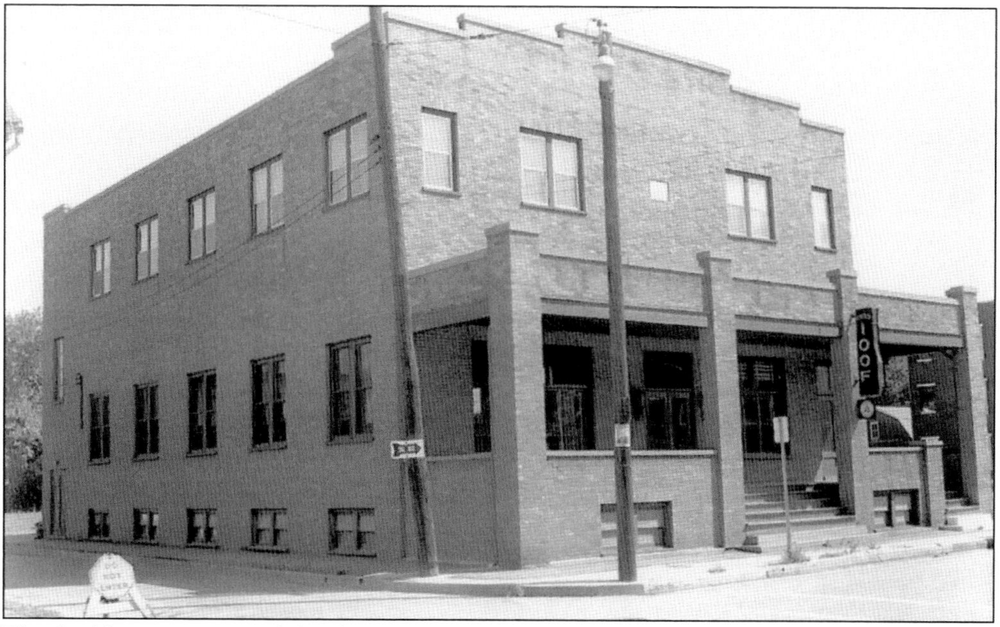

This building, constructed for the IOOF in 1928–1929, stands where the Gamble Hotel once stood. The organization dates back to before 1745 in England, and the first lodge in America was established in 1820 in Baltimore. The first lodge in Lycoming County was established in Jersey Shore on January 23, 1845, with H. H. Martin as Noble Grand. The 1883 fire on South Main Street destroyed all prior records, and the departure of the New York Central Railroad in 1931 was hard on this organization.

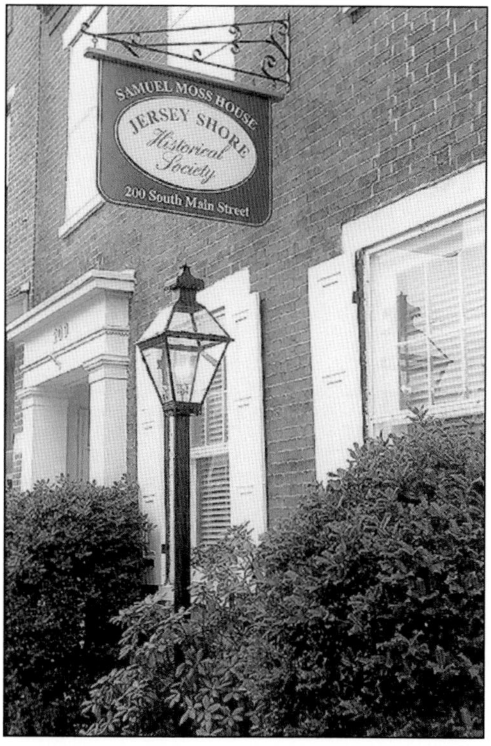

The Jersey Shore Historical Society was formed in 1963 with meetings first held in private homes. Then a room at the Broad Street School was used for museum purposes before acquiring the 1846 Samuel Moss House at the corner of Smith and South Main Streets in 1972. Samuel Moss was a merchant, mail carrier, and stagecoach driver on the Coudersport Pike.

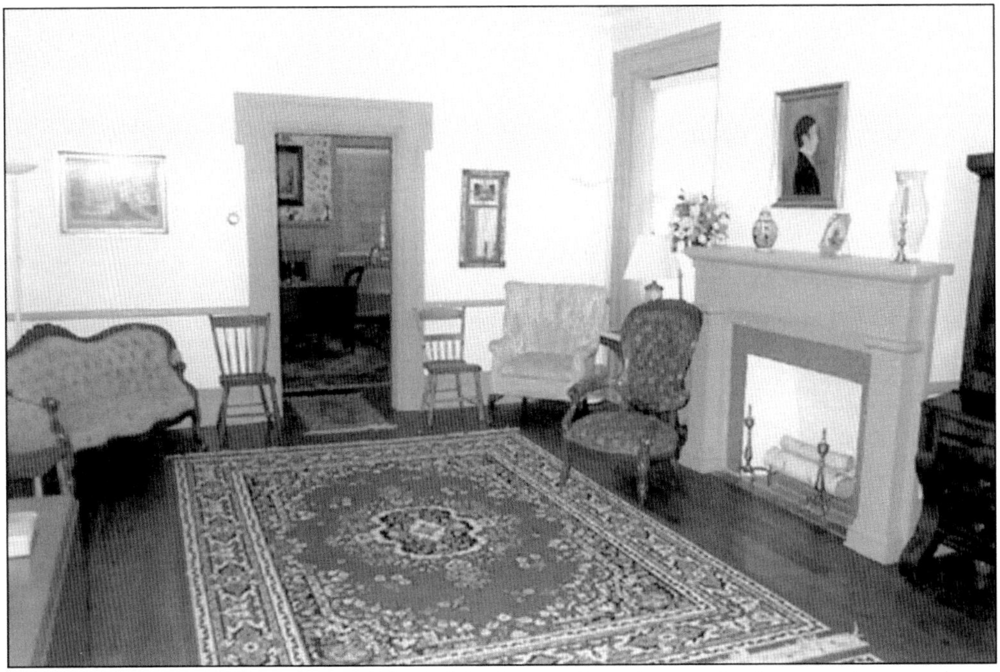

The deeply recessed doorway, typical of older Jersey Shore homes, leads into a foyer and two large rooms downstairs. These rooms have been little modified since 1846 and show three fireplaces, wide pine floors, original wood trim, Lincoln doors, locks, chair rails, and decorative ceilings. The first room one sees, called the "Waynesburg" room, was the parlor and the second room the kitchen.

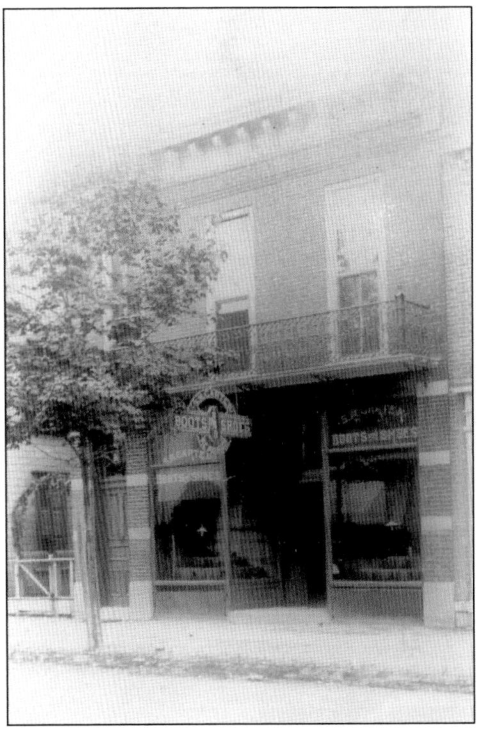

The Samuel M. Carter Shoe Store shared a common wall with the Samuel Moss house. Sam was a prominent merchant in Jersey Shore, conducting a shoe business for 36 years. The South Main Street fire of 1917 severely burned this building, but not the Moss House next door.

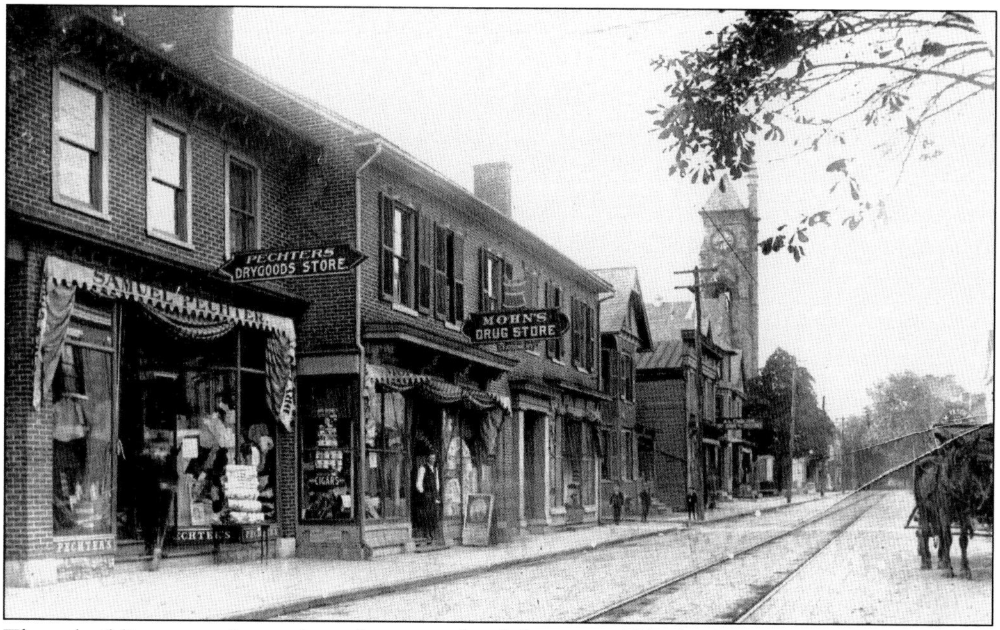

These buildings were located on the east side of the second block of South Main Street before the fire of 1917. The first building housed Zettle's Bakery and Sam Pechter's Drygoods Store, followed by the large brick Dr. Uriah Reed Building, which housed Mohn's Drug and Stationery Store and a millenary shop. Around the corner and on the alley was a set of apartments known as "the Seven Kitchens," and across the alley English's brick home and store followed by Lewis Probst's Meat Market.

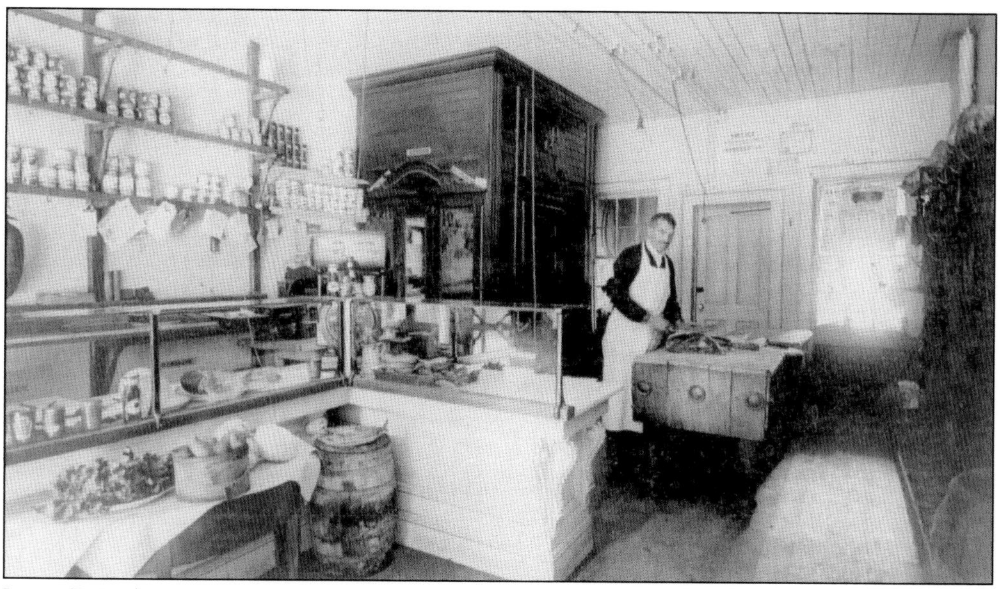

Lewis E. Probst's Meat Market at 229 South Main Street began before 1896 and operated until the flood of 1936. After being closed for 40 years, Dale and Carolyn Wolfanger purchased the market and restored it to its near original appearance. The store opened on November 21, 1977, as Dale's Market "the Meating Place." In 1980, Paul Mays ran the business, and Erv Rauch purchased the place in 1985.

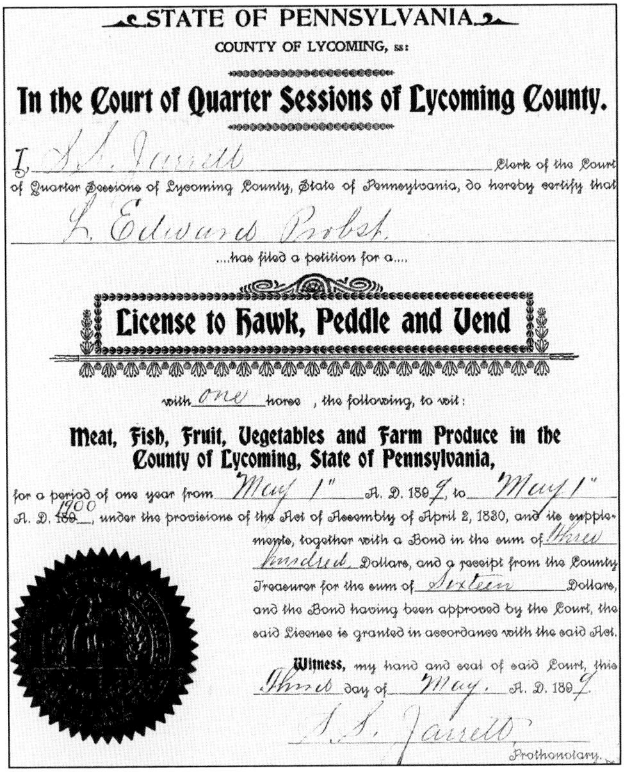

STATE OF PENNSYLVANIA

COUNTY OF LYCOMING, ss:

In the Court of Quarter Sessions of Lycoming County.

I, S. S. Jarrett Clerk of the Court of Quarter Sessions of Lycoming County, State of Pennsylvania, do hereby certify that L. Edward Probst,

...has filed a petition for a....

License to Hawk, Peddle and Vend

with one horse, the following, to wit:

Meat, Fish, Fruit, Vegetables and Farm Produce in the County of Lycoming, State of Pennsylvania,

for a period of one year from May 1st A. D. 1899, to May 1st A. D. 1900, under the provisions of the Act of Assembly of April 2, 1830, and its supplements, together with a Bond in the sum of Three hundred Dollars, and a receipt from the County Treasurer for the sum of Sixteen Dollars, and the Bond having been approved by the Court, the said License is granted in accordance with the said Act.

Witness, my hand and seal of said Court, this Third day of May, A. D. 1899.

S. S. Jarrett, Prothonotary.

Shown here is Lewis Probst's 1899 "License to Hawk, Peddle and Vend" with one horse: meat, fish, fruit, vegetables, and farm produce in the county of Lycoming, State of Pennsylvania, under Act of Assembly of April 2, 1830. His license required a $300 bond.

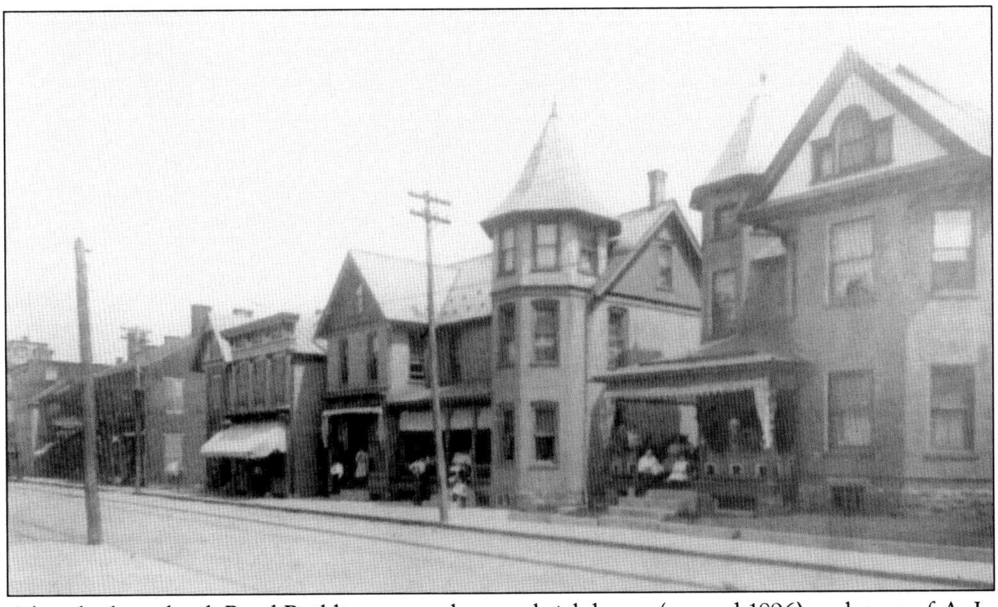

After the large brick Reed Building came the new brick home (around 1896) and store of A. L. English. The house was complete with lights, central heat, and hot and cold running water. In 1856, he was paid $21 a year for tending the town clock in the steeple of the Presbyterian church across the street. Following English was the Probst Market and home and the Presbyterian parsonage that replaced the Robert McGowan home at this site. The 1917 fire burned all buildings up to the Probst home.

The first Presbyterian church in the area was built on Pine Creek near the Tiadaghton Elm in 1792. From here they joined the Baptists in building a more substantial church at the corner of Broad and Seminary Streets in 1832. In 1850, they built this church on South Main Street across the alley from the water company today. It burned on September 19, 1893, from a fire that started in an adjoining building. In 1850, the population of the town was 608 including 112 families.

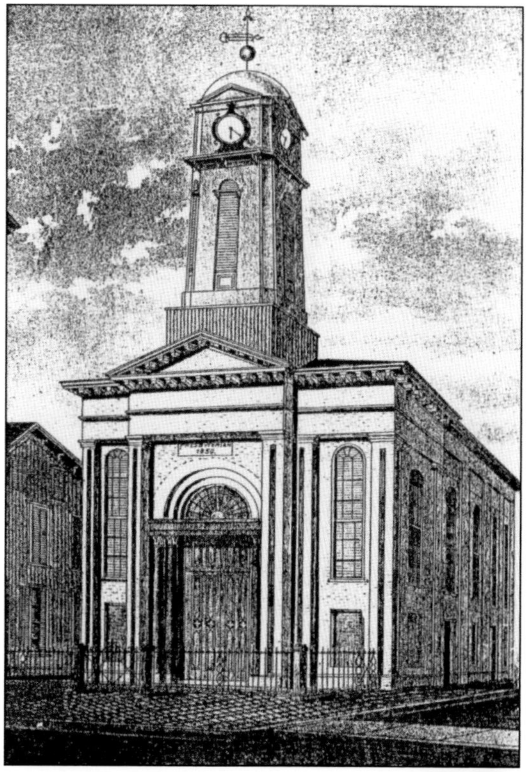

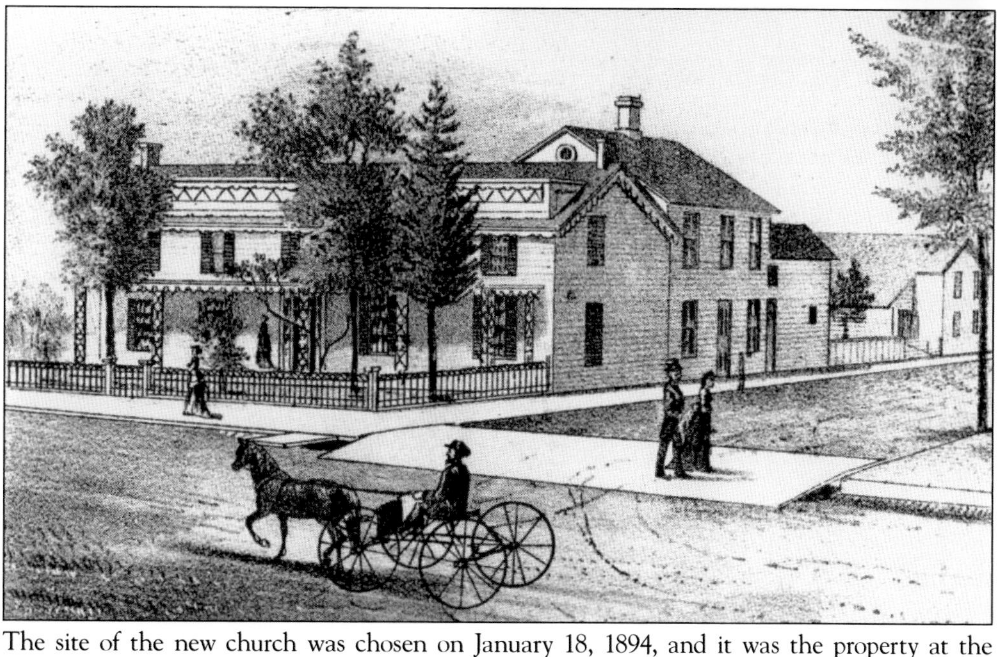

The site of the new church was chosen on January 18, 1894, and it was the property at the corner of Thompson and South Main Streets. L. L. Stearns had lived here before rafting his business to Williamsport. The decision to move downriver came with the town's rejections of the Philadelphia and Erie Railroad and the lumber industry. In 1872, Dr. M. Koenig was living in a house where the Masonic temple was built on Allegheny Street but later moved to this location.

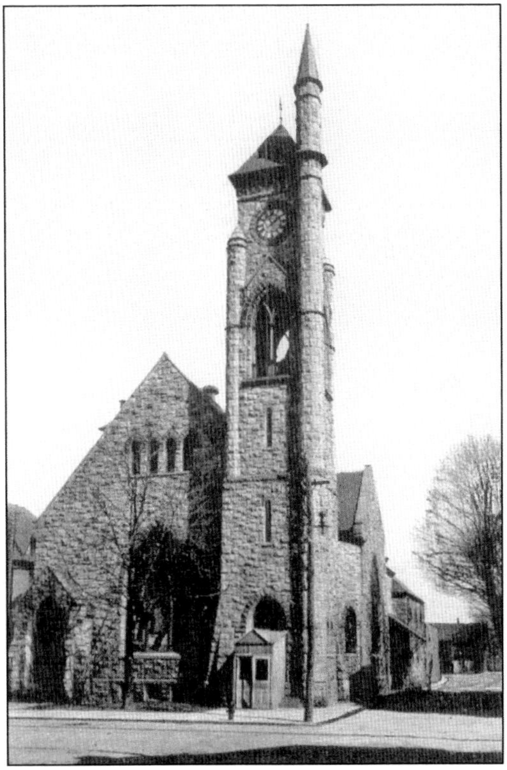

The cornerstone of this new Presbyterian church was laid on September 12, 1894, and the church was dedicated on July 14, 1895. The total cost of church and furnishings was $35,000. This Gothic structure, made of sandstone, has a seating capacity of about 700 with oak pews arranged in amphitheater form.

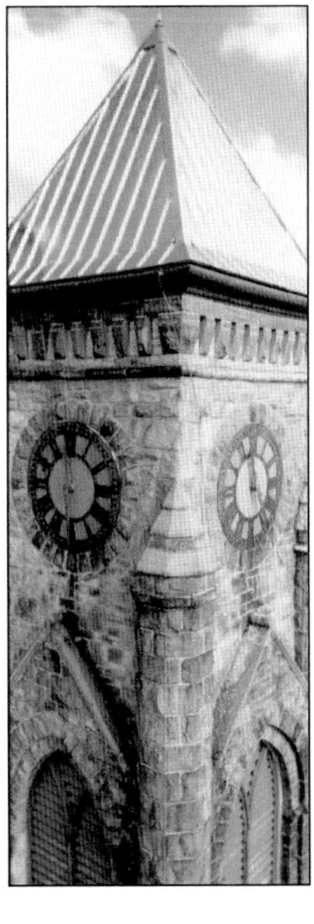

This photograph shows the tower of the Presbyterian church from 60 feet above the street. It is 16 feet square and rises 102 feet. The large hands on the clock faces are made of wood.

The Borough of Jersey Shore paid $625 for placing a clock in the tower of this church. The clock was purchased from the E. Howard Watch Company of Boston on September 3, 1895. It began operation on November 12, 1905. The winding and care of the clock was given to W. W. Davis at a salary of $25 a year. In 1854, borough council levied a special tax for the purchase of the first town clock, which was placed in the tower of the former Presbyterian church.

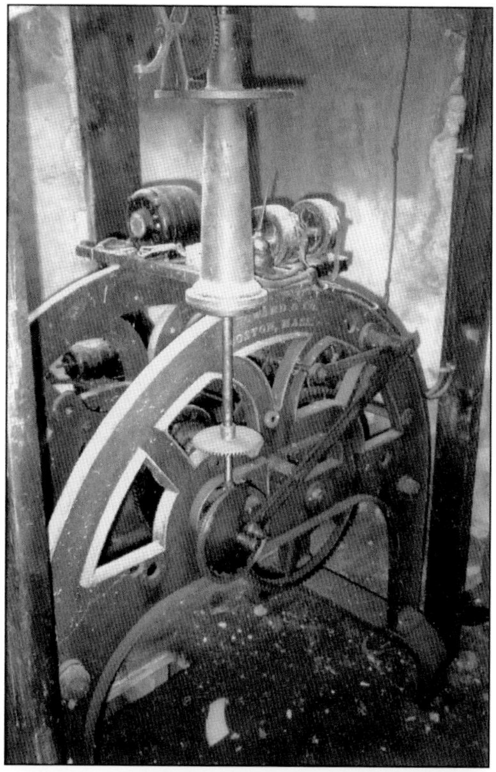

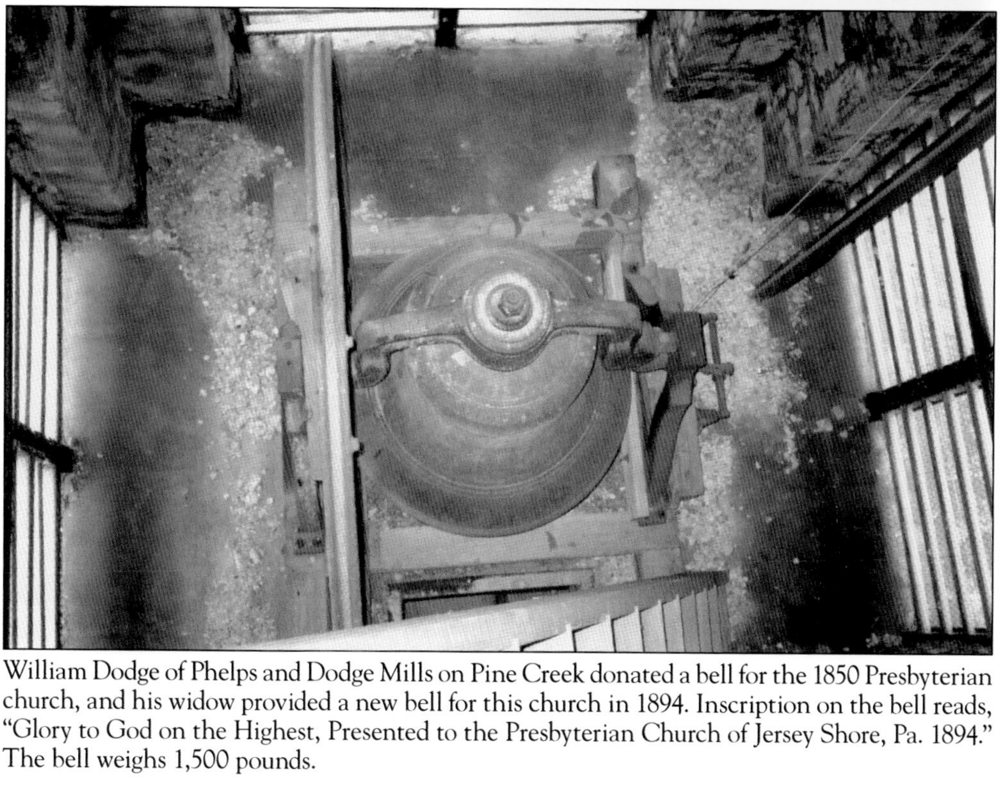

William Dodge of Phelps and Dodge Mills on Pine Creek donated a bell for the 1850 Presbyterian church, and his widow provided a new bell for this church in 1894. Inscription on the bell reads, "Glory to God on the Highest, Presented to the Presbyterian Church of Jersey Shore, Pa. 1894." The bell weighs 1,500 pounds.

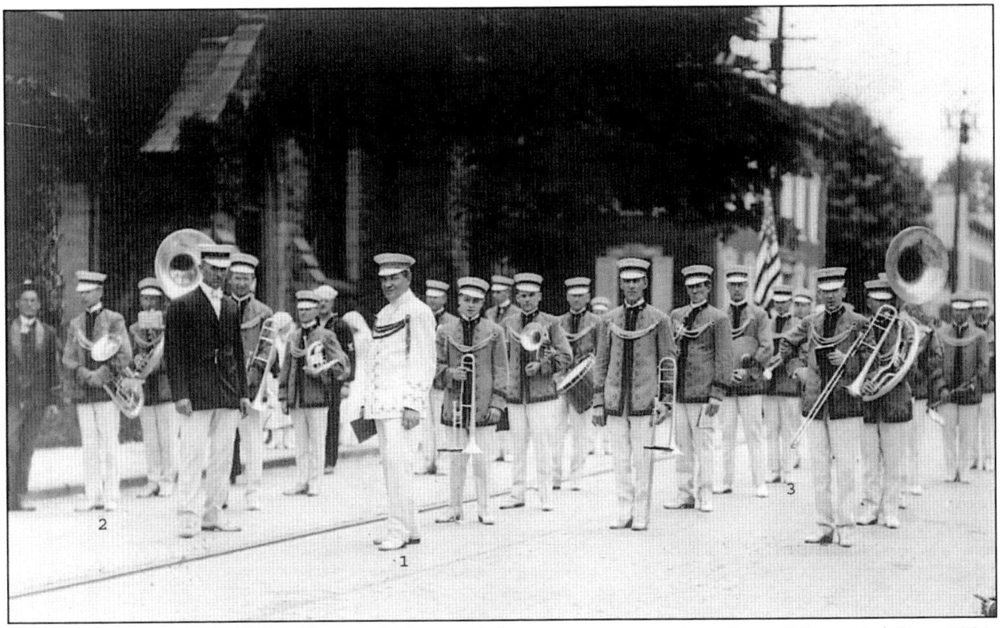

The New York Central Band rests in front of the Presbyterian church on Memorial Day 1921. Frank Schoendorfer was the director and his two sons, Carl and Frank, are in the picture. The large brick structure beyond the church was built by Alexander Smith for Samuel Humes in 1852. It was a combination home and store. Humes was a director of the Jersey Shore National Bank and the Jersey Shore Bridge Company. He also served as postmaster for a time.

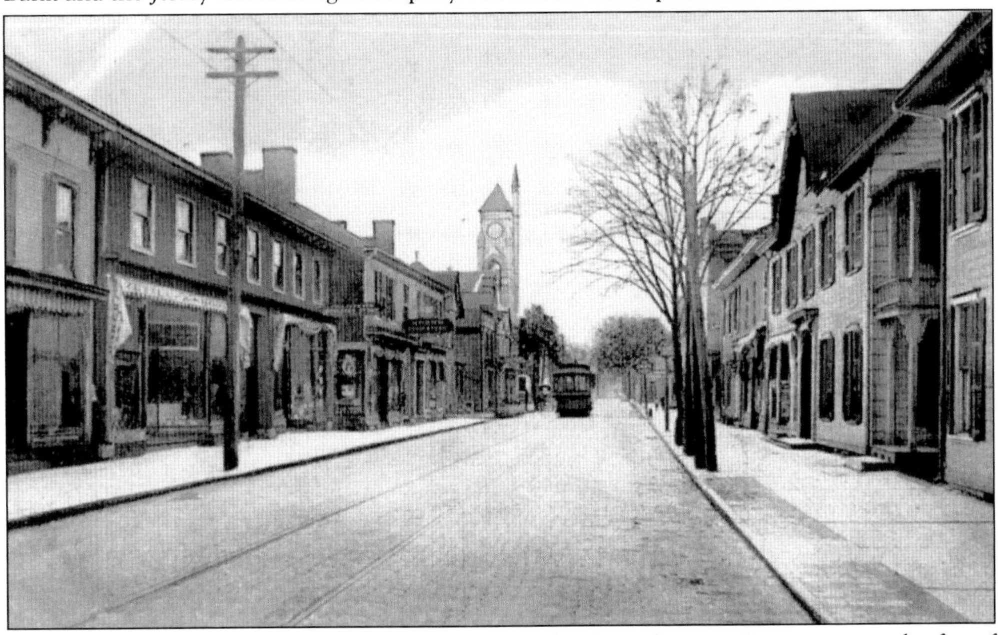

This is a view of the buildings that lined the west side of South Main Street prior to the fire of 1917. Most everything in this block burned. The first house on the right was the John Kelchner residence followed by Sam Henry's home and tailor shop. Next was an apartment building and McCullough's store, where the fire began on that cold December night in 1917. Beyond this is the opera house, or former Presbyterian church that partially burned in 1893.

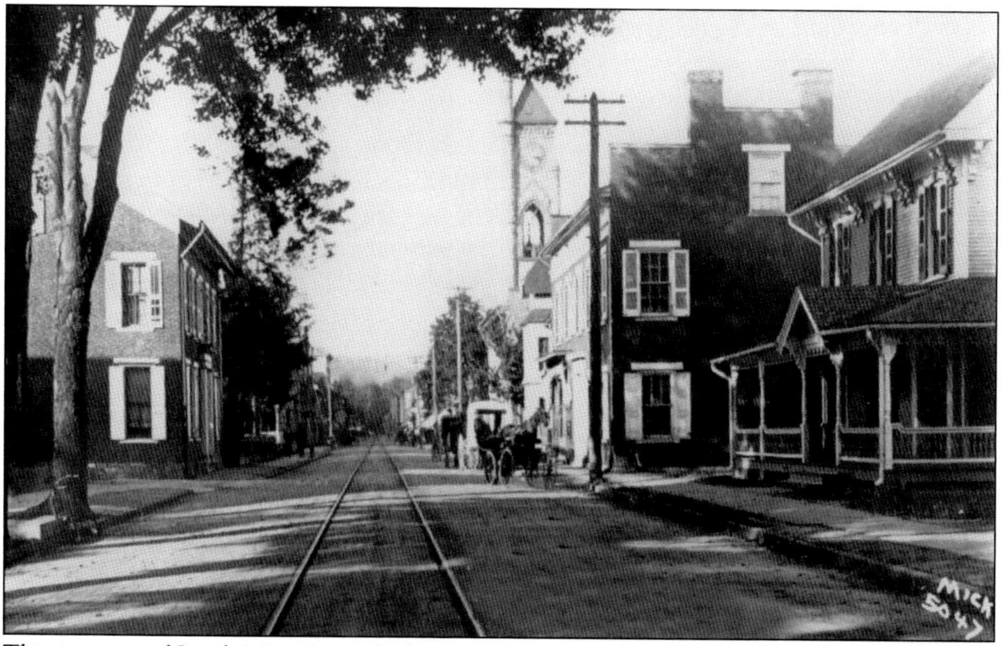

This is a view of South Main Street looking north toward Thompson Street and the square prior to the fire of 1917. The home to the left was that of Thomas Waddle, and down the left side was the Seeley home and Crawford Hotel with the old Blackwell store (built in 1854) owned at this time by Gheen and Spigelmyer. A major fire in August 1857 threatened the Waddle home when the stables of Brown and Ramsey, Waddle, and Gamble burned. "The groans of the poor animals were heart-rendering."

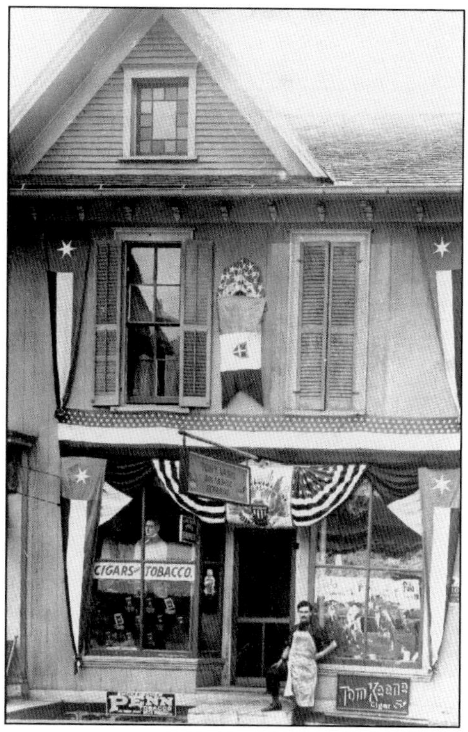

On the south side of the 1850 Presbyterian church was the home of Alexander Brown. He was born in Ireland in 1836 and came to America in 1847, establishing a shoe business in 1856 and a livery business in 1863. This 1912 photograph shows Tony Vairo standing in front of his shoe business, which was located in the right half of Brown's house. Tony immigrated from Felitto, Italy, in 1910 and was a likeable, hard-working, highly skilled craftsman who made many friends here in Jersey Shore.

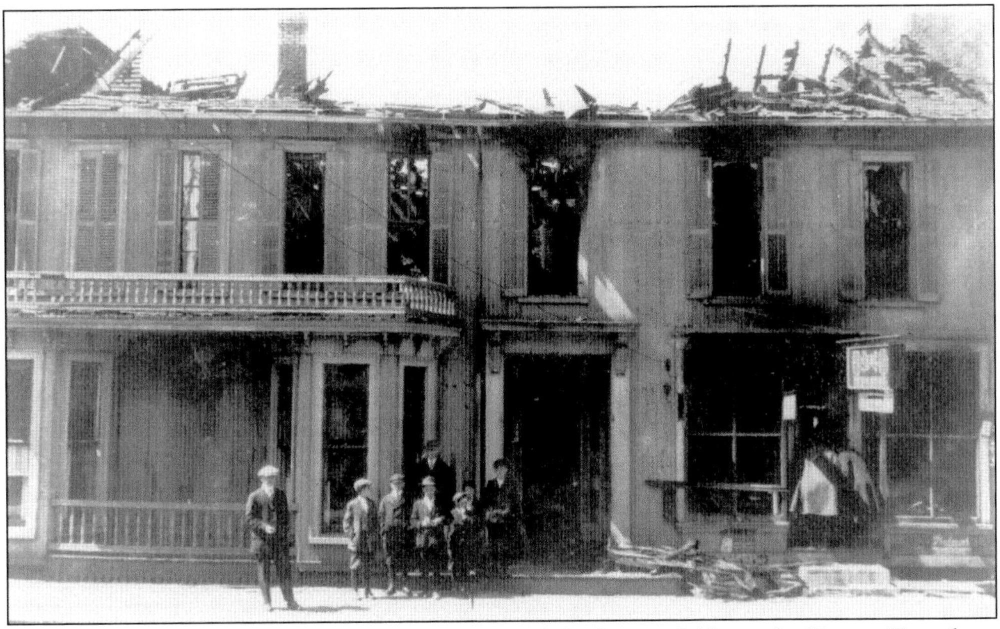

In 1913, a fire destroyed Tony Vairo's shoe shop and the home of Alexander Brown. From here Vairo moved his business down the street to the Reed block and was burned out again in the fire of 1917. He then had a shop at the corner of South Main and Locust Streets. In 1946, Bill Sechrist moved Vairo's shop from 135 Market Street to 115 South Broad Street. The business was taken over by his son Charles in 1950.

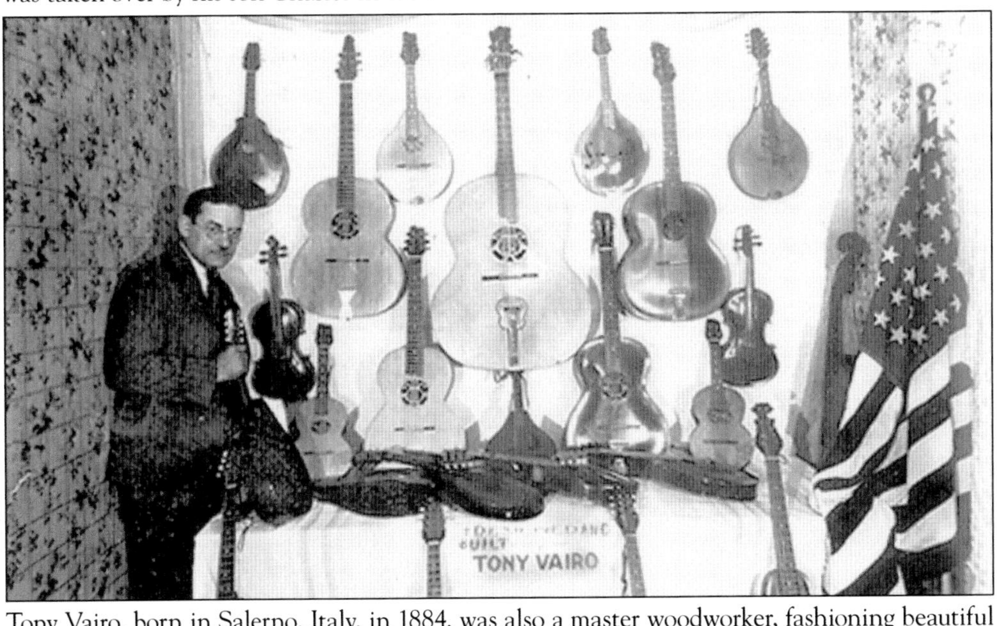

Tony Vairo, born in Salerno, Italy, in 1884, was also a master woodworker, fashioning beautiful furniture and constructing 150 violins, guitars, cellos, and mandolins. He learned the skill by watching such craftsmen in Italy and getting ideas from books. Vairo was also a good musician, learning to play the clarinet, flute, baritone horn, and cornet and later the violin and mandolin. His favorite wood for mending string instruments was well-seasoned walnut, which he obtained from old furniture.

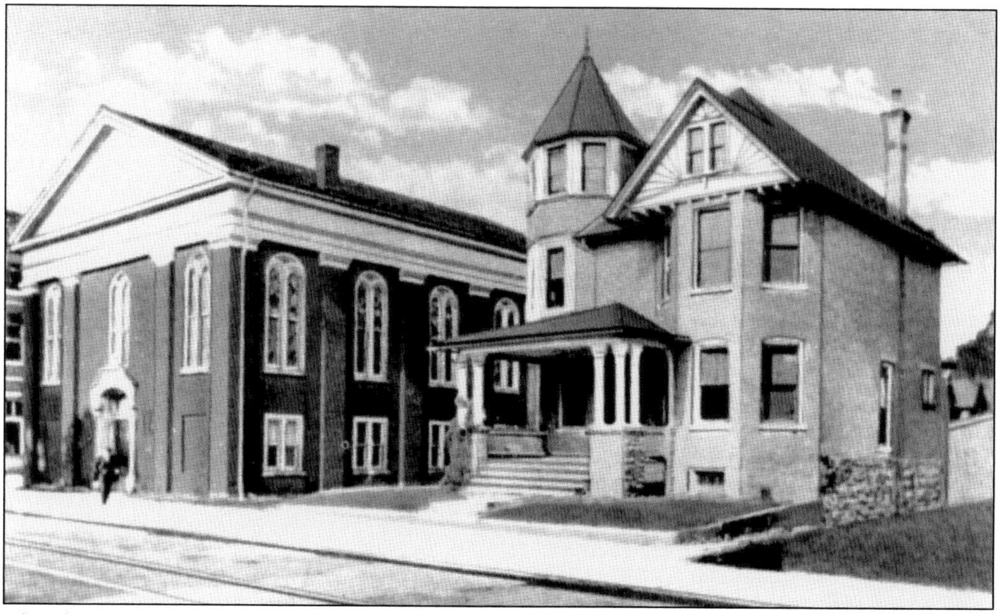

The charter for the Methodist Episcopal Church of Jersey Shore was granted in September 1843. Construction began in 1845, and the dedication was in 1847. Timber for the building was floated down Pine Creek from English Center. The church parsonage was built and furnished in 1900 at a cost of $5,000.

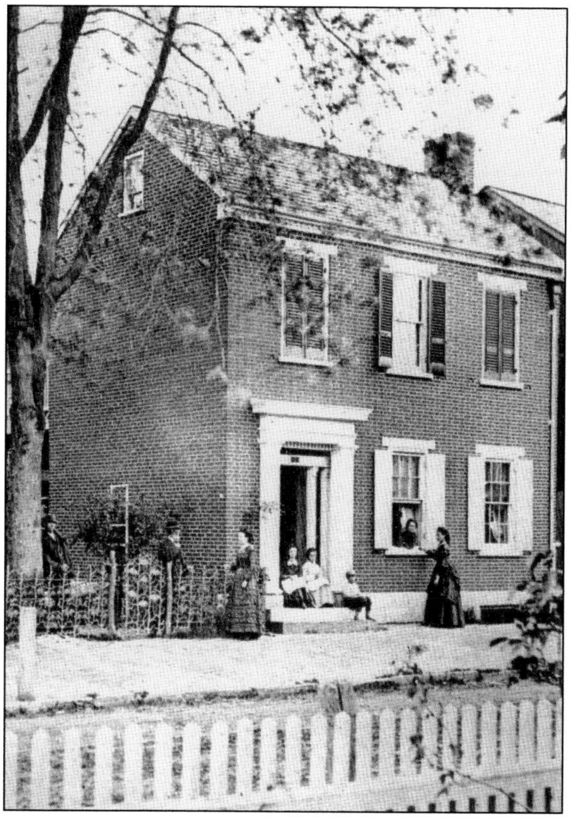

This was the home of George P. Nice. It stood where the Methodist parsonage was built. George owned the Excelsior Carriage Works, and his son, John F. Nice, was an early Jersey Shore photographer or daguerreotypist.

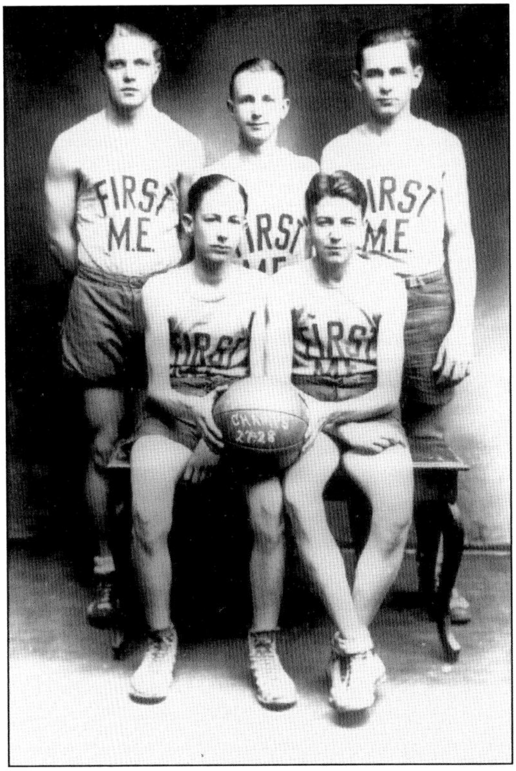

These were the Methodist church basketball champs of 1927–1928 that defeated the Presbyterian players from across the street. Pictured here from left to right are as follows: (first row) Charles Crist and Hilton Campbell; (second row) Charles Farley, Cliff Messiner, and Roy Hartzel.

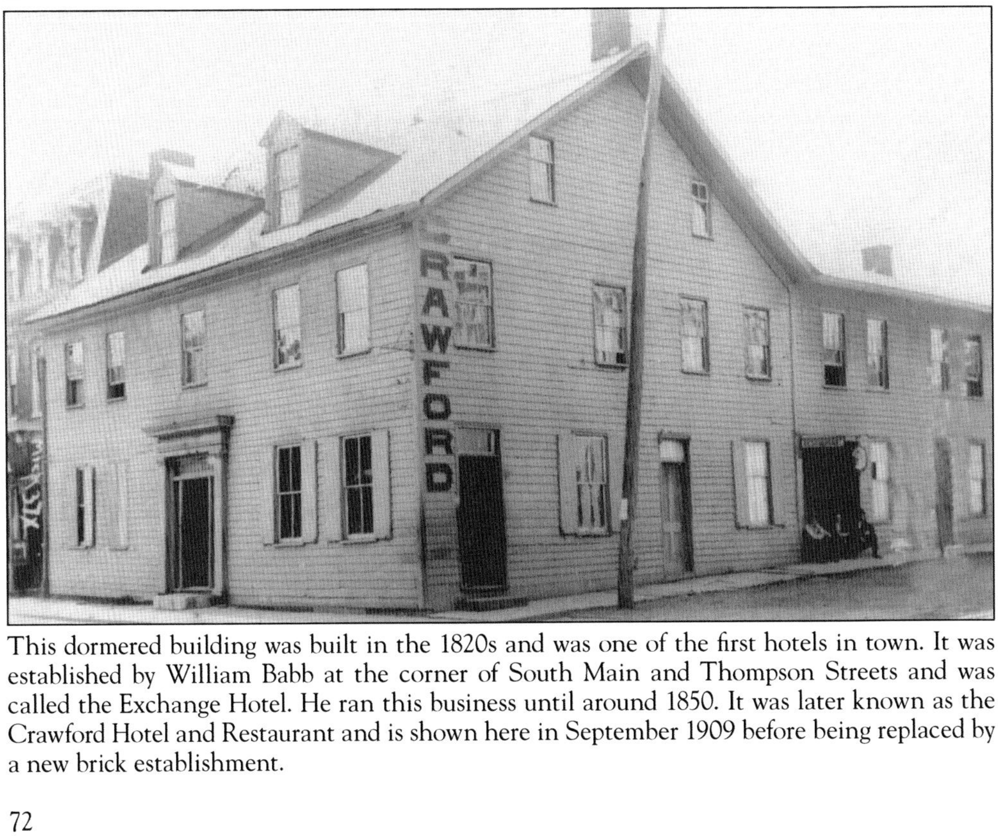

This dormered building was built in the 1820s and was one of the first hotels in town. It was established by William Babb at the corner of South Main and Thompson Streets and was called the Exchange Hotel. He ran this business until around 1850. It was later known as the Crawford Hotel and Restaurant and is shown here in September 1909 before being replaced by a new brick establishment.

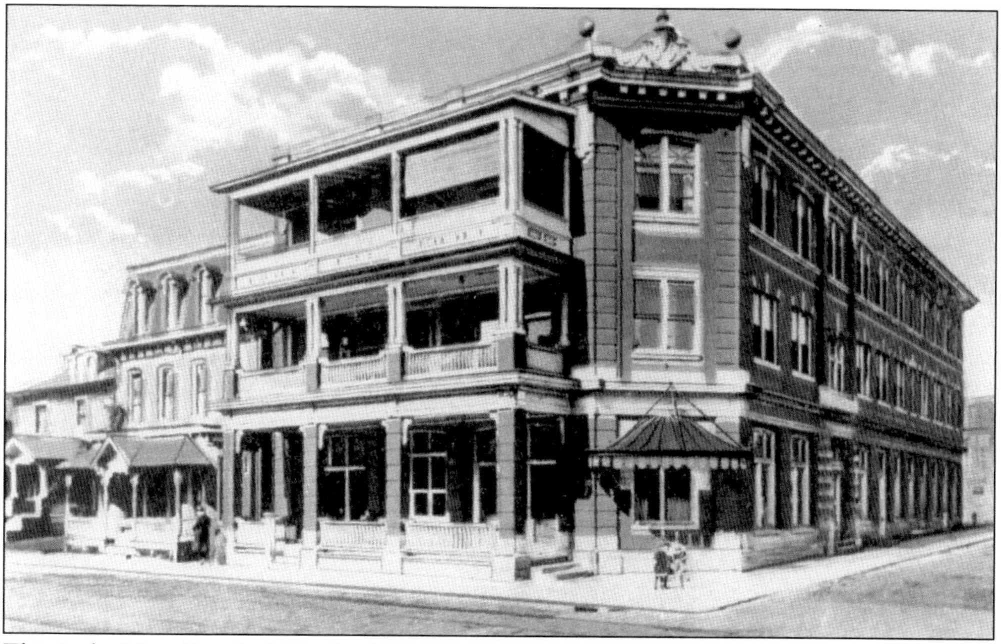

This is the New Crawford Hotel, which was built in 1910 and over the years was known as the Macklem and Hiller apartments. It burned in January 1974. The fired caused the destruction of 17 apartments, and 32 people were left homeless. The Seeley home is left of the hotel, and the home of the first public library is next to it. The house that stood on the library site was moved by horses to the corner of Cemetery Street and South Lincoln Avenue where it stands today.

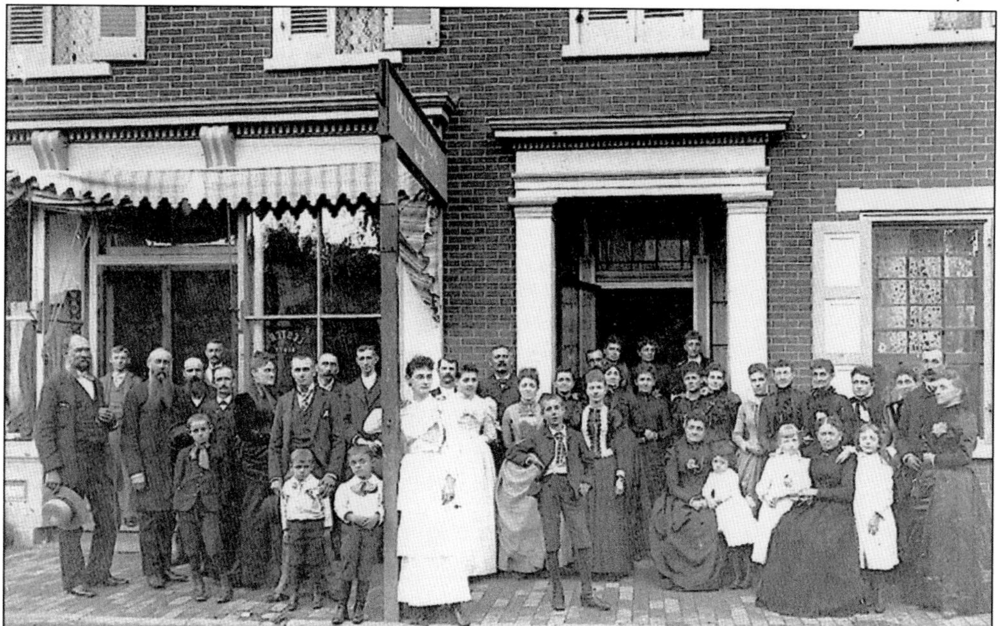

This building has been used as a store longer than any other in Jersey Shore. The land was purchased by John Webb in 1836. He later built the structure and operated a store here until 1885. Over the years, Uriah Reed, Samuel Junod, Miles Sallada (as seen here in 1890), and John Brownlee ran various businesses out of this building.

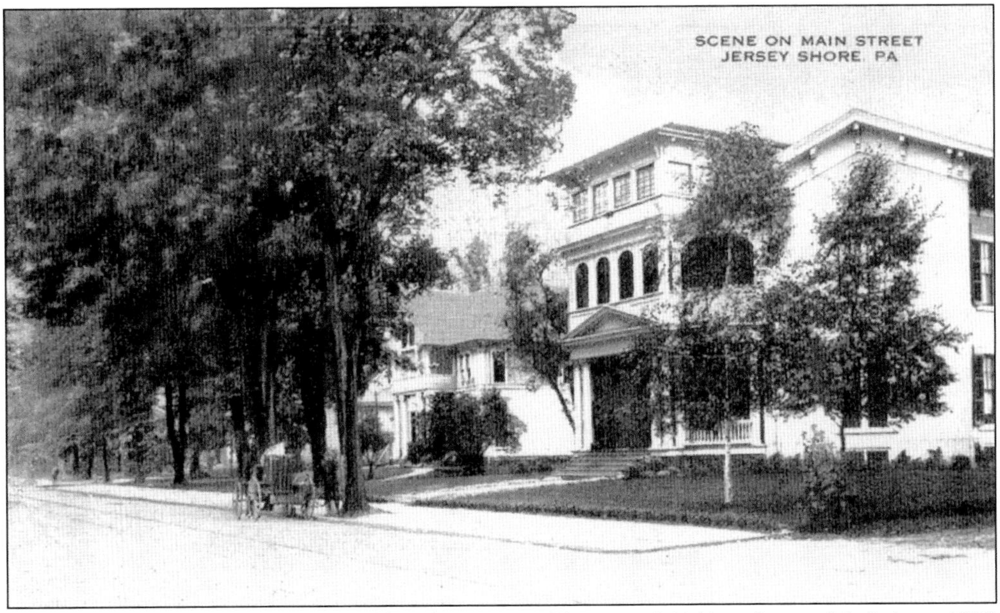

This home was built for the Honorable John A. Gamble around 1860 and remodeled about 1900 by the Humes family. It has also been known as the Krom/Collins place. John was admitted to the bar in 1833 and began law practice in Jersey Shore in 1836. He served as a member of the state legislature from 1842 to 1855 and returned to Jersey Shore. He became president judge of the Lycoming District in 1868 and moved to Williamsport.

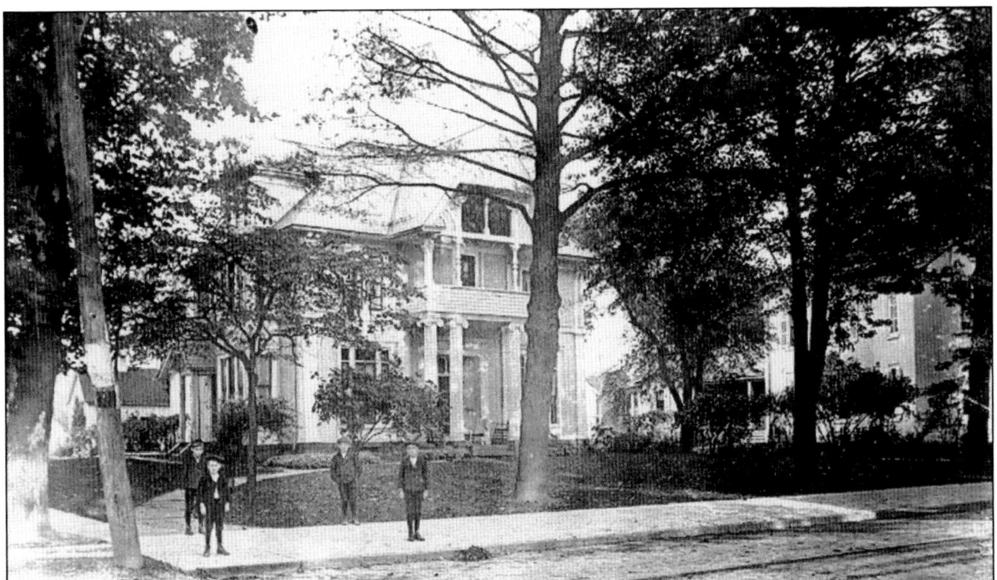

This home started in the early 1850s as a single-story Greek Revival dwelling built for a well-known surveyor and civil engineer named Alexander H. McHenry. It was greatly altered around 1885 by the second owner, Dr. D. H. Cline. Many area surveys of this area were produced by McHenry. He began his life's work in 1836 field surveying and became involved with the Fallbrook Railroad, the Jersey Shore Bank, and the gas company. He served in the Civil War. He died in Jersey Shore in 1892.

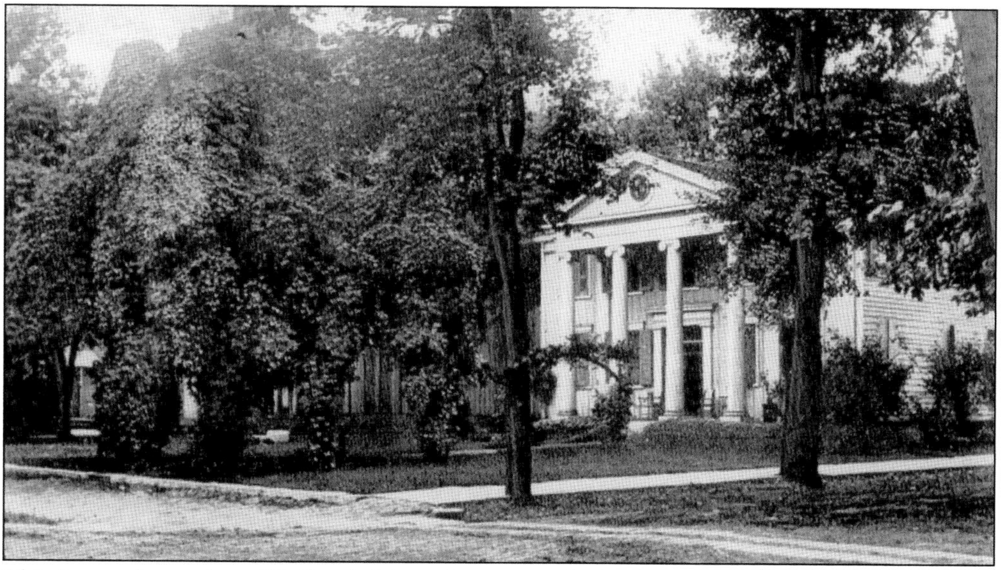

This house, located at 400 South Main Street, was built about 1845 for Mark Slonaker. He donated land for a new cemetery, which was laid out into 432 lots by A. H. McHenry. Dr. Uriah Reed donated 10 acres soon after. Cemetery Hill was called Mount Pleasant and would serve to replace the old Broad Street Cemetery, which later became Richmond Park. Mark's father, John, was a member of the first Jersey Shore Borough Council.

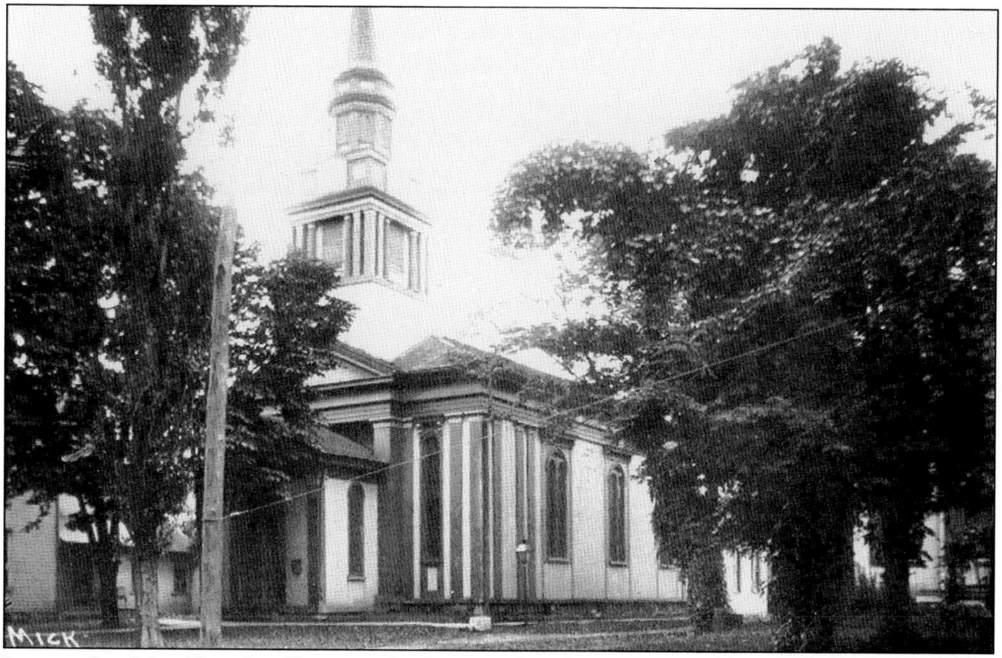

Just south of the Slonaker House is the Baptist church, which was dedicated on December 25, 1844. The work began on December 26, 1842, when Peter Bastress, Andrew Plotner, and Aaron Keyser broke a path through the snow on Bald Eagle Mountain south of Antes Fort to quarry stone for the foundation. Twenty other men soon joined them. A 625-pound bell was placed in the steeple in 1846 and removed in 1918 when the church was drastically altered from one of Colonial to Spanish architecture.

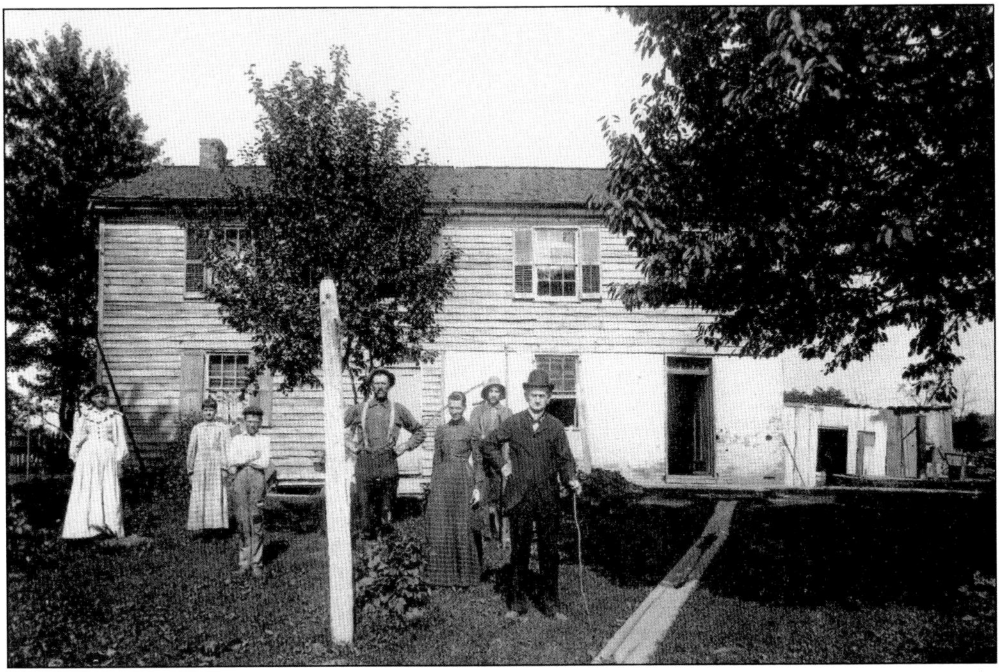

The old River Road runs through beautiful farm country to the Silver Bridge over Pine Creek. This farm, just outside Jersey Shore, belonged to the Morrisons in 1785, and afterward to Andrew Ferguson (1812), John Slonaker (1817), John Pfouts (1818), Rev. Joseph Stevens (1862), Asher Bubb (1919), and Robert M. Bubb (1949). The kitchen area is built of brick and may have been a tollhouse on the canal.

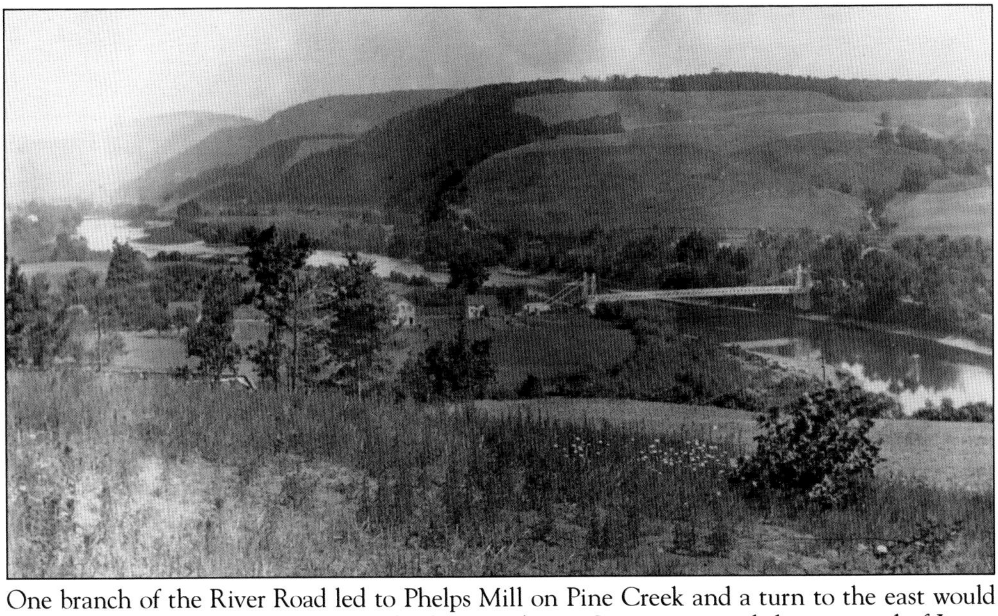

One branch of the River Road led to Phelps Mill on Pine Creek and a turn to the east would take one over this suspension bridge back into Glen or Stavertown and the west end of Jersey Shore. Since 1834, there have been at least 11 bridges built over the lower end of Pine Creek. A covered bridge was built at this site in 1857 by Anson Phelps and was replaced by this suspension bridge before 1889. It was 270 feet long and 16 feet wide and lasted until 1924.

Five

Beyond the River

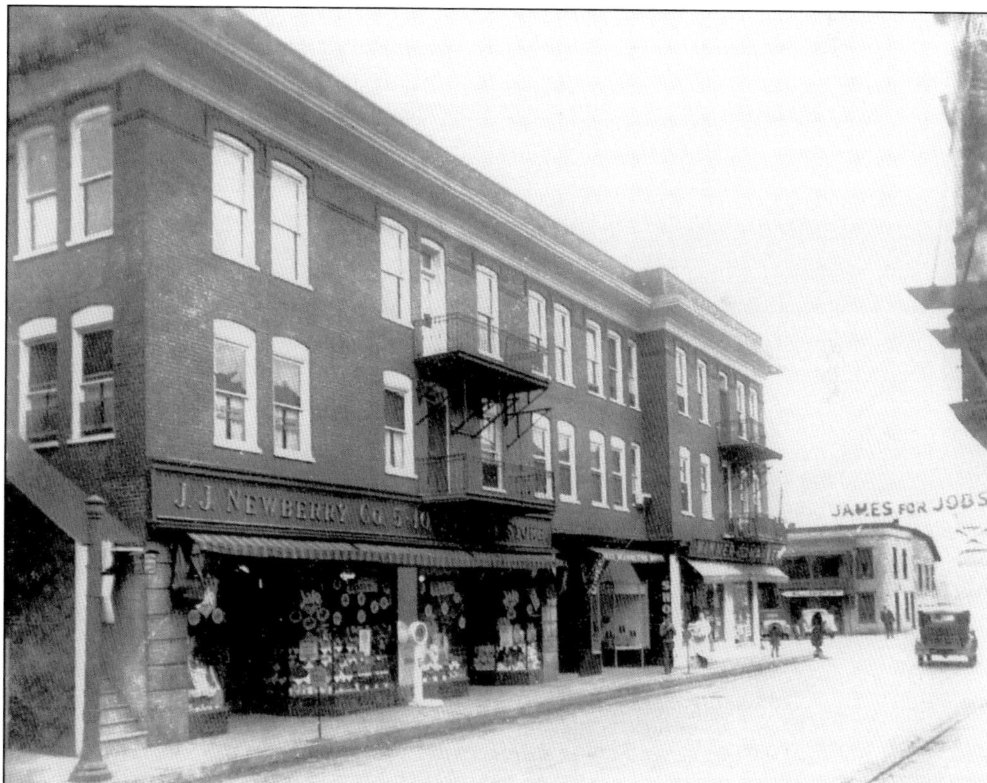

This large brick building at the square was known as the Mamolen Building, which replaced the Hepburn Building at this site around 1900. J. J. Newberry opened here in 1921 and replaced the 5¢ and 10¢ store run by Walter Muir. Next is the shoe store of Max Mamolen, who came to town in 1898 and established himself in the shoe business. Winner Meats is on the corner, and the old tollhouse and trolley building are across the square.

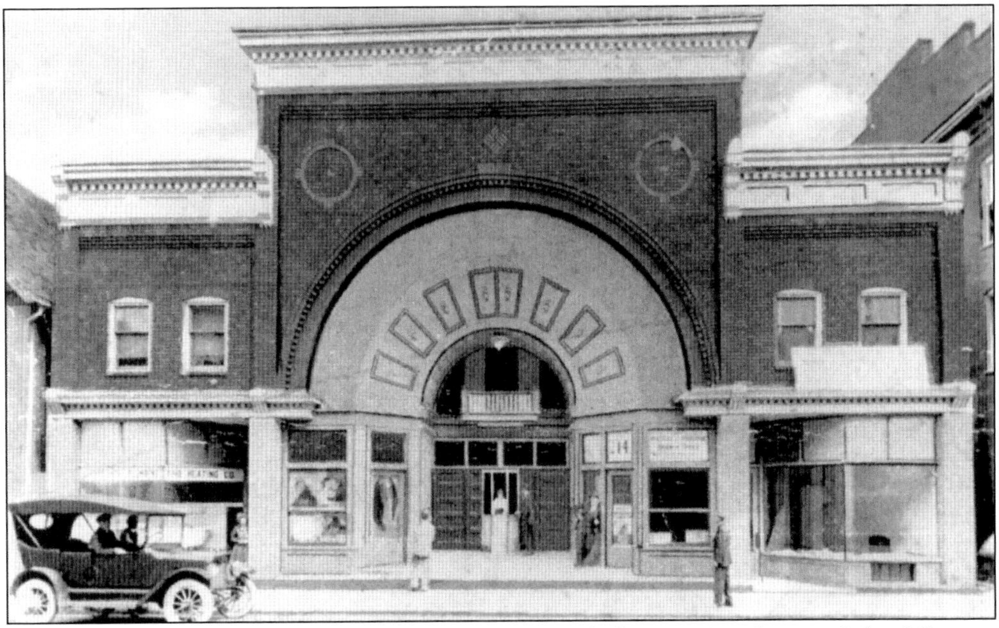

The Victoria Movie Theatre was built by Dr. S. E. Bickell in 1916 and opened the following year. Prior to this, the empty lot was occupied by Traveler's Cafe, and before that it was a small apple orchard. The theater seated 565 people. Raymond Tate managed this theater for years. A Saturday matinee, for the kids, would cost 10¢. Two features were run plus cartoons and a newsreel. An ice-cream parlor, called the Villa, was located here as well.

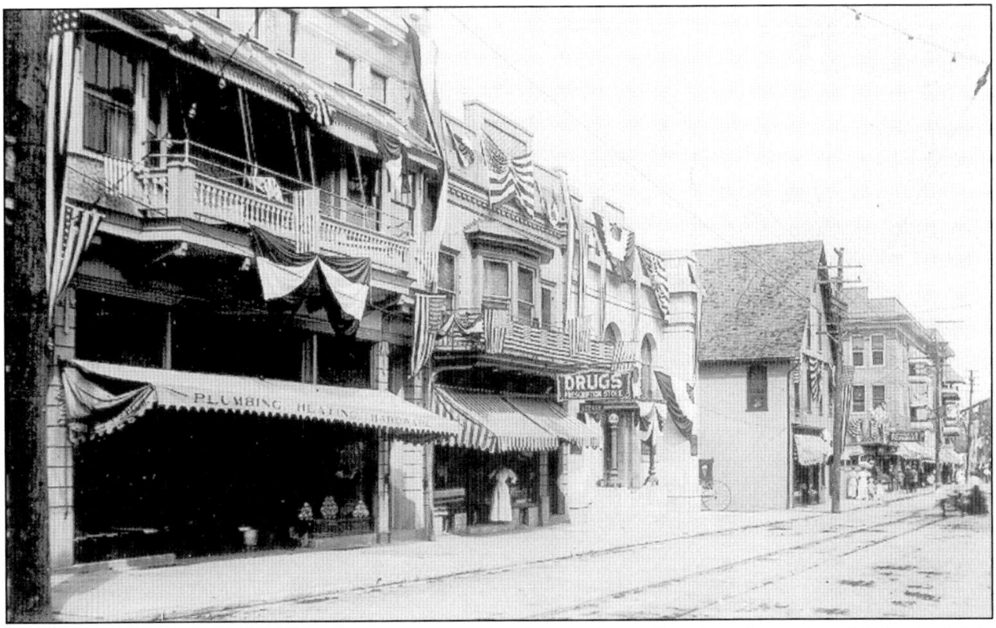

This picture, taken before the theater was built, shows Kerns Jewelry Store (established 1901); the National Bank, shown rebuilt after the 1910 fire; Nevins Drug Store (established 1883) at this time run by his son George; and the hardware store of Crowe and Stenner. The first electric clock in town was displayed at Kern's Jewelry August 23, 1928. The master clock for this area was at the Power and Light Company at Williamsport.

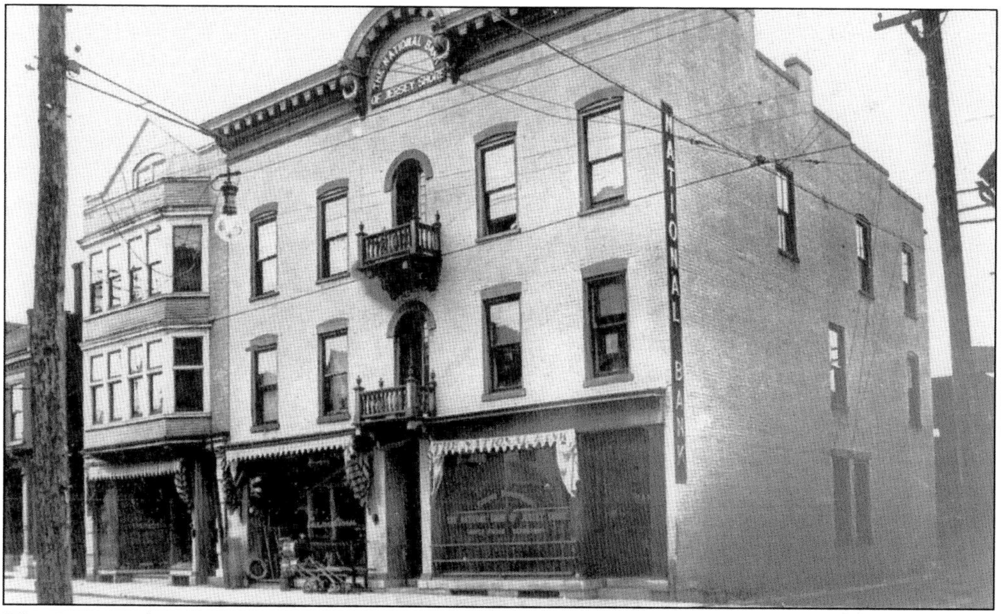

The National Bank of Jersey Shore began operation on March 12, 1902, in this building formerly operated as a millinery shop. The bank remodeled the building, but fire destroyed it on February 9, 1910, along with other structures seen here. In June 1927, this bank consolidated with the Jersey Shore Trust Company on Main Street, and a new Union National Bank was chartered on July 2, 1928. The first president was Daniel P. Miller, and the first account with the bank was that of Dr. P. A. Bay.

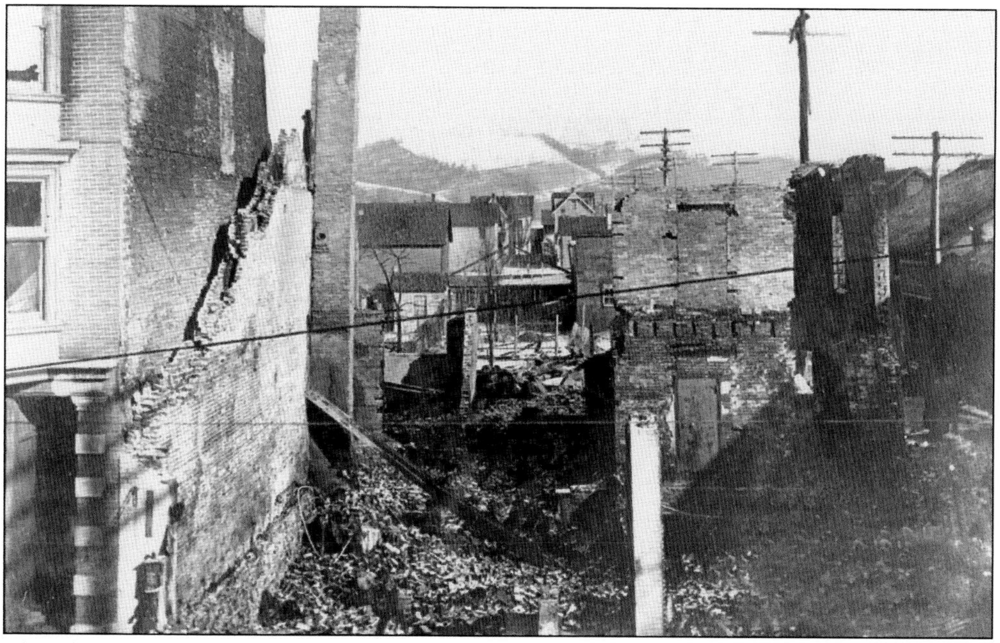

This photograph shows the aftermath of the bank fire of 1910. The site is where the bank stood with a view looking north toward Seminary Street. The bank vault door is visible in the center of the burned building. Nevins Drug Store, in the W. T. Ferrar building, is to the left. Three lives were lost in this fire.

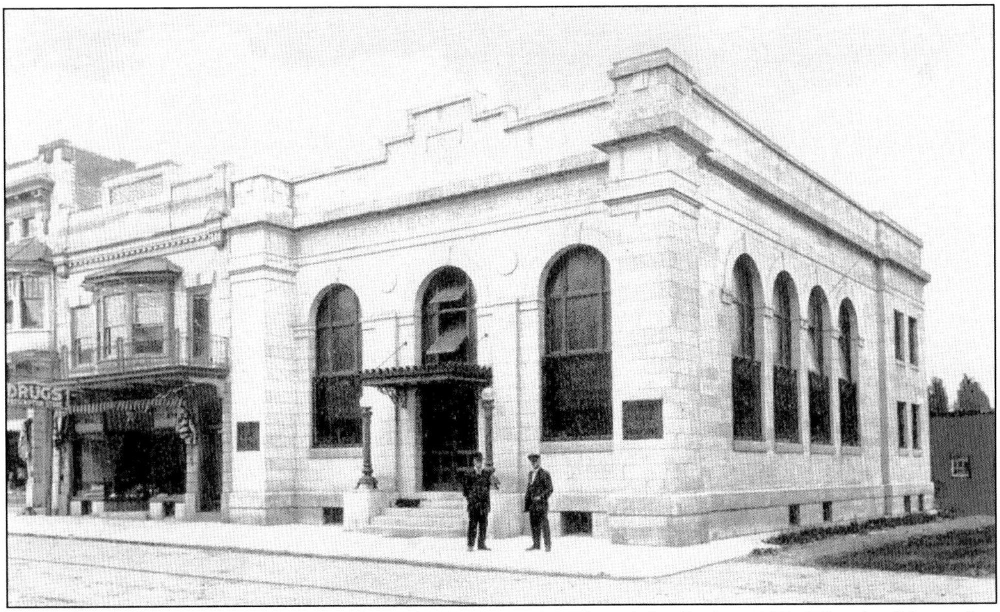

Construction of the new National Bank was completed on March 11, 1912. This building also housed the Union National Bank, which opened for business on July 2, 1928. Charter members included John G. Smith, J. P. Bower, Benjamin Atherton, and Dr. Samuel Carter. Danny Miller was its first president, followed by Benjamin Atherton and Dr. Samuel Carter. This bank merged with Commonwealth Bank and Trust Company in 1969.

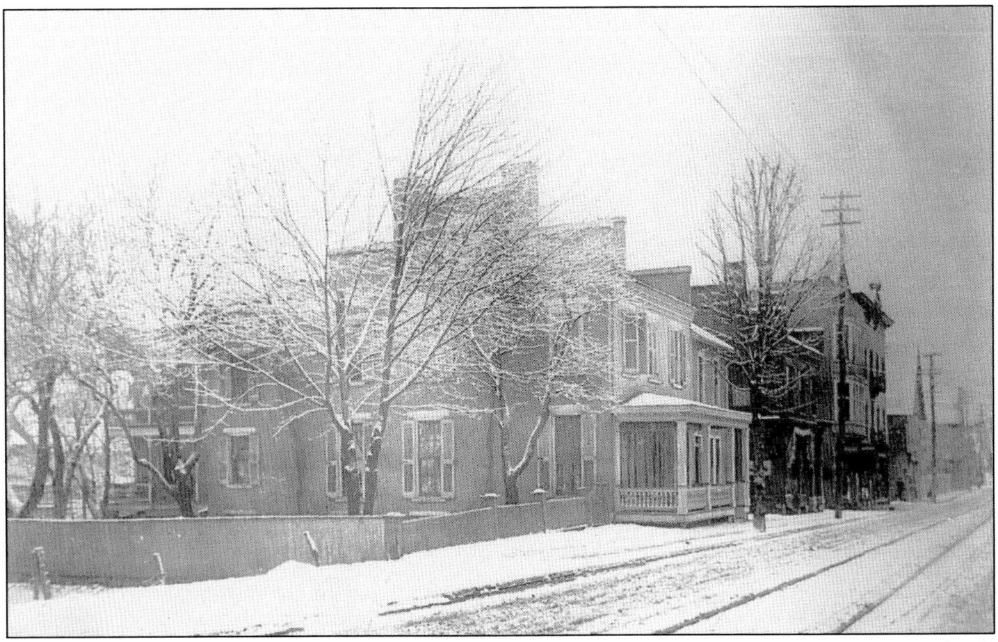

This is a view showing the north side of Allegheny Street from the canal. The large brick building was formerly the home of Peter D. Bricker, former Civil War soldier, lawyer, and mayor of Jersey Shore. On July 21, 1938, the federal government allotted $88,000 for the construction of a new post office building at this site. World War II postponed the construction for 22 years, but the new post office was finally built and dedicated on May 7, 1960.

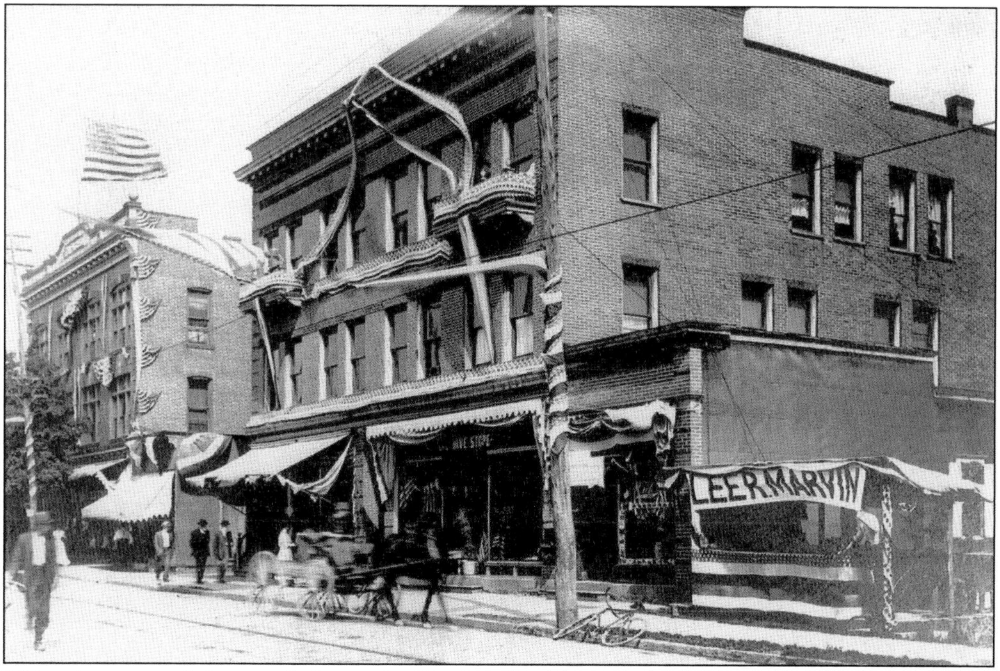

This view west of the canal shows the Patchen Building to the left and the Oechler Building soon after the beginning of the 1900s. These buildings housed many apartments, with stores on the first floor. The Oechler building burned on March 4, 1927, with the loss of the Blue and White Restaurant, the Men's Quality Shop, Star Grocery, Mick's Photo Shop, and five apartments. The Patchen building became known as the J. C. Penny Building in 1929 and was originally the site of the home of Rev. John H. Grier.

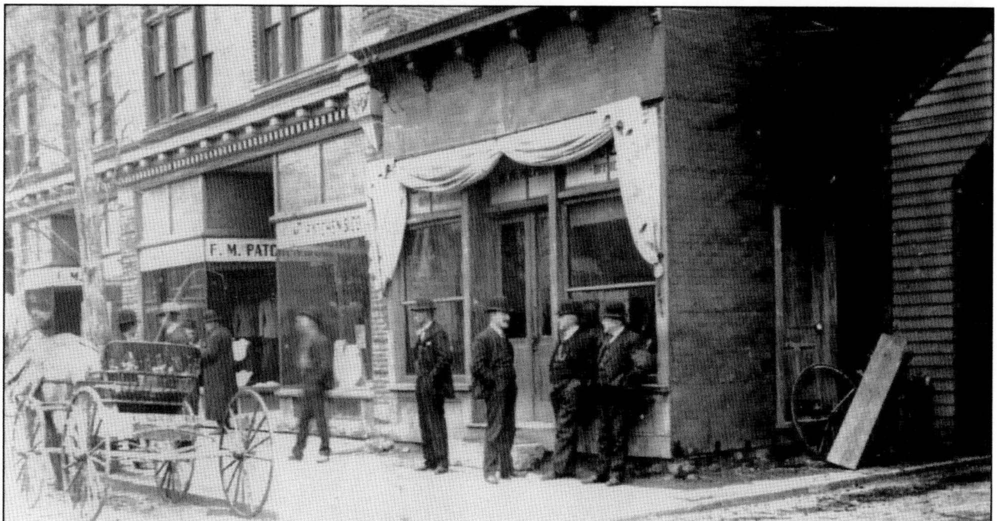

Between the Patchen and Oechler buildings was the livery and coal office of William H. Hepburn. Large sheds stored the coal as during canal days. In 1900, Hepburn built a large, three-story barn out back that he used as a livery stable. Here he kept carriages, spring wagons, and traps on the first floor, horses on the second, and hay and straw on the third. At this time, an old abandoned canal boat still laid in ruins along the canal.

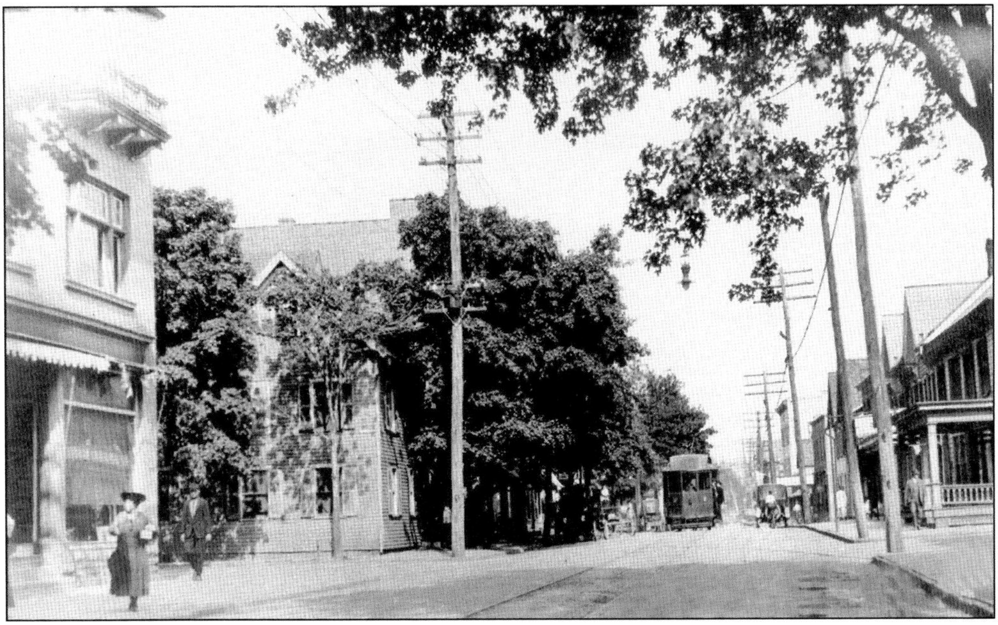

A trolley heads uptown near the corner of Allegheny and Broad Streets. The Charles King home occupied the corner until construction of the Herald Building in 1925. A corner of the Danny Miller Building shows to the left. The home of Andrew Gaus is on the corner to the right, followed by Ford's Restaurant and the Allegheny House.

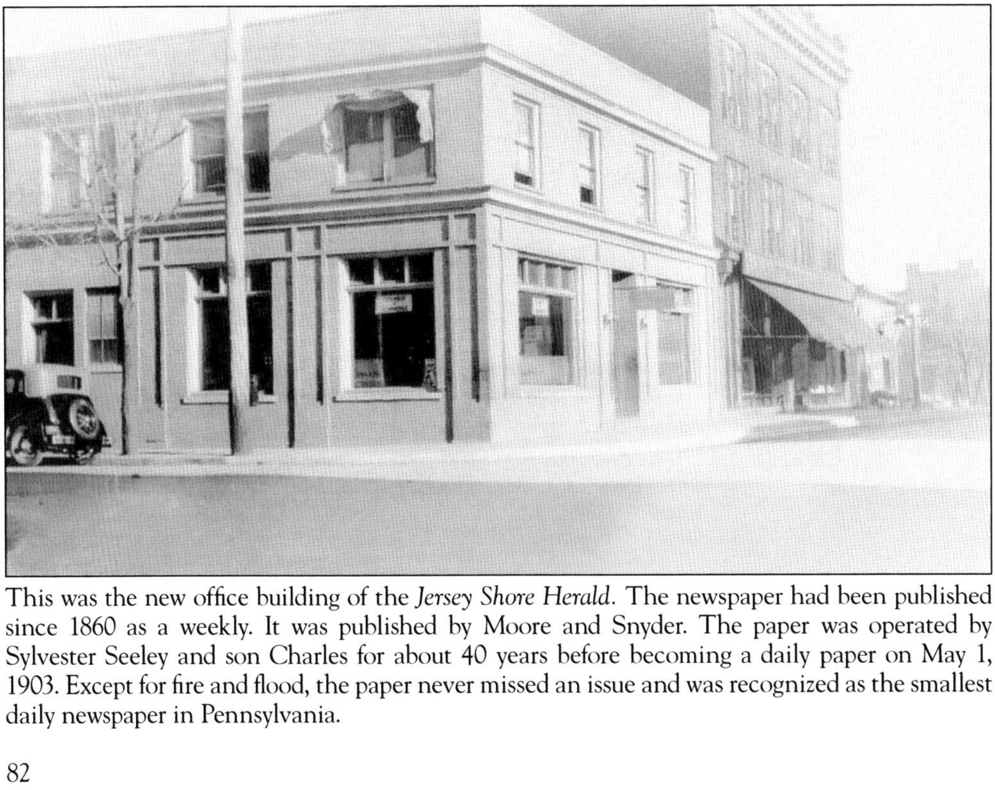

This was the new office building of the *Jersey Shore Herald*. The newspaper had been published since 1860 as a weekly. It was published by Moore and Snyder. The paper was operated by Sylvester Seeley and son Charles for about 40 years before becoming a daily paper on May 1, 1903. Except for fire and flood, the paper never missed an issue and was recognized as the smallest daily newspaper in Pennsylvania.

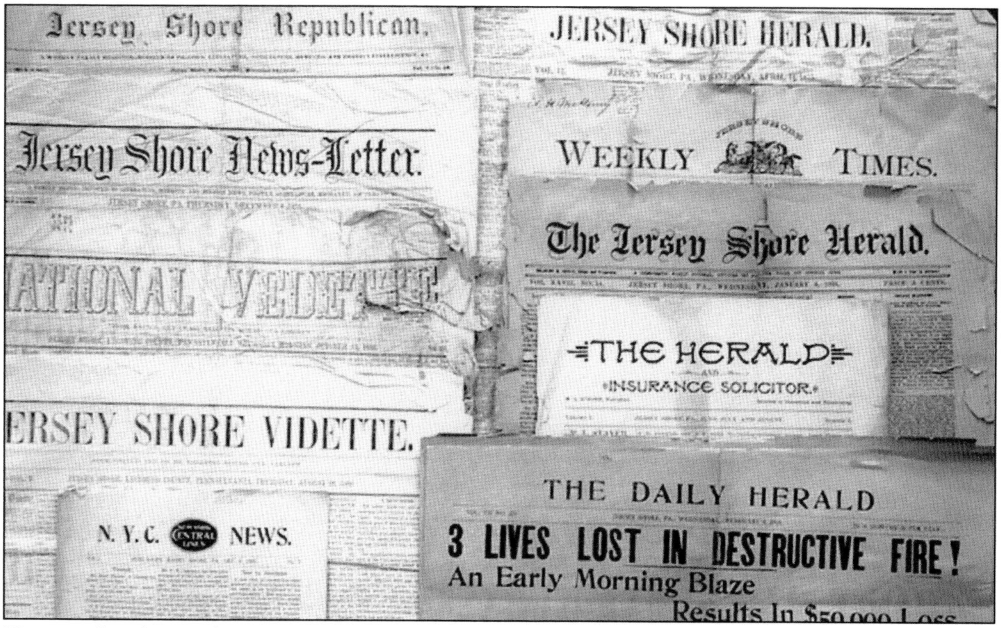

Here are headings of various newspapers published in Jersey Shore over the years. The first paper published in Jersey Shore was the *West Branch Courier* that began in January 8, 1827, by Daniel Gotshall. In 1960, the name of the *Jersey Shore Herald* was changed to the *Evening News*, and on July 30, 1961, it was bought out by the *Lock Haven Express*. The *Express* ceased publication of a separate newspaper for Jersey Shore on October 10, 1969, but John Rasmussen remained editor of the Jersey Shore section.

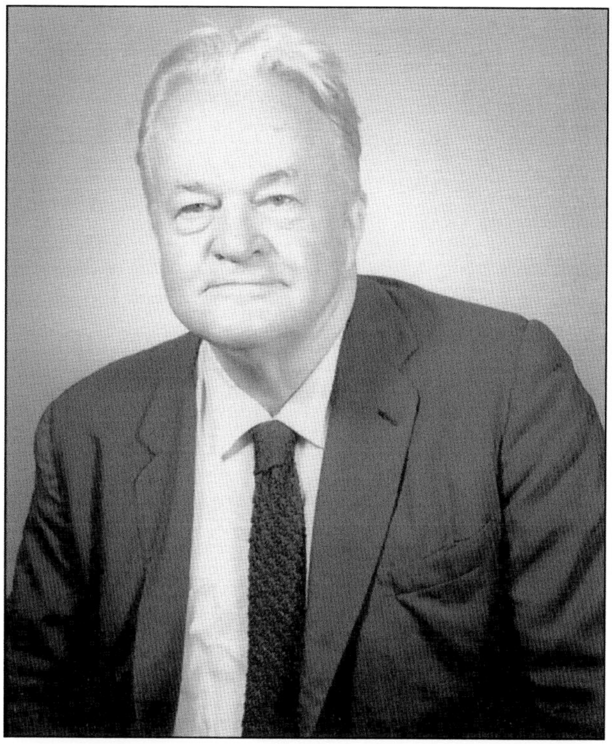

Joe Cox was author of the *Jersey Shore Herald's* "Shore Lines" from January 15, 1946, to his death on January 6, 1972. For 25 years he wrote about historical events in Pennsylvania, the West Branch Valley, and Jersey Shore. Joe was born in Emporium on October 27, 1897, son of Harry and Amelia Cox, and was raised on Pewterbaugh Mountain. He wrote a good history of the town for its 125th anniversary in 1951.

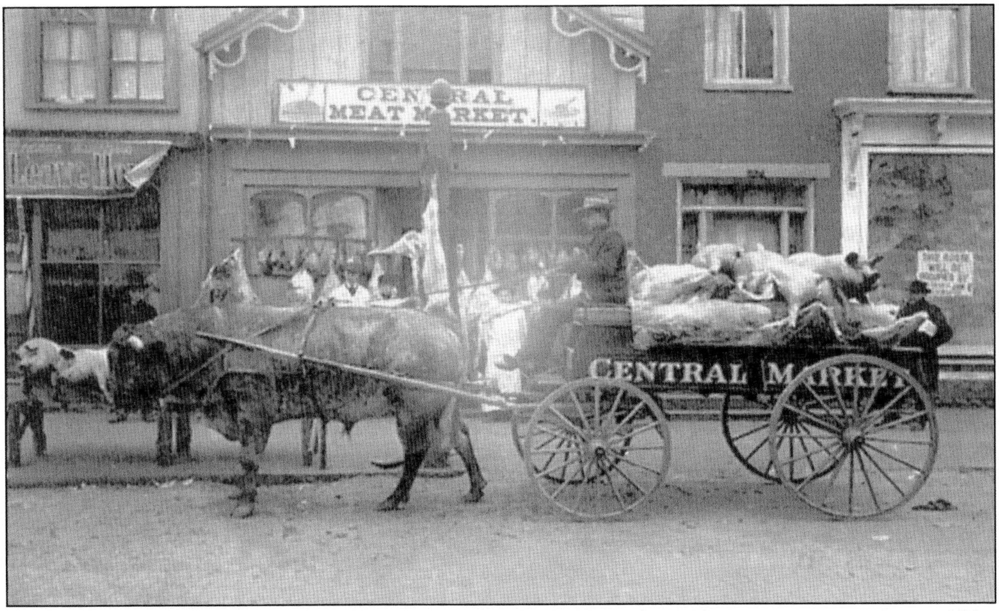

Winner Market opened its first store in Jersey Shore in 1863 where the Masonic temple would be built in 1916. This photograph shows the front of their store on Allegheny Street in 1900.

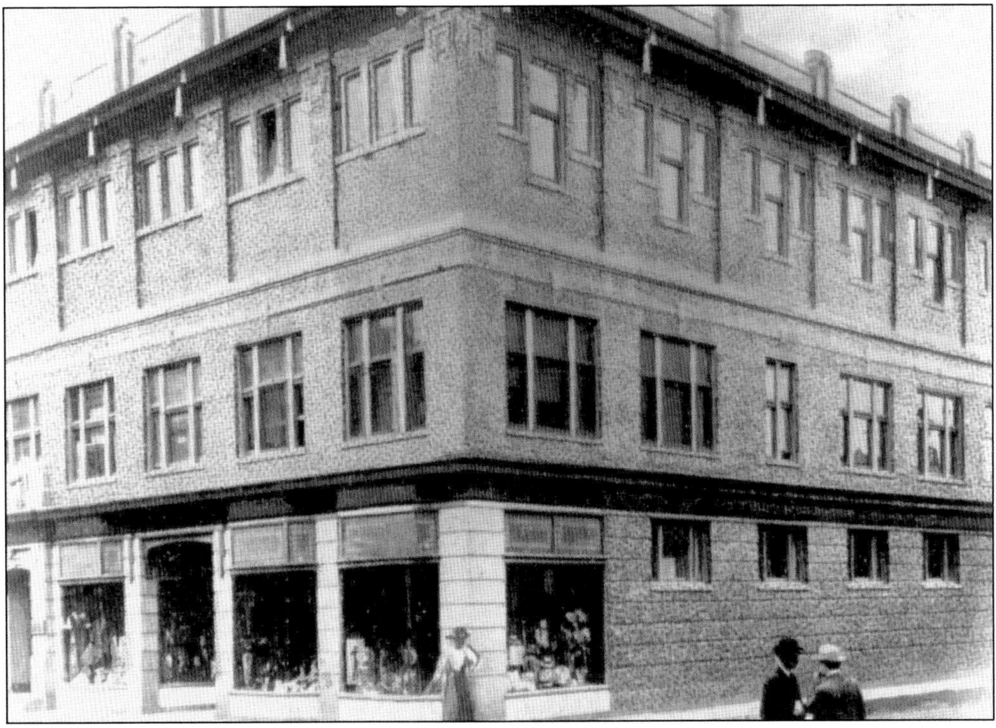

This was the first Masonic temple in Jersey Shore. It was built in 1911 and burned on December 18, 1916. The first Masonic lodge west of Williamsport was established in Jersey Shore on February 8, 1827, and was called Lafayette Lodge No. 199. It eventually went "underground" and moved to Lock Haven on November 11, 1845. The first floor of this building was occupied by the Allen Clothing Store with offices on the second floor for Dr. Angle and lawyer W. R. Peoples.

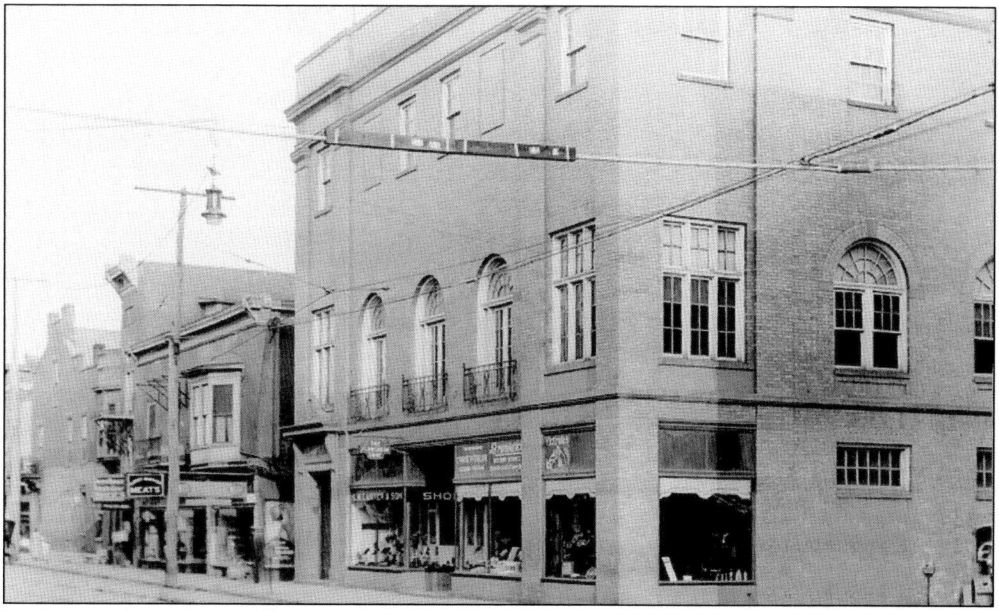

In 1848, eight Masons pulled out of the Lock Haven Masonic lodge and applied for a new charter in Jersey Shore called La Belle Valee, which was established on June 22, 1848, with John A. Gamble as worshipful master. A new temple was built in 1923 on the site of the first. This was one of the locations of Weis Market, which first opened in Jersey Shore in 1919.

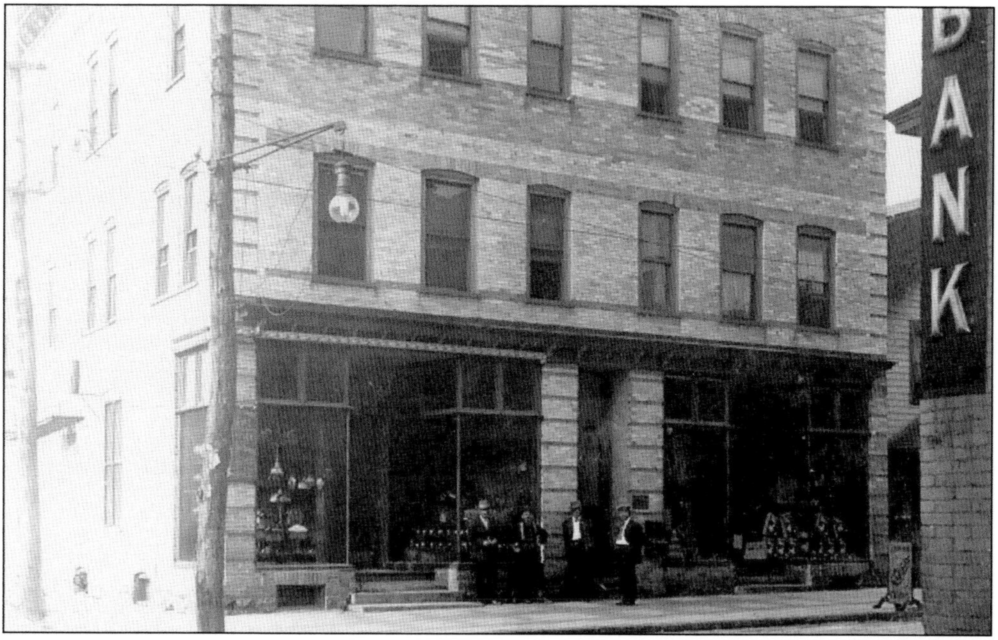

This structure was built as the William T. Ferrar Building and was later known as the Neefe and Johnson apartments. Robert Neefe graduated from the Pennsylvania School of Forestry in 1913 and worked for the State Department of Forest and Waters until 1922, at which time he came to Jersey Shore and started the Riverfront Garage on North Main Street. His business partner was his brother-in-law, E. R. W. Johnson. At first they sold Durant, Dodge, Buick, and Reo automobiles, but switched to Chevrolet in 1930.

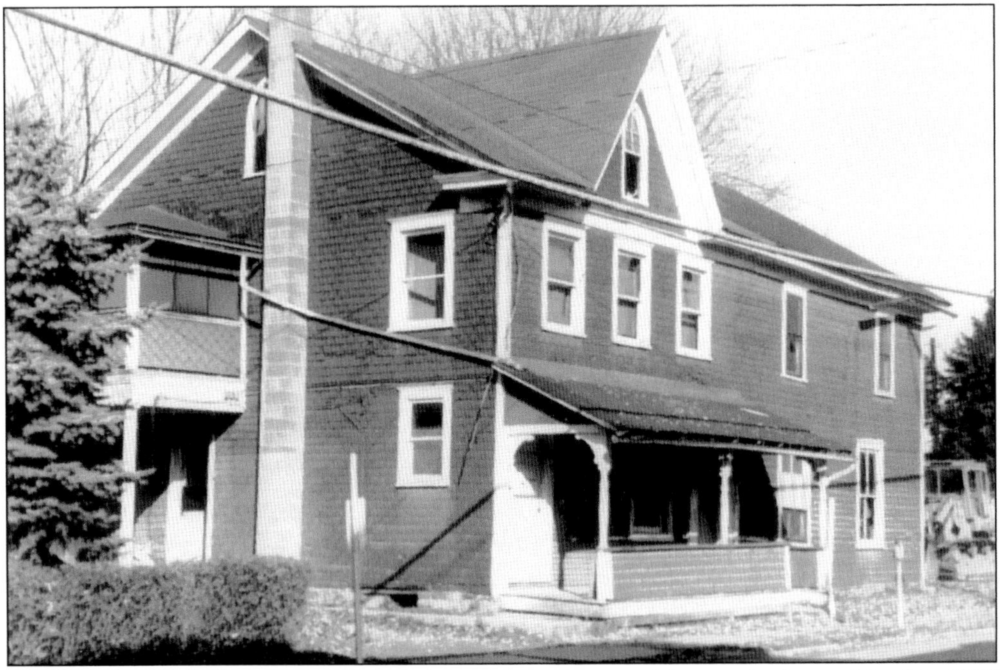

This was the Frank Gray house that was moved from the site of the new Pickering Hotel in 1909 and located here at 132 Market Street. At one time, it was used as the funeral parlor of John Kelchner and the home of the Fraternal Order of Eagles and the home of Arnold Sundberg Sr. It was one of the first homes demolished in the town's urban renewal program that began on October 28, 1974.

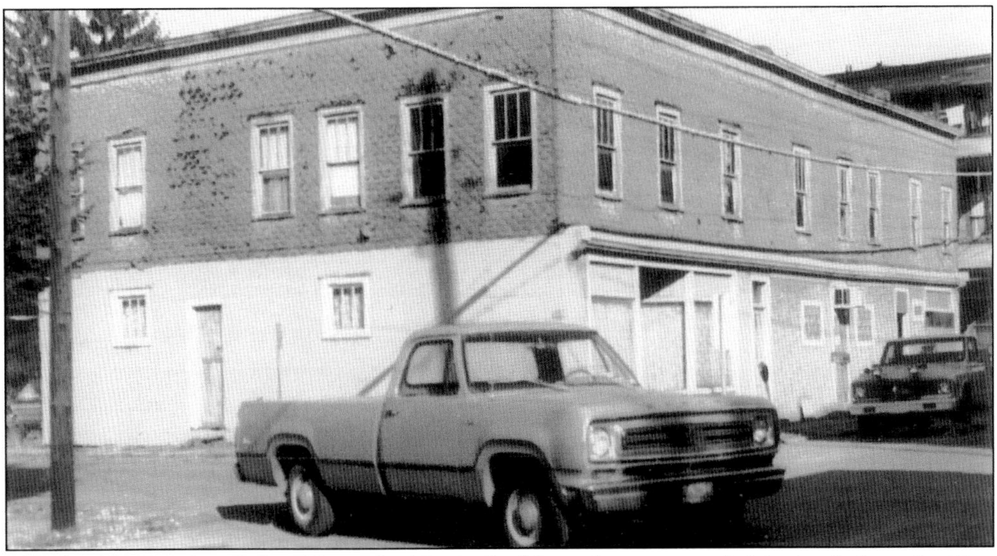

This building replaced the Alexander Zettle Building that occupied this site before the Dan Bower fire of 1902, which destroyed some 14 homes and a hotel and stores. By 1913, this section of Cherry Alley was widened and became Market Street because the outlying farmers would set up here and sell their produce. This building once housed Harrison's Meat Market, Joe Seeto's Steam Laundry, and the American Legion.

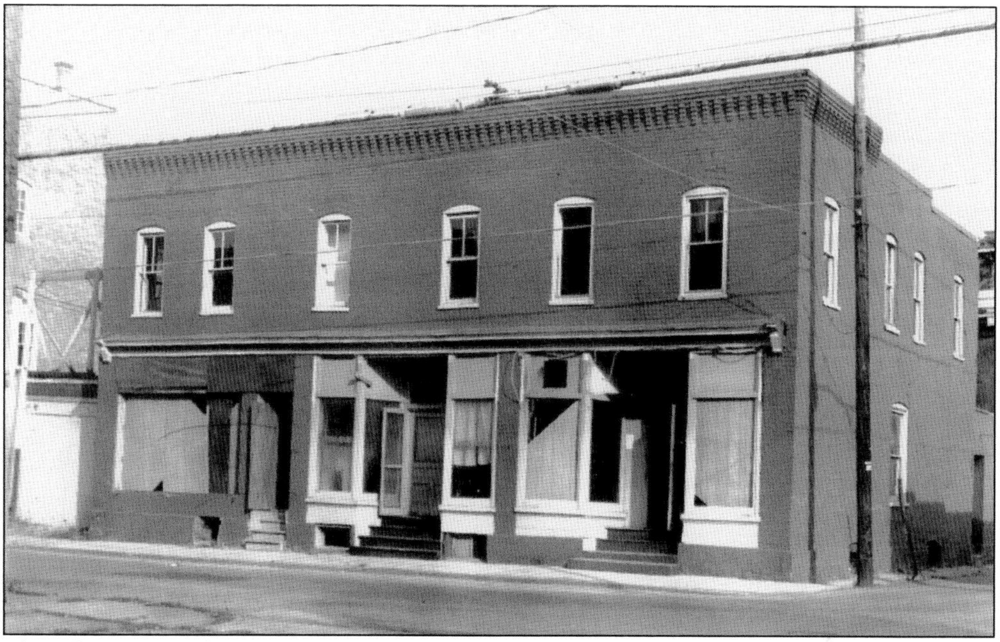

This place on Market Street once housed a bakery with large ovens attached to the back, a furniture store, Bower's Coal, and the Dixie Grill—"The place you see double and feel single." The business belonged to Ted Lehman from June 6, 1946, to August 1976. Prior to this it belonged to Pete Follmer and John Curns. The name "Dixie" was the result of John's winter trips to the south.

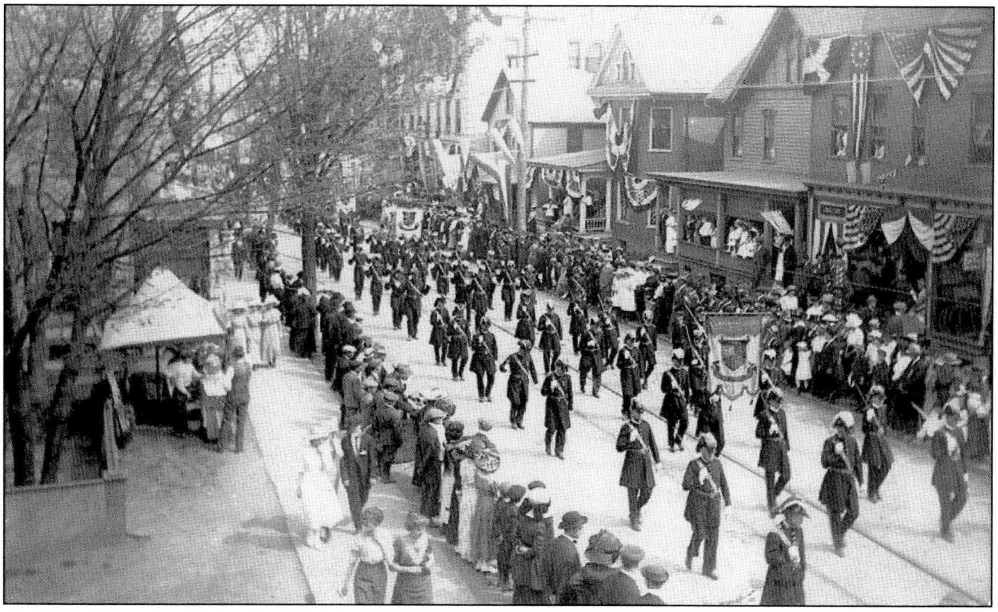

Celebrations involving bands, uniforms, and parades were the order of the day. This parade was for the Odd Fellows Convention held in 1913, and the scene is at the corner of Canal and Allegheny Streets. The wooden building to the right had been John Irvin's Jersey Shore Cycle Company but was bought by Benjamin F. Burtnett in 1898 and was turned into a sporting goods store, which added guns, ammunition, powder, and gun repair to the business.

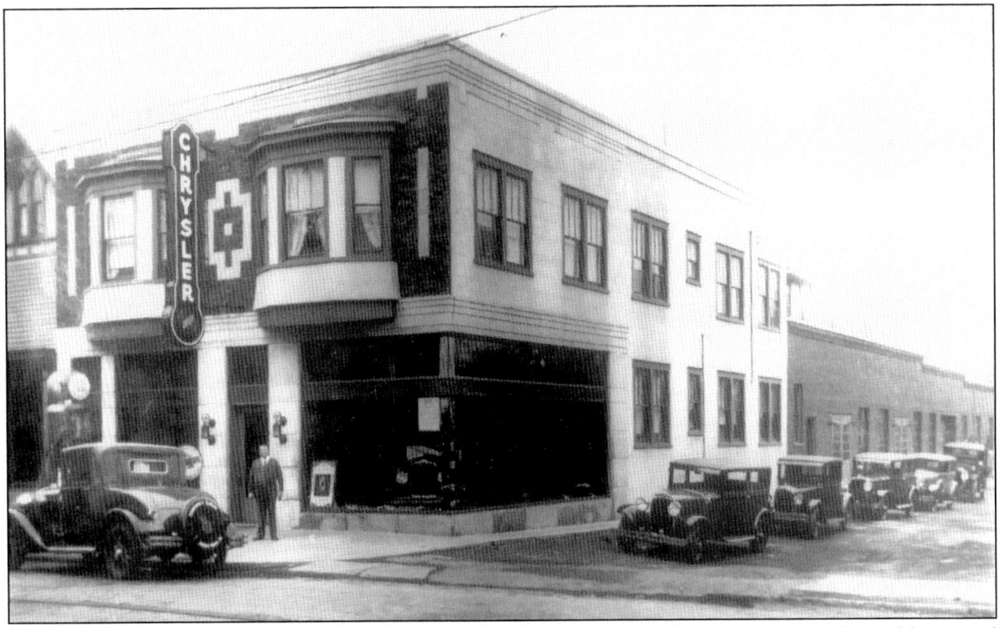

L. C. Thompson replaced the wooden sporting goods store with this new brick building and attached it to the preexisting structure to the rear. As the front symbol indicates, this was a Chrysler dealership, but Hudson, Essex, and Paige automobiles were also sold here. Later Elmer Weaver sold Dodge and Plymouth. The Blue Moon Restaurant was also located here, and later it housed an A&P market, which over the years had four different locations on Allegheny Street.

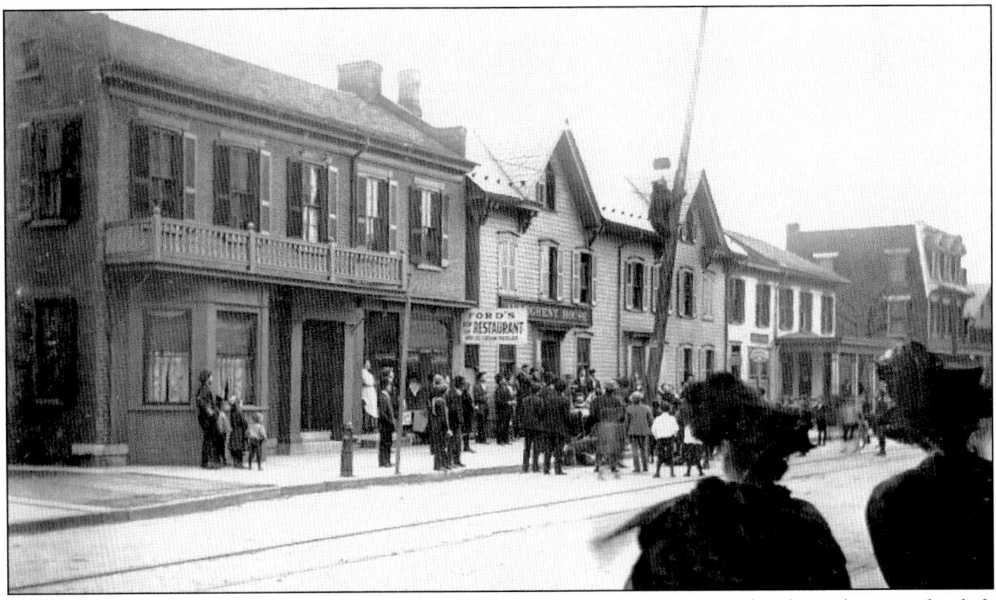

All of these buildings remain today. Andrew Gaus at one time owned the first place to the left and the house at the corner of Broad Street. The one in the middle is the Allegheny House, which was built by Christopher Oechler in 1868 and operated by him until his death in 1897, at which time his son Philip took over. Joseph Feerrar was proprietor of this place from 1908 to 1950 when he retired. His son Jack ran the business next.

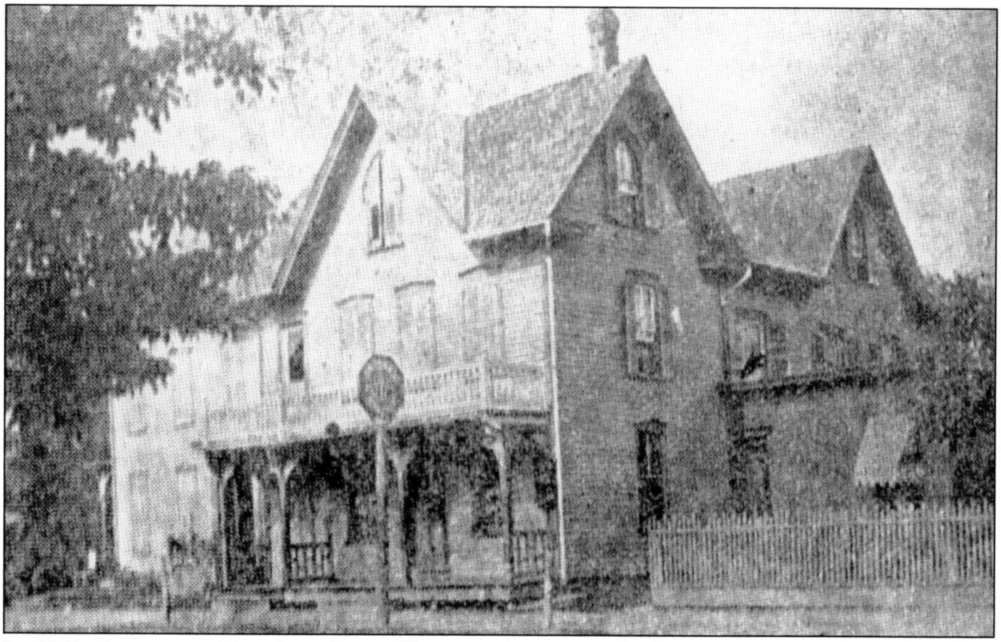

In 1873, there were 4 hotels in Jersey Shore, making a total of 10 over the years. This one, the National Hotel, began as a rooming house called Mrs. Schielie's Hotel. The date is 1815, at which time Methodists were holding service here. Gottfried Schiele ran it in 1873. In 1896, John Green was proprietor of what was then called the National Hotel and thoroughly renovated the building. By 1910, William Turkington was proprietor and George Betzer was drayman.

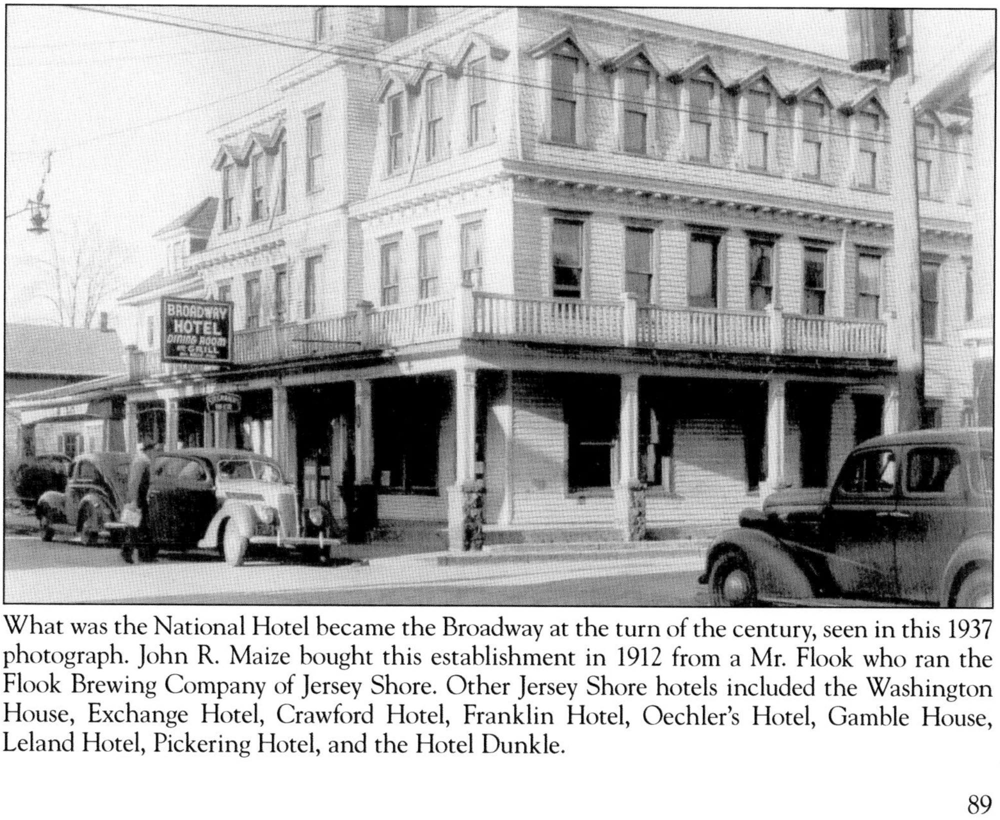

What was the National Hotel became the Broadway at the turn of the century, seen in this 1937 photograph. John R. Maize bought this establishment in 1912 from a Mr. Flook who ran the Flook Brewing Company of Jersey Shore. Other Jersey Shore hotels included the Washington House, Exchange Hotel, Crawford Hotel, Franklin Hotel, Oechler's Hotel, Gamble House, Leland Hotel, Pickering Hotel, and the Hotel Dunkle.

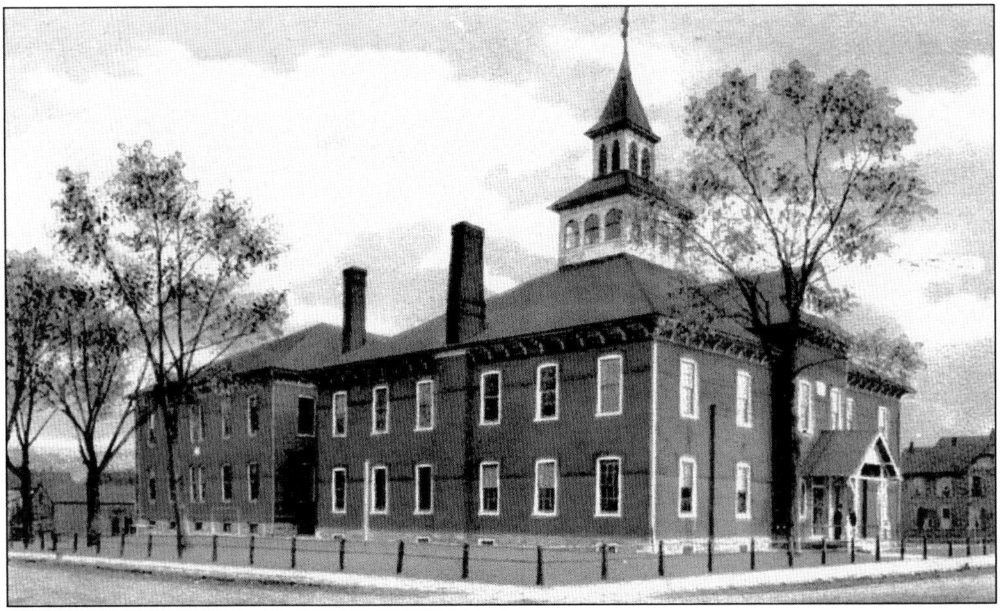

This new Broad Street School was dedicated on October 15, 1885, and at that time included only the front half of the building. The rear section, not being built until 1905, was used as the high school. The contractor was William Levegood, and the total cost was about $15,000. In 1885, John Moyer was principal and teacher of the high school students and four women were the elementary teachers. There were 225 students that first year, and the total salary for the teachers was $1,768.

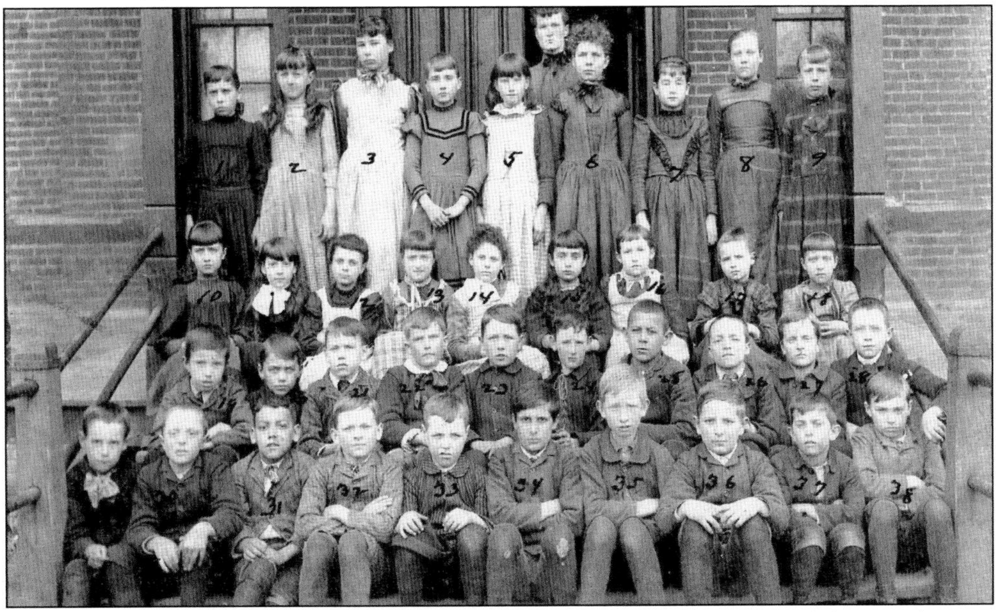

This class of 38 elementary students was photographed on the front porch of the Broad Street School. The teacher was Laura Williamee. In 1892, there were eight schools in the Jersey Shore District and eight teachers, two men and six women. The school year was 7.25 months, and total enrollment was 346 students. The first commencement from the Broad Street Public High School was held at Staver's Hall on May 16, 1889, for 11 graduates.

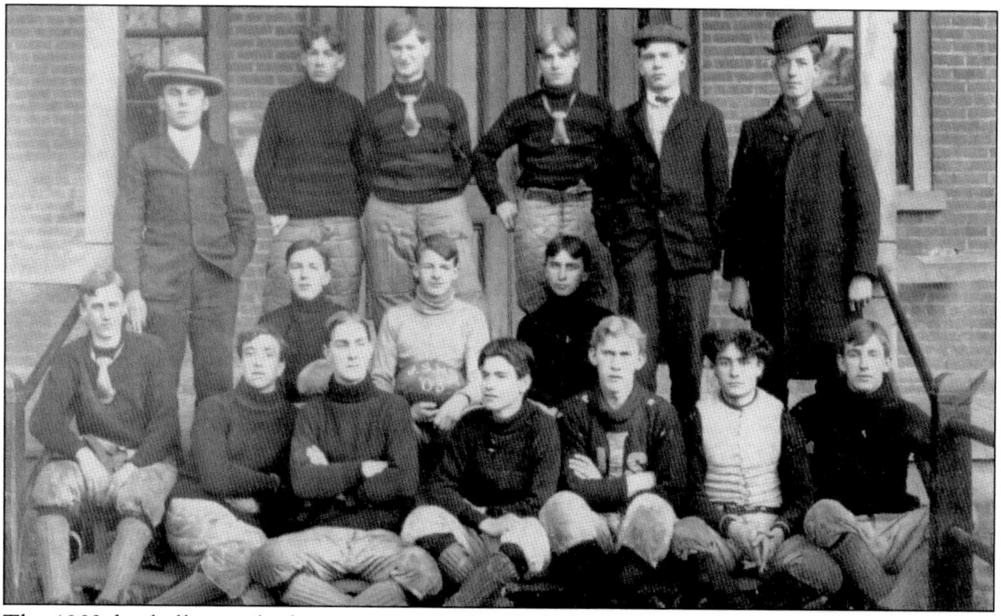

The 1903 football team had an average weight of 130 pounds. Nevertheless, they won all their games but one. They beat Williamsport twice, 6-0 and 24-0; Lock Haven, 12-0; and Muncy, 11-0. The oldest picture of a football team, with names, found to date is 1895, with local games played on Long Island. Jersey Shore's first official football team was recognized on September 25, 1920; they traveled to Williamsport on Mr. Richard's coal truck and beat the powerful Millionaires 30-0. Clyde Baltzer was coach.

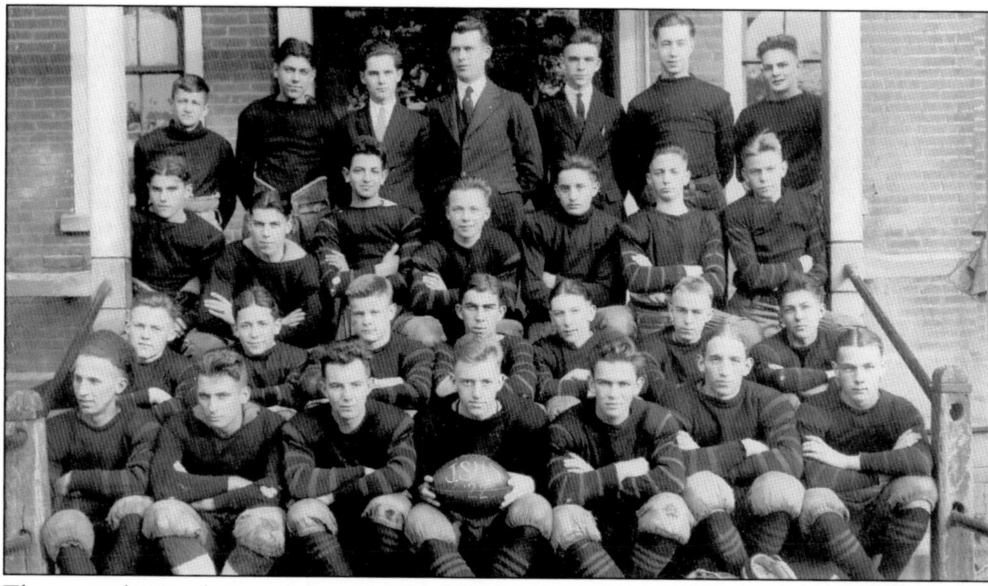

These are the 28 players of the powerful 1922 Jersey Shore football team. In eight games they scored 575 points to their opponents' 0. The results of the games were as follows: Galeton, 56-0; Bellefonte, 46-0; South Williamsport, 127-0; Mansfield, 77-0; Bloomsburg, 101-0; Mansfield, 9-0; Shamokin, 44-0; and Carroltown, 113-0. The name of the teams changed from the Tornadoes to Orangemen and Bulldogs in the 1930s in reference to a mascot, named "Jerry," loaned to the team for games and parades by Harry and Dorothy Thompson.

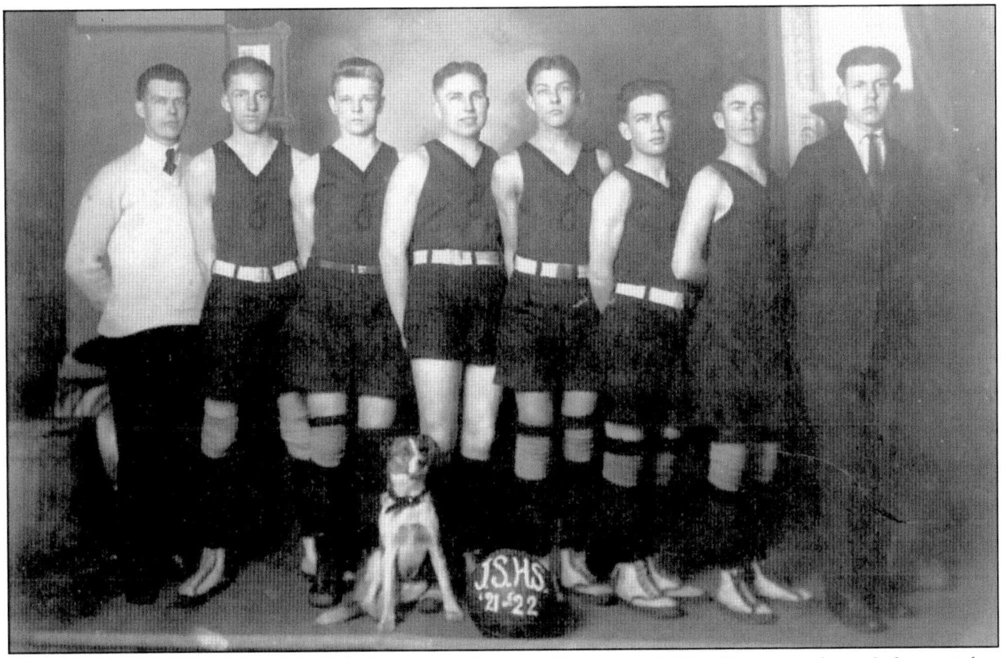

This is the championship basketball team of Jersey Shore in 1922. They are, from left to right, Clyde Baltzer, coach; George Young; Fred Sweeley; Alec Brown; Lee Bowes; Gordon Singer; Lee Triebels; and George Weiler (manager). Games were played at the YMCA since there was no court at the Broad Street High School.

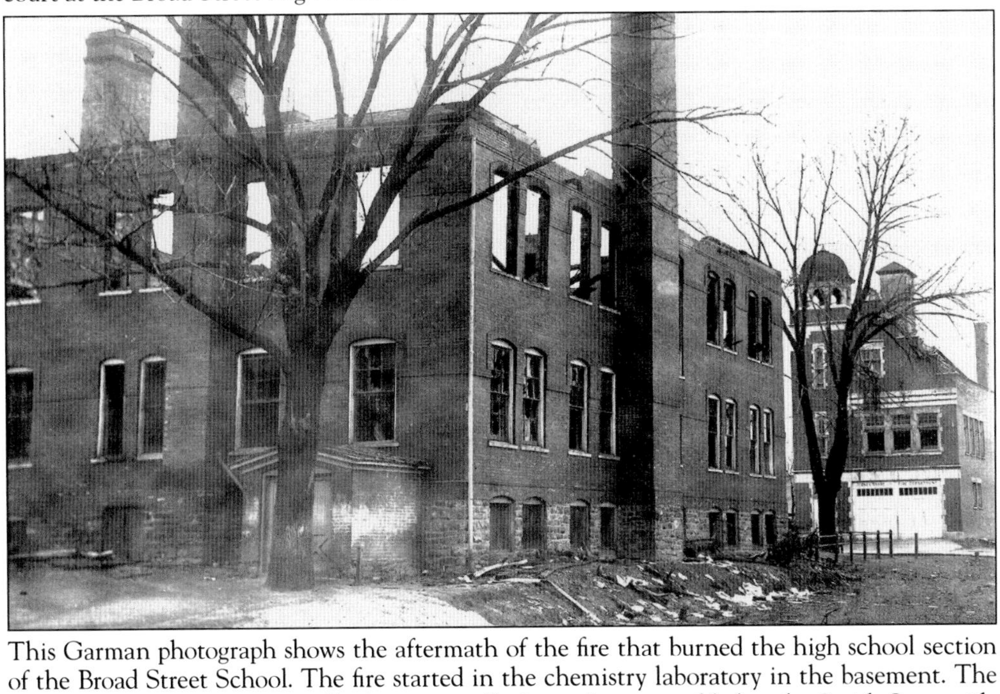

This Garman photograph shows the aftermath of the fire that burned the high school section of the Broad Street School. The fire started in the chemistry laboratory in the basement. The wing was rebuilt using essentially the same walls, but a door was added to the Smith Street side near the 1905 marker, which indicates the original year of construction. Across the street is the municipal building and fire station, which still retained its bell and hose-drying towers.

This was the photography shop of William H. Garman, or actually Cohick and Garman in 1898 when this photograph was taken. William was born on Pine Creek in 1861 and died at age 77 in 1938, the same year as his competitor, Joseph Mick. His South Main Street shop was destroyed in the fire of 1883 after which he moved to 311 Smith Street, and continued in the profession of a photographer for 56 years. He also operated a grocery and confectionery store here near the Broad Street School.

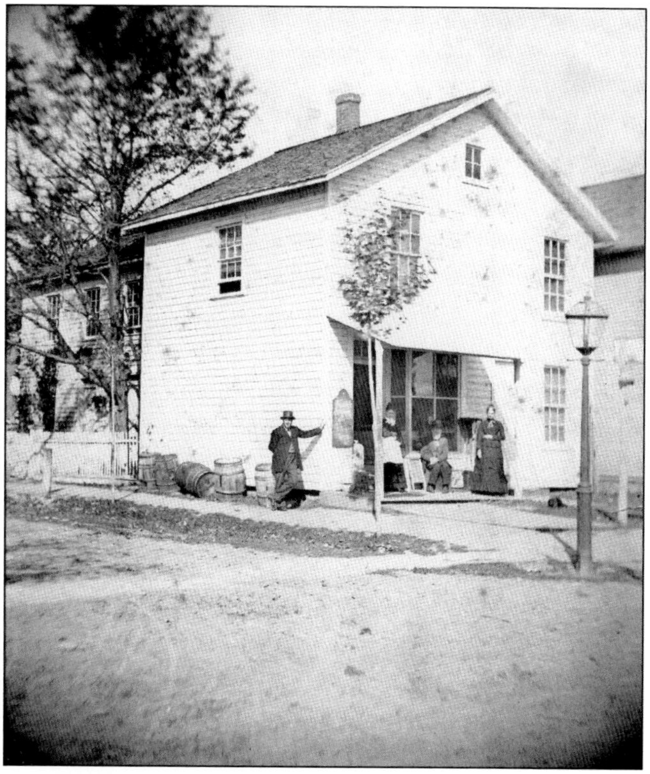

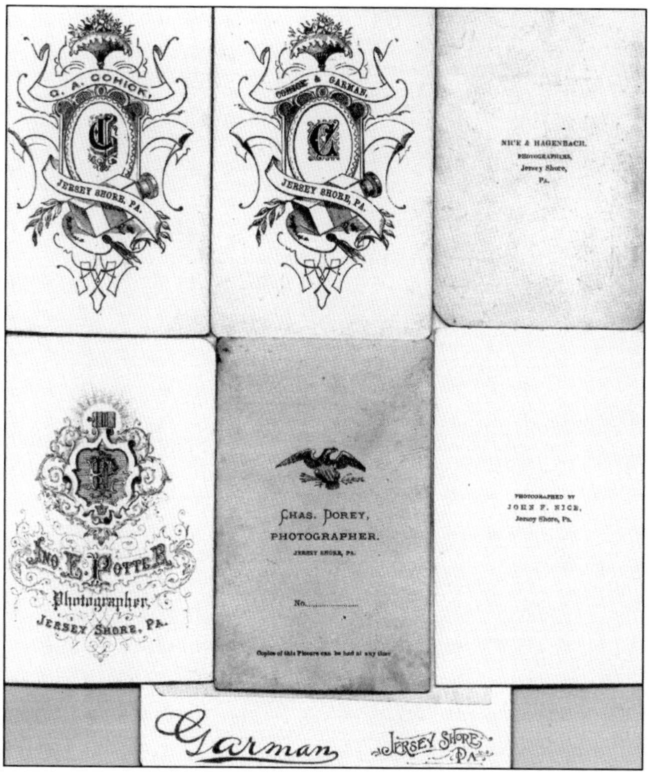

These are samples of photograph backings advertising the photographer who took the picture. The last professional photographers in Jersey Shore were Charles (until 1972) and Robert Harer (until 1994). Practical photography began in 1839 with the daguerreotype, and the photograph soon became the most powerful form of communication since invention of the printing press. It is easy to understand why a picture is often worth more than a thousand words. Tintypes came into use in 1852, and photography as a profession was established by 1860.

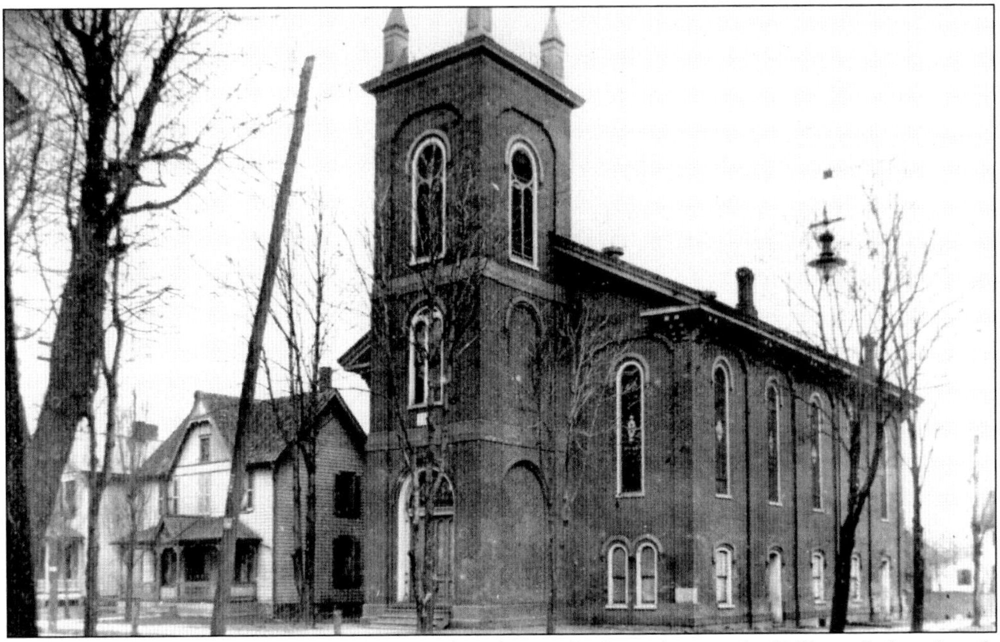

The cornerstone of St. John's Lutheran Church was laid on August 8, 1868, and the church dedication was held in 1871. A Sunday school room was dedicated in 1869. The parsonage was built by 1871. A tall steeple was completed in the same year, and pews, pulpits, and choir furniture were in place. Total cost of the church was $11,000. The steeple blew down in 1891. New stained-glass windows were installed (1891–1898), and the old coal oil lamps were replaced with gas fixtures.

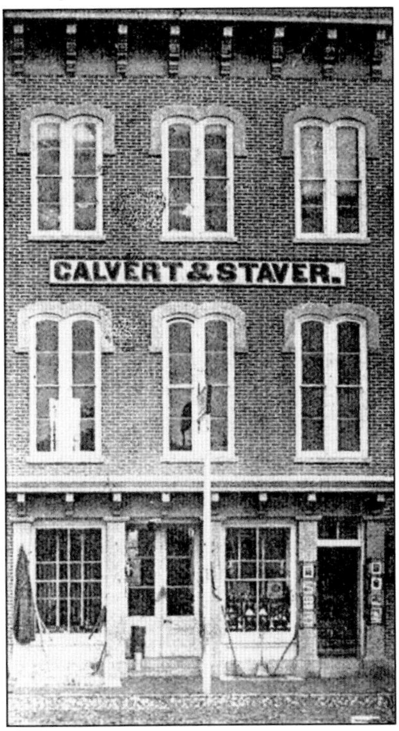

Members of St. John's Lutheran Church held their first services in this building on South Main Street in 1867. John Staver was the driving force behind the building of the new church on Broad Street. He was a liberal contributor, and he solicited building funds, superintended construction, and furnished teams for hauling materials. This building was damaged in the 1871 fire on South Main Street and was completely destroyed by the 1883 fire.

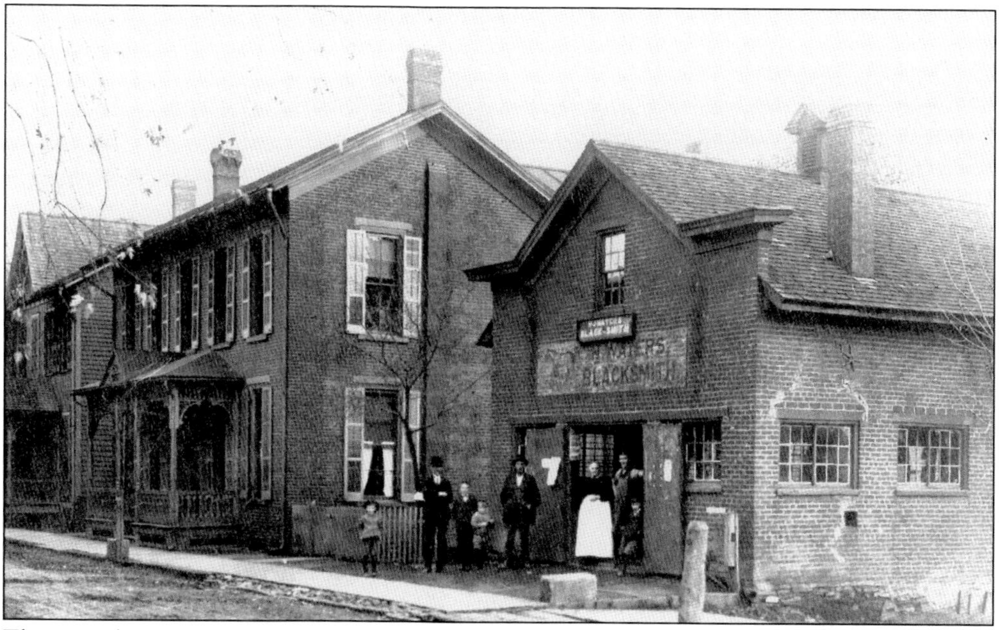

This was the Hiram J. Waters's blacksmith house and shop at 225 Thompson Street. He was born in Lewisburg, Pennsylvania, in 1836 and died here in 1914. In 1860, at the age of 25, he was one of six blacksmiths on the tax records for Jersey Shore. He was married to Sarah Brown, daughter of William Brown who came to this country in 1848 from County Tyrone, Ireland. Their son Frank took over his father's business.

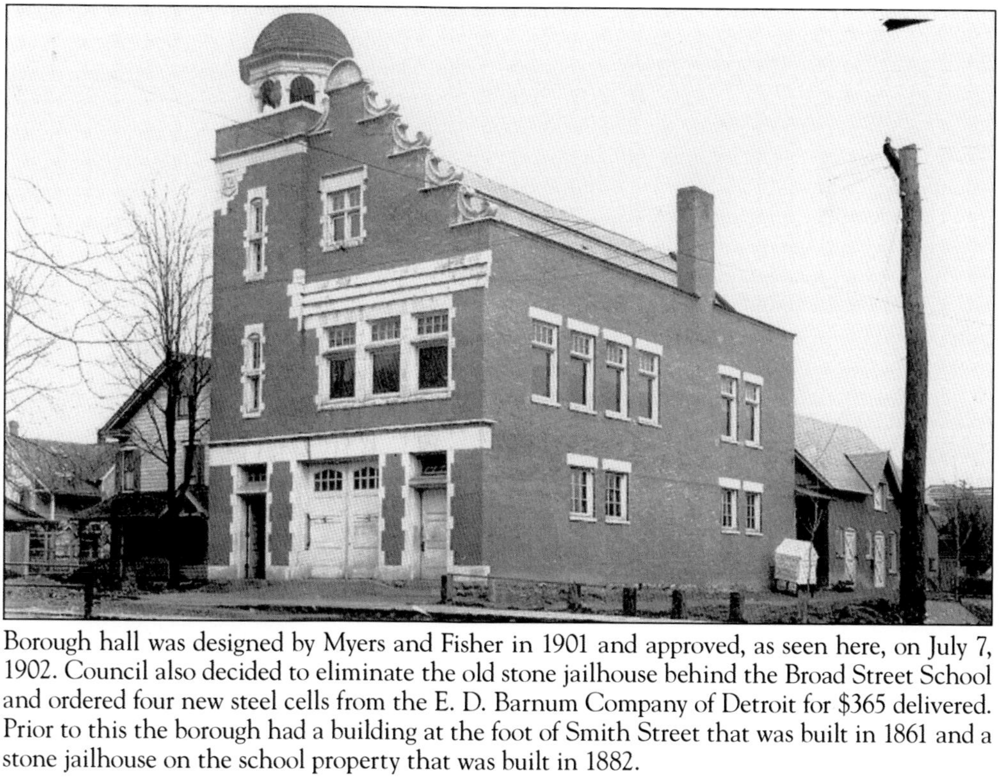

Borough hall was designed by Myers and Fisher in 1901 and approved, as seen here, on July 7, 1902. Council also decided to eliminate the old stone jailhouse behind the Broad Street School and ordered four new steel cells from the E. D. Barnum Company of Detroit for $365 delivered. Prior to this the borough had a building at the foot of Smith Street that was built in 1861 and a stone jailhouse on the school property that was built in 1882.

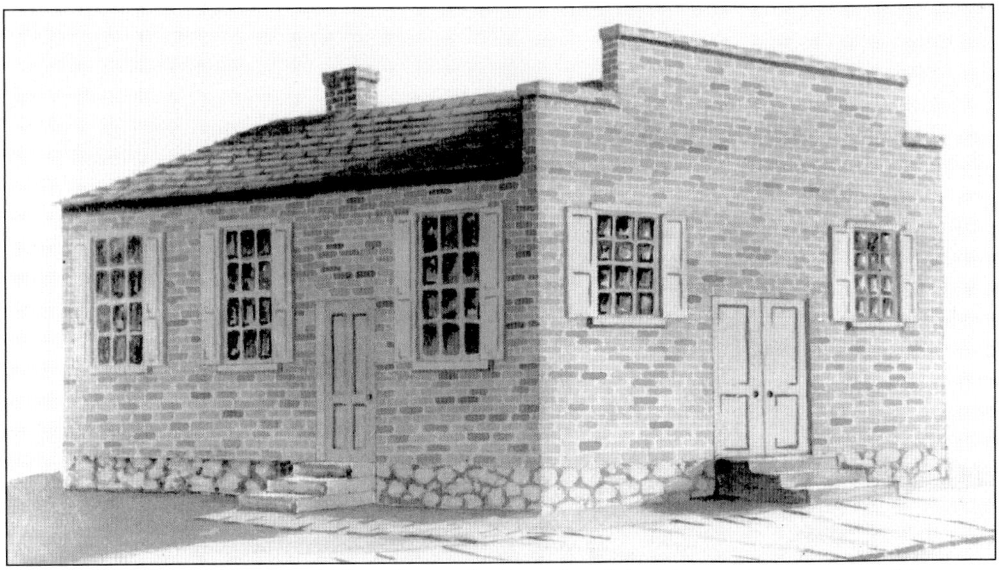

This First Methodist Episcopal Church was the first church building to be constructed in town. It was built in 1830, along the canal where borough hall now stands. It was 35 feet square and would hold about 150 people. It was vacated and sold about 1845 when the Methodist congregation moved to its new church on South Main Street. This drawing was done by Grant Morrow in 1930.

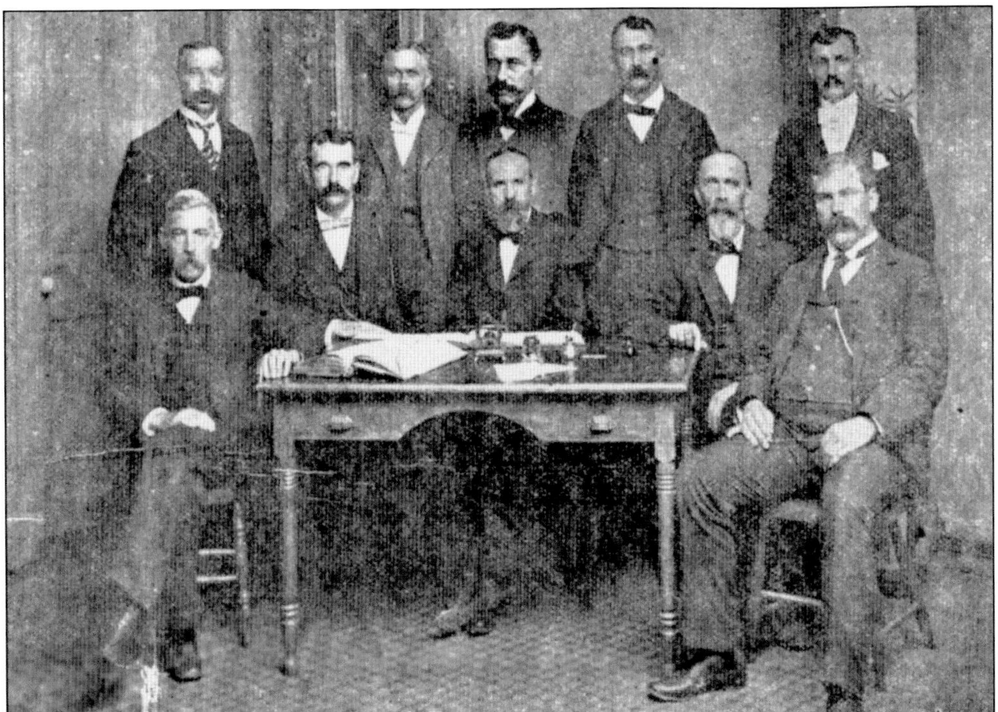

The borough councilmen in 1899, as seen from left to right, are Charles Shoup; M. I. Sallada; W. A. Selts; J. G. Scarborough; Robert McCullough, burgess (seated); P. J. Luce; F. N. Brown; E. K. Fiester; Dr. S. E. Bickell (seated); and E. M. Gann.

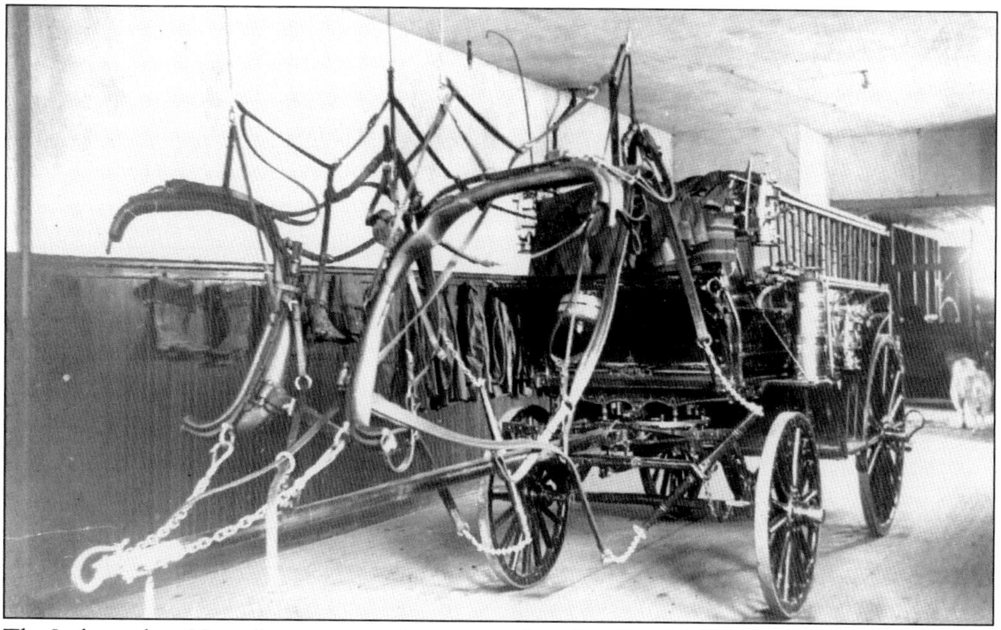

The Independent Hose Company was incorporated on October 2, 1902. At the time the borough only owned two hand-drawn hose carts, but in 1905, an American LaFrance hose wagon was purchased with harnessed teams and drivers furnished by the liveries of Joe Feerrar and Dan Bower. In 1906, the fire company purchased its own team and this automatic drop harness. The use of horses ended in 1918 when the first fire truck was purchased.

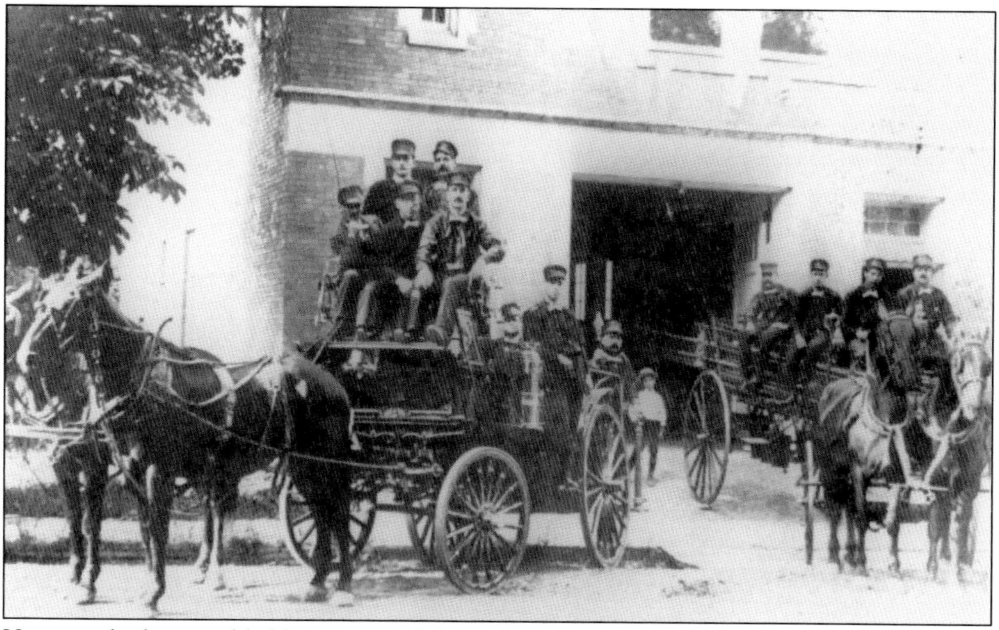

Here are the hose and ladder wagons of the Jersey Shore Fire Company. They are, from left to right, as follows: (hose wagon) William Neff, Morris Myers, Robert Shadle, chief; (back seat) Joe Mick, and A. L. Dingler; (standing on side) Joe Feerrar; (rear) Charles King, George Lewis, and a boy, George Dingler; (ladder wagon) Fred White, Al Britton, George Dingler Sr., and W. J. Corson. The 1860 fire company was called the Neptune Fire Company.

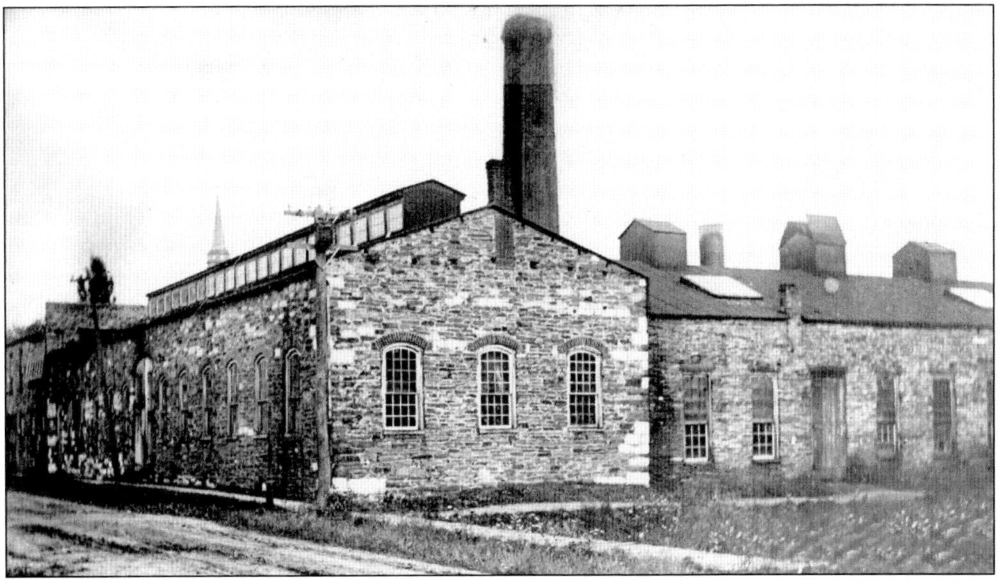

A foundry business was established here by the W. R. Wilson Company in 1851, but the place soon burned and this one made of stone took its place. The business was originally built to manufacture farm machinery, but over the years made bells, parts for railroad engines, automobile parts, ammunition for World War I, and television antennas. There were 450 men employed at the foundry during its most prosperous times. The place burned on July 26, 1980.

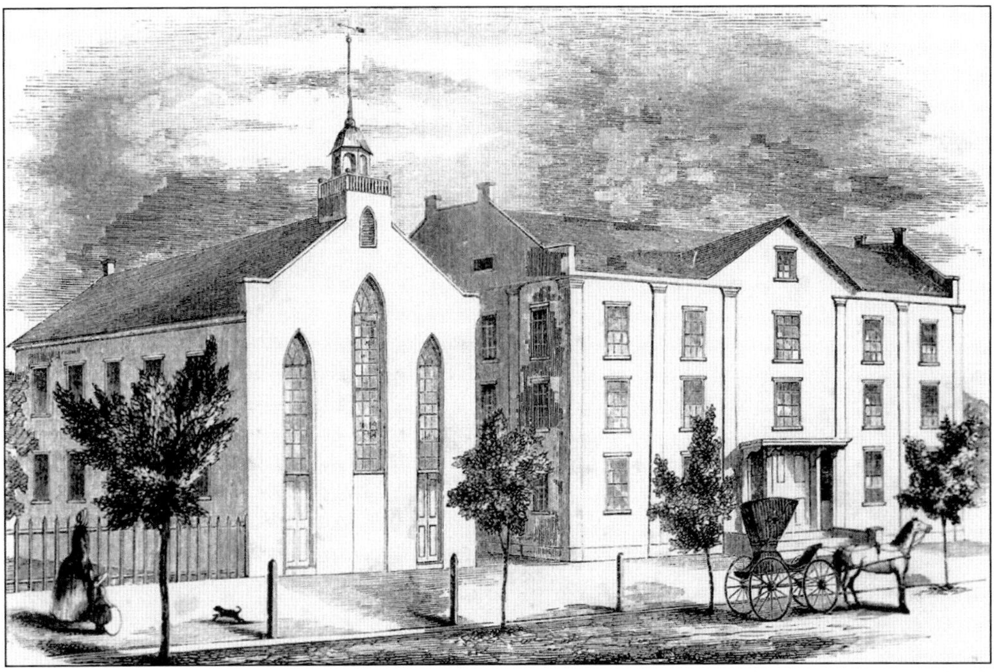

This structure was originally built as a church in 1832, and by 1852, became a private high school, which was incorporated in 1855 as the West Branch High School. The dormitory could hold up to 100 students. Many very successful and influential local people went to school here. A 10-month term, including room and board, cost $200. This school closed in 1884, and the Presbyterians sold both buildings in 1891.

Six

Railroading

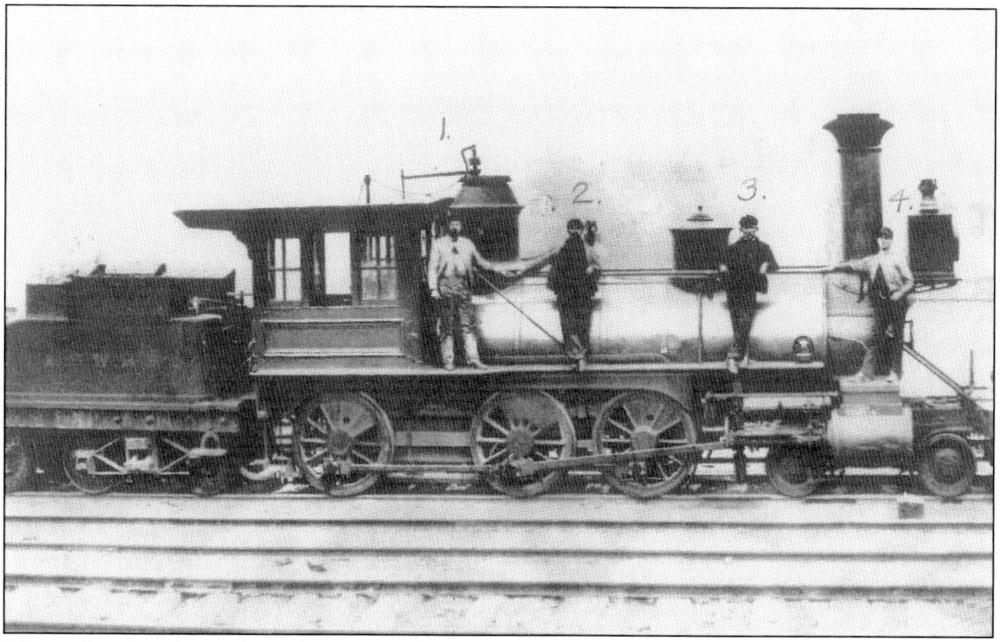

The railroad industry brought a groundswell of good paying jobs to the area beginning with the Beech Creek line in 1884. The first paying run occurred on May 15, 1884, with a train of 15 coal-laden cars delivered to the Fallbrook line at Jersey Shore Junction. This locomotive, engine No. 2, went into service in 1883. It was bought secondhand from the Pennsylvania Railroad and had been manufactured by Baldwin in Philadelphia. The last Beech Creek engine in service was No. 1627.

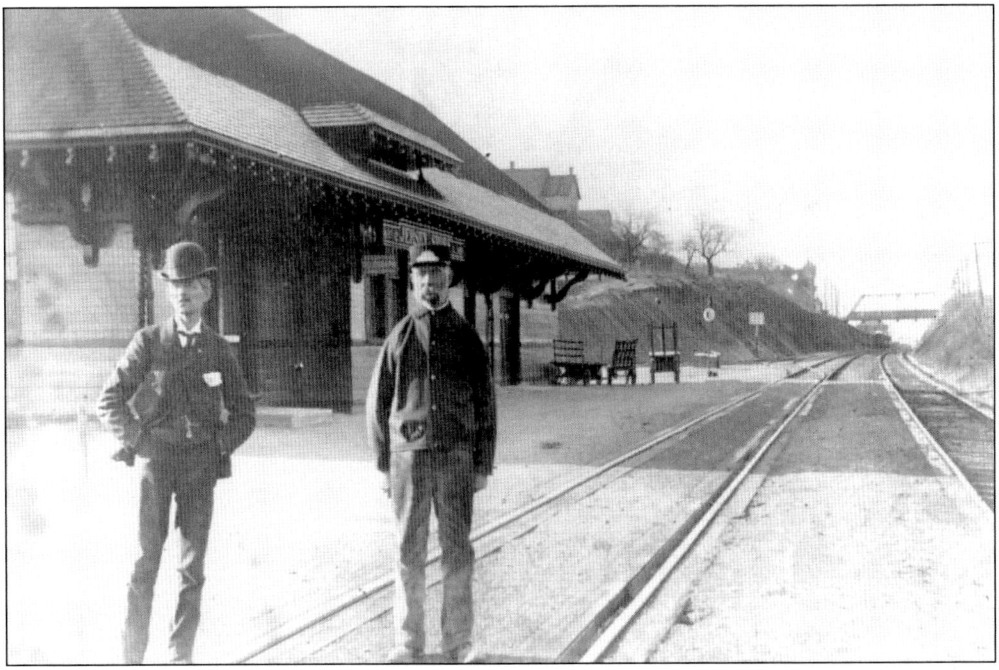

The first passenger train ran between Williamsport and Beech Creek on July 1, 1884. There were stations at Williamsport, Newberry Junction, Linden, Larry's Creek, and Jersey Shore. The distance to Williamsport was 15.8 miles and another 20.8 miles on to Beech Creek. Passenger service ended in February 1933 due to the increased use of the automobile. Bridge Street is seen in the distance with the large Torbert House to its left.

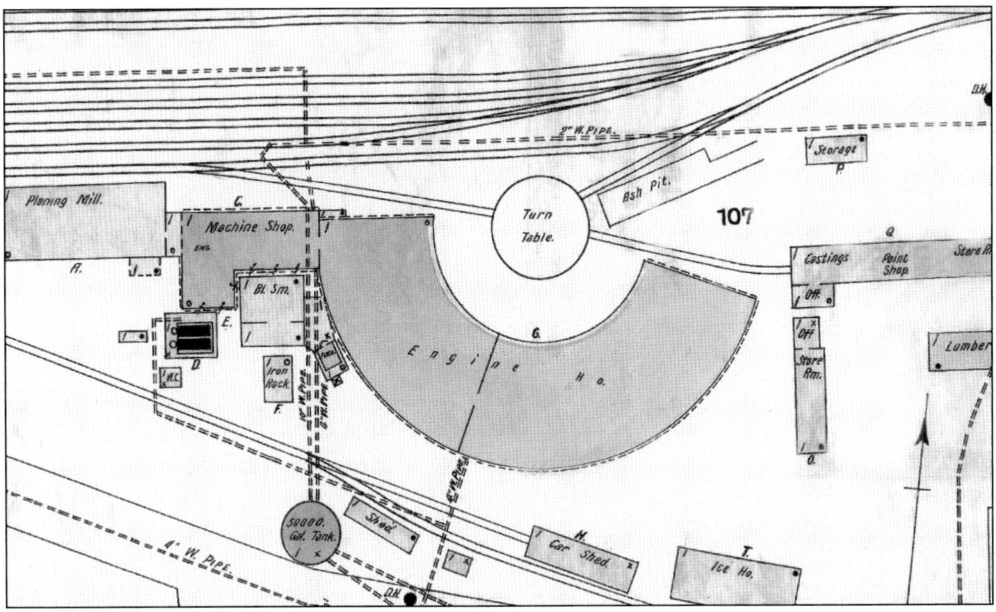

This Sanborn map of 1906 shows the extent of the old Beech Creek yard and maintenance facilities that were established at "uptown" Jersey Shore in 1884. Railroad employment doubled the population of the town and started a building boom that did not end until July 1931, at which time the locomotive repair works at Avis was transferred to West Albany.

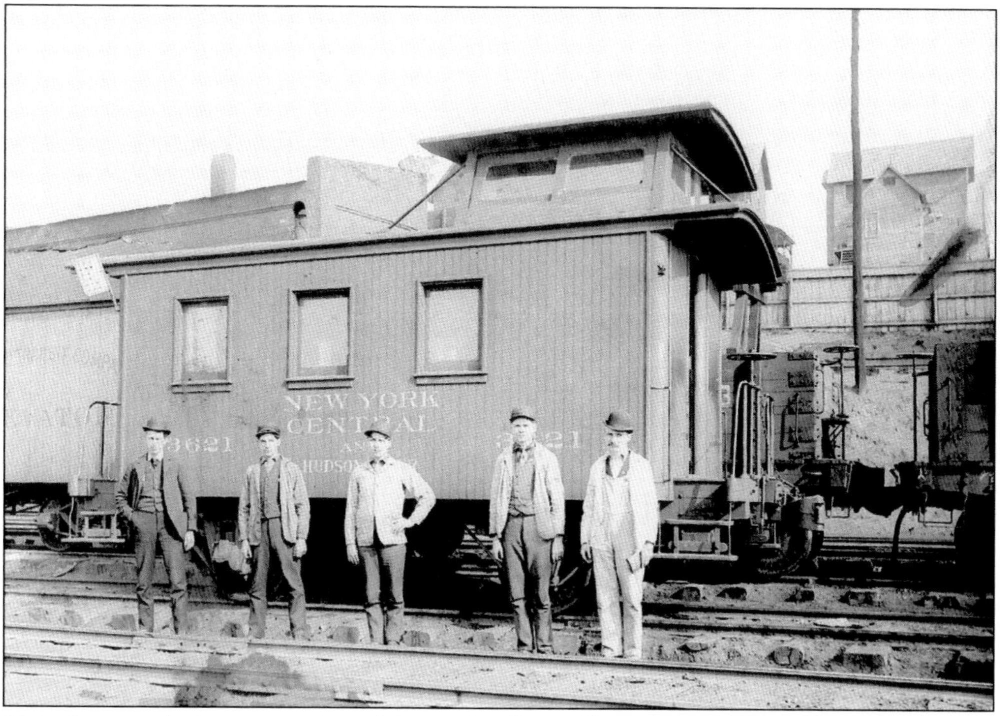

This photograph shows a section of the yard at Jersey Shore Junction with houses in the rear on Allegheny Street. Between 1902 and 1913, the New York Central built a new repair yard in South Avis. There was constant improvement of equipment, and the size of the engines and cars got bigger and bigger. The Jersey Shore yard repaired wooden cars, but the Avis shops worked on both wood and steel cars.

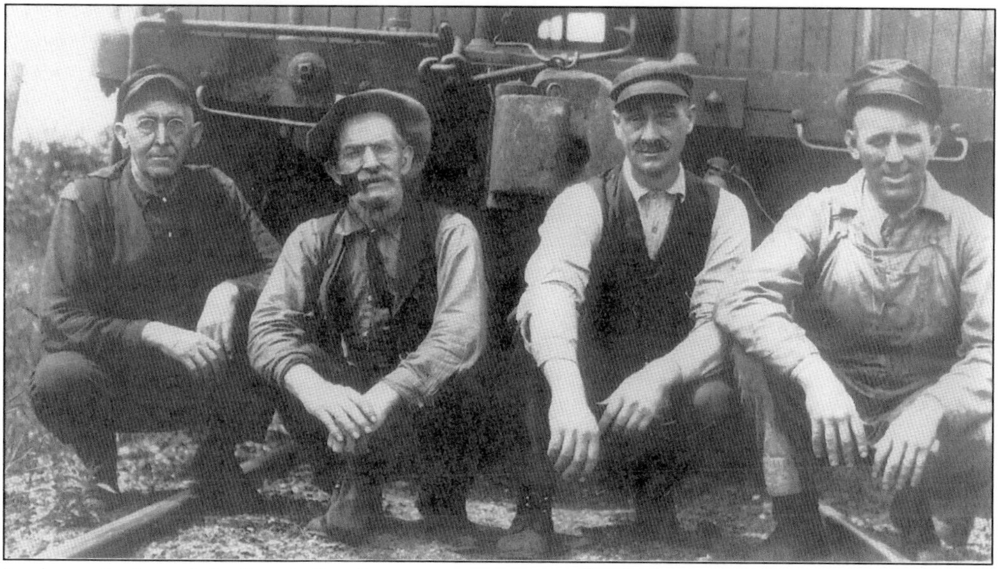

In the early days of the Beech Creek it was a common sight to see employees severely wounded or killed, and it was passed off as the fortunes of work. The old link and pin couplers and deadwoods were two such dark spots. Dewey Douglas of Maple Street came to Jersey Shore as a road fireman in 1893 and retired at age 70 on May 29, 1930. Retirement was mandatory at age 70.

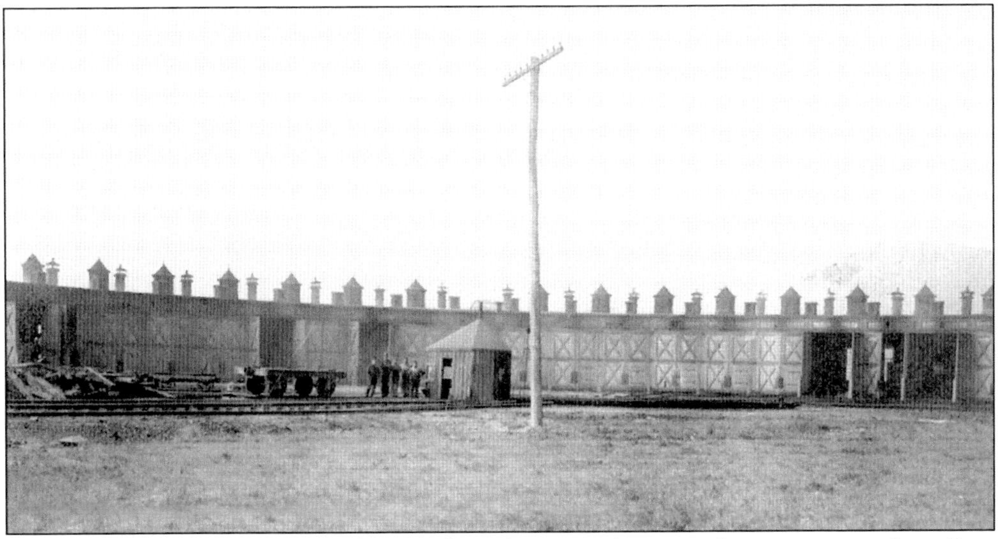

In 1902, the roundhouse was built as well as the power house and engine repair shop. Four hundred acres of land around this railroad development site were purchased by Sen. J. Henry Cochran and others and were used to build a community for the workmen. The place came to be called Avis, named after Henry's wife and daughter. This land was formerly the farms of J. Harris McKinney, Thomas Crawford, and George Shaw.

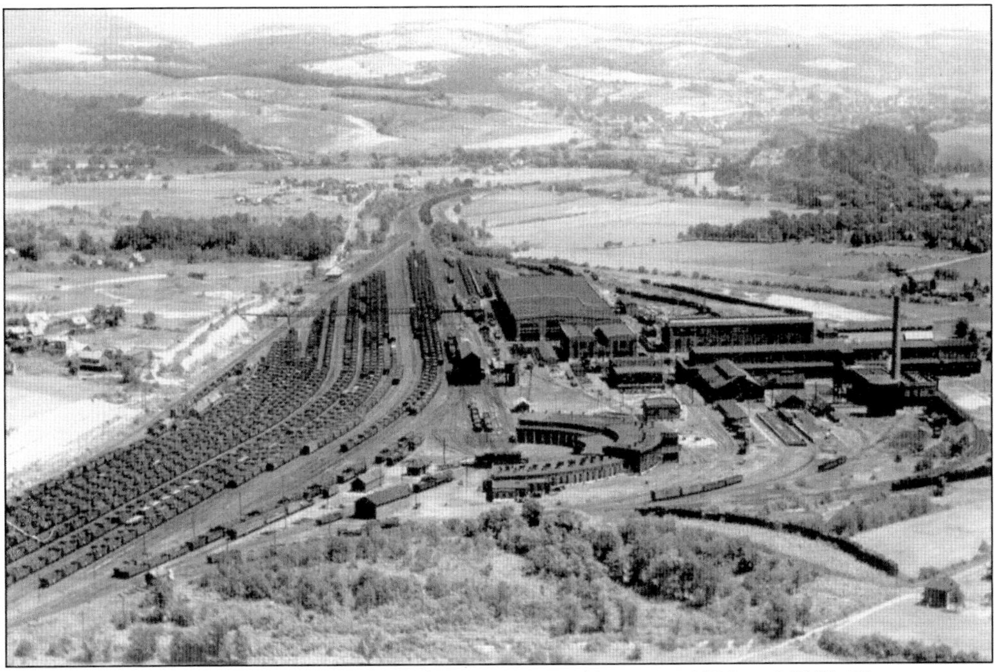

The large New York Central Yard at South Avis operated between 1903 and 1955. The car repair shop was added in 1910 and measured 200 feet by 850 feet. "The car repair plant will nearly double the size of the operation and will furnish employment to many men. Our town will soon enjoy its most prosperous time in history," reported the *Jersey Shore Herald* on March 10, 1910. In 1953, it still employed 350 men, and the Jersey Shore Steel Mill, which began operation in 1938, occupied the old locomotive shop.

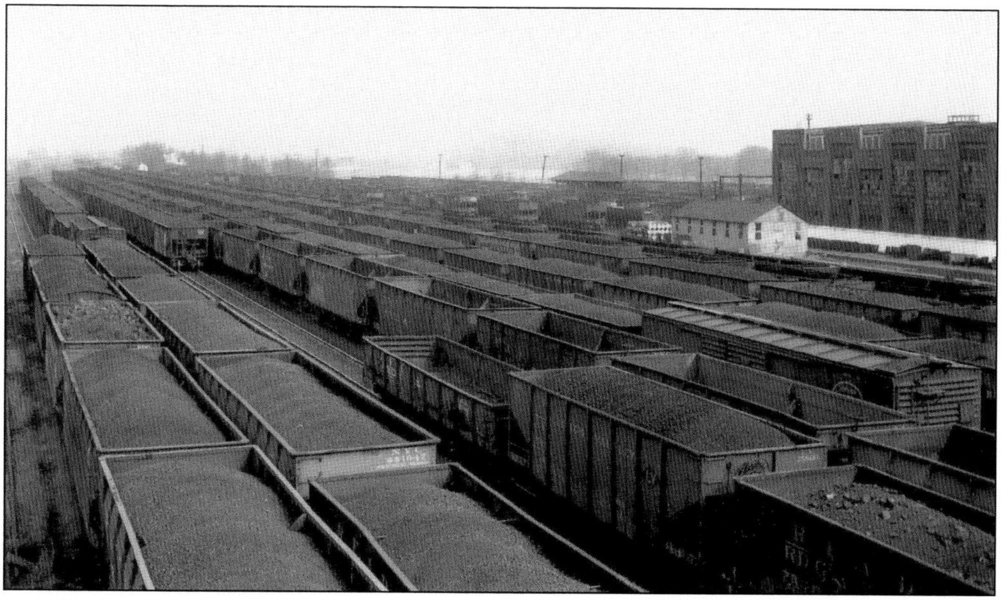

In 1930, the Avis yard was extremely busy repairing steam locomotive engines and cars. The yard had over 100 tracks and was often crowded with coal trains as seen here. In 1926, American railroads earned $3,587 per employee and paid an average of $1,527 per employee. Subtracting all other investments, the railroads were left with five percent profit, and since 1919, their taxes amounted to more than the dividends paid to stockholders.

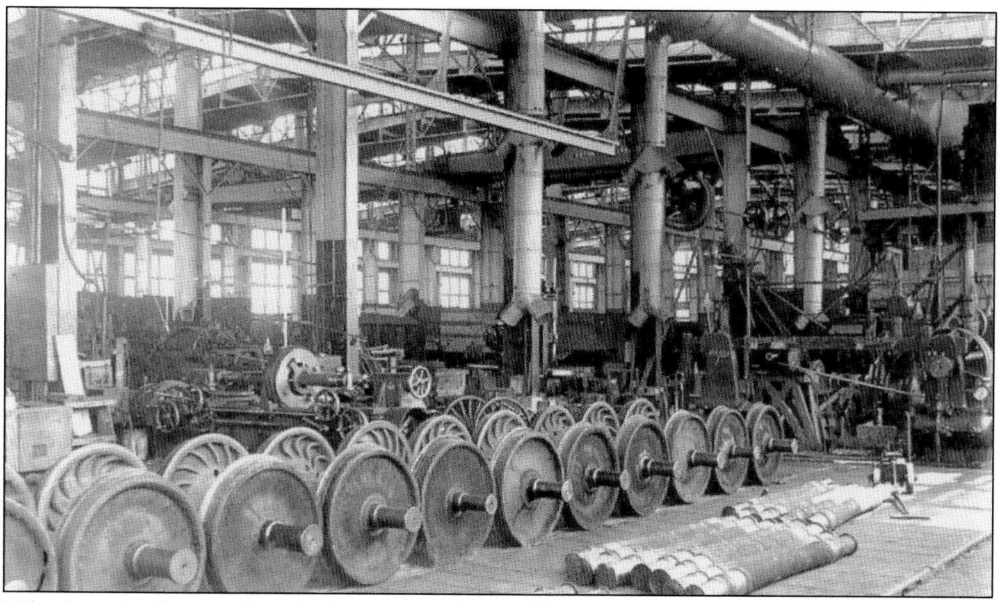

Wheels and axles stand ready for repair and assembly. The axles hold the wheels to gauge and transmit the load from the journal boxes to the wheels. Gauge was first determined by measuring the distance between carriage wheels with a little room for play, setting gauge at four feet and eight and a half inches. The first iron rail was made in 1831 and consisted of strap metal nailed to a timber stringer. The first "T" rail was made in 1834.

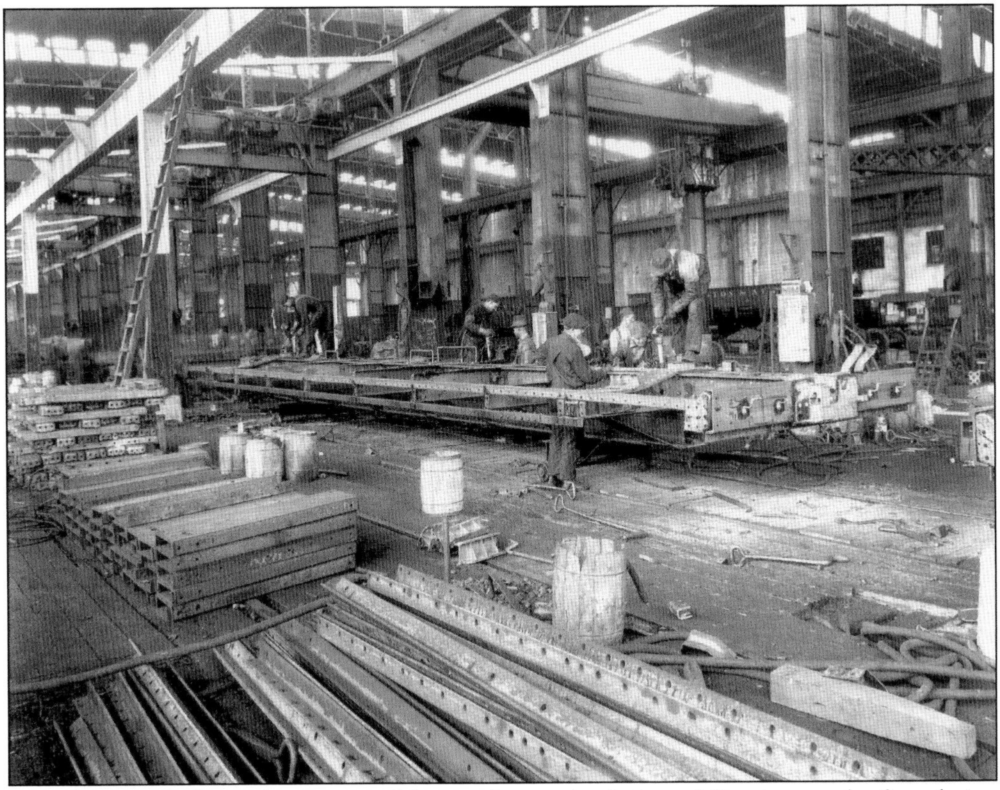

This photograph shows the interior of the car shop at the Avis yard. Fundamentals of car design had been adopted by the Association of American Railroads (AAR) for guidance in building freight cars. A book called the *Car Builder's Dictionary* was first published in 1879 with 18 revised editions published by 1951. In 1922, the name was changed to *Car Builder's Cyclopedia.*

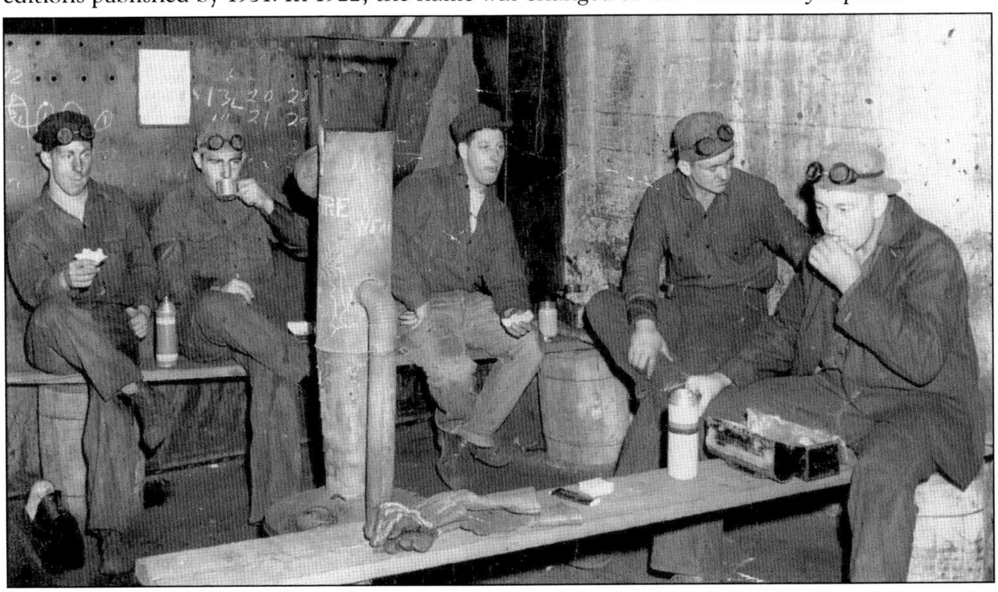

Here are a few "car knockers" at lunch break during the early 1950s. They are, from left to right, Jack Thomas, ? Eckenstine, Bob Bay, Pete Thomas, and John W. Karstetter.

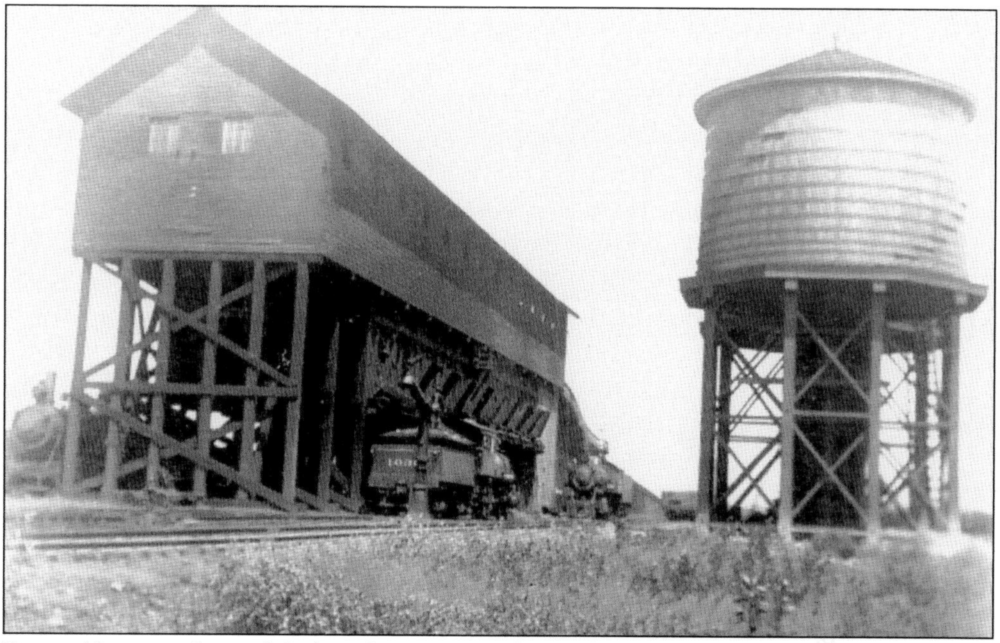

Pictured here are the coal dock and water tower during the days of steam power. The tower was made of cedar wood held together with steel strapping. Water was pumped from the creek or river, and it was not uncommon to find fish inside. In 1860, distance was measured in miles per cord of wood and per pound of pork, which was used in place of oil at that time.

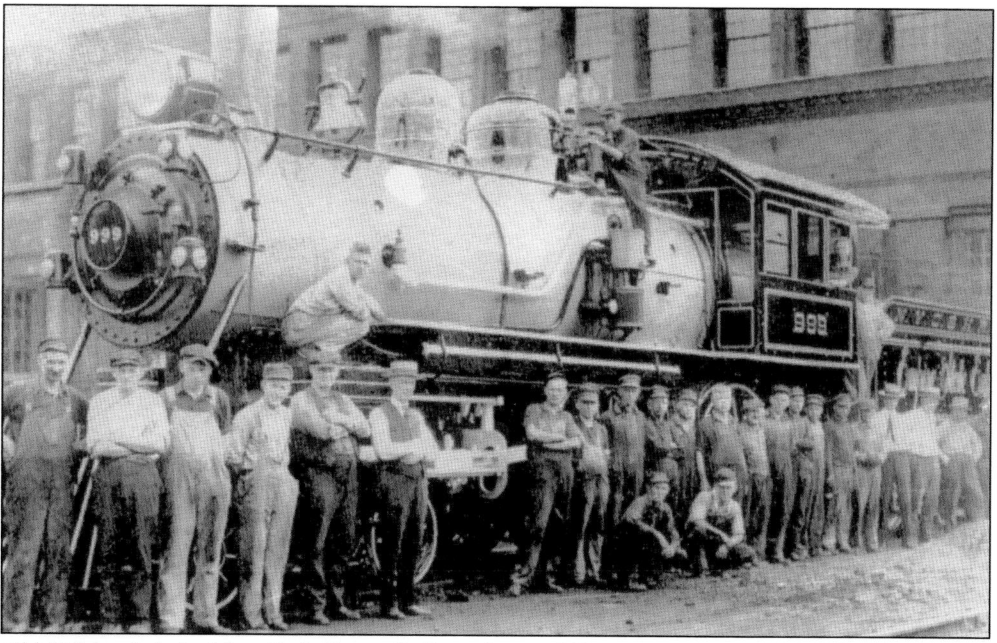

Old 999 hauled the New York Central's State Limited Express train at 112.5 miles per hour on May 10, 1893, and broke the world record for speed. The driving wheels were 86 inches high. Charlie Hogan was the engineer. It lost its number in 1913, was renumbered 1086, and used to pull passenger trains between Jersey Shore and Clearfield. Old 999 was taken out of service in 1921 and restored by this crew at the Avis Shops.

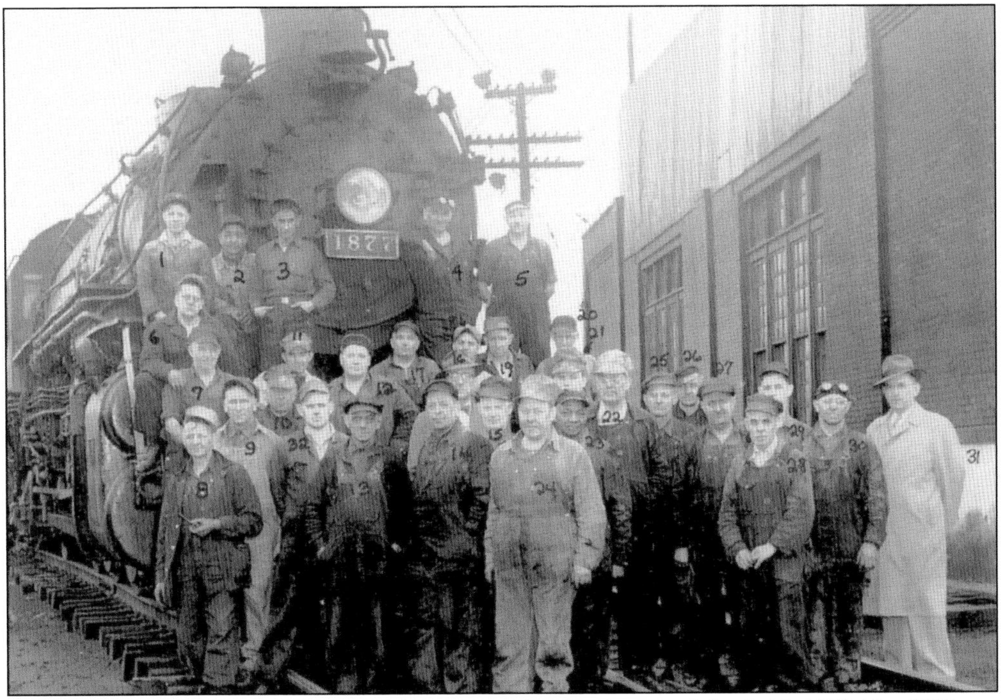

This was the last steam engine out of the Avis yard—the date was March 23, 1953. No. 1877 was used in the Avis yard and on occasional freight runs between Jersey Shore and Williamsport. Gone was the sound of the steam whistle echoing across the valley. Both the New York Central Railroad (April 17, 1826) and the town of Jersey Shore (March 15, 1826) originated the same year.

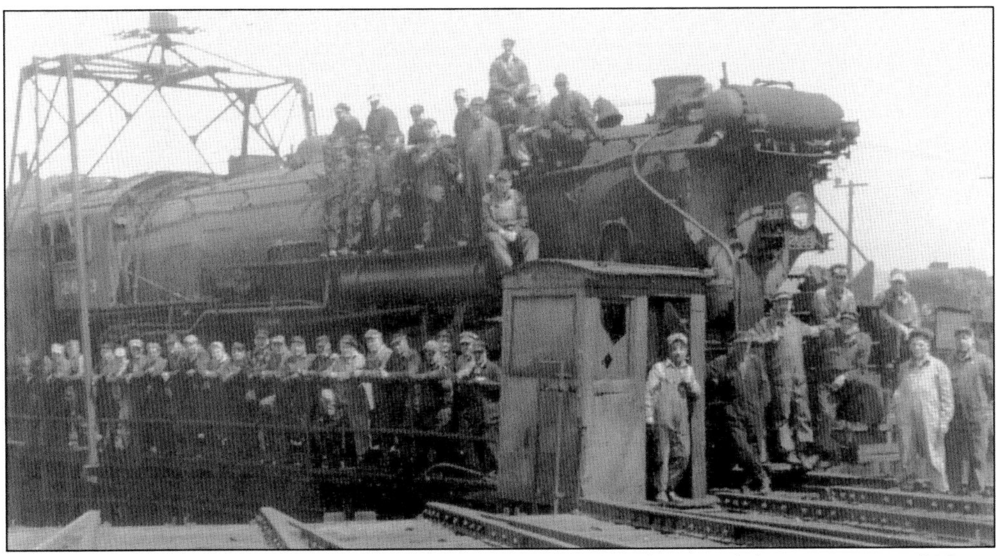

The roundhouse crew and engine on the turntable posed in honor of the retirement of Harry Shellenberger on May 5, 1950. The table was turned by two large electric motors down in the pit. The railroad shop completely closed down on August 2, 1955, and dismantling operations were completed on September 16. The Pennsylvania and New York Central Railroads merged in April 1966.

Frank Schoendorfer was born in Austria in 1867, studied at the Vienna Music Conservatory, and immigrated to the United States in 1887. In his early career he was baritone soloist for John Philip Sousa's band and in 1911 took charge of the New York Central Band in Avis. He made it one of the finest bands in the east. He retired from the railroad in 1932 and became music instructor and assistant conductor of music at Mansfield and played with the Williamsport Symphony Orchestra.

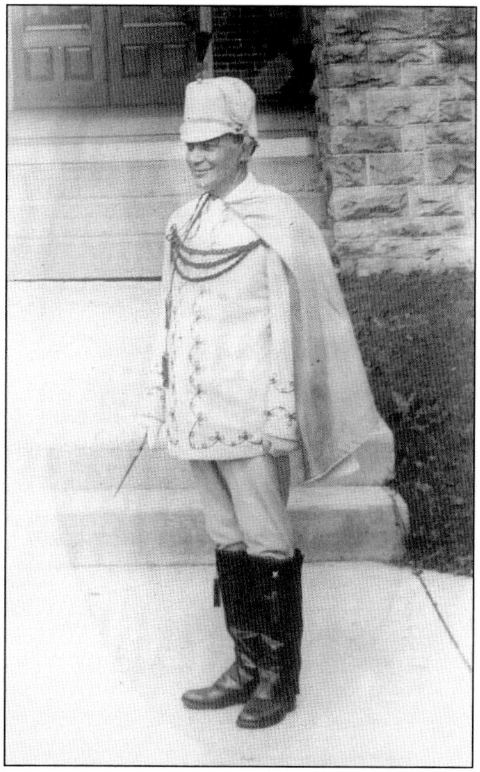

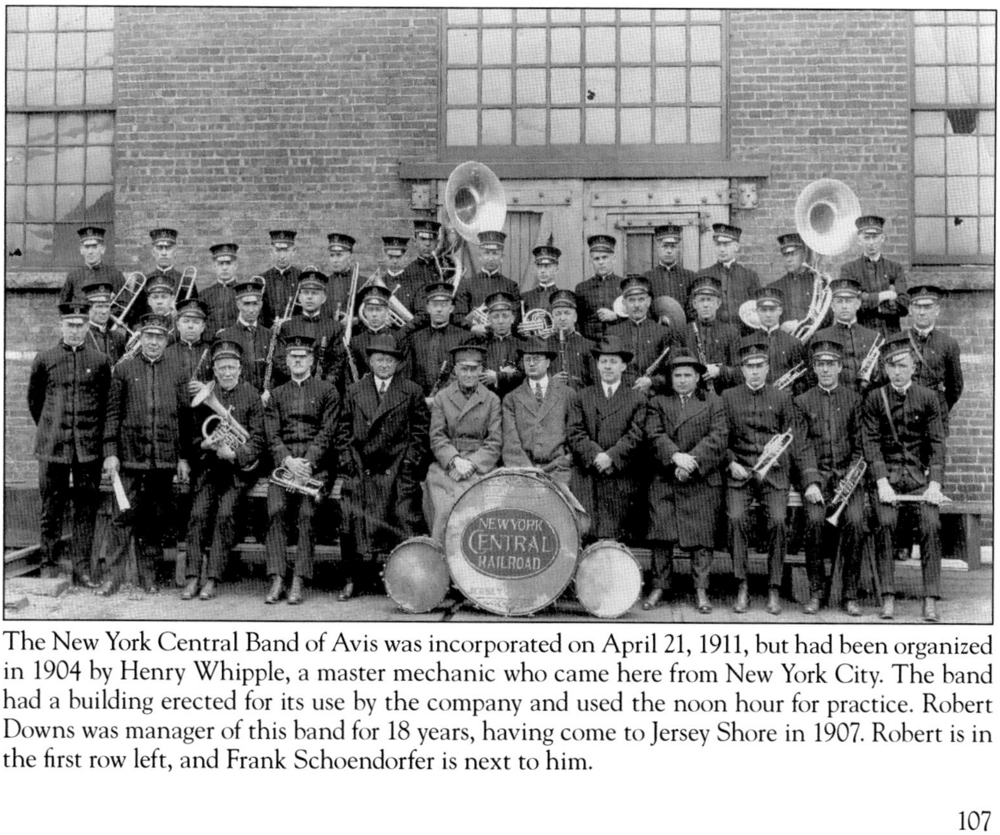

The New York Central Band of Avis was incorporated on April 21, 1911, but had been organized in 1904 by Henry Whipple, a master mechanic who came here from New York City. The band had a building erected for its use by the company and used the noon hour for practice. Robert Downs was manager of this band for 18 years, having come to Jersey Shore in 1907. Robert is in the first row left, and Frank Schoendorfer is next to him.

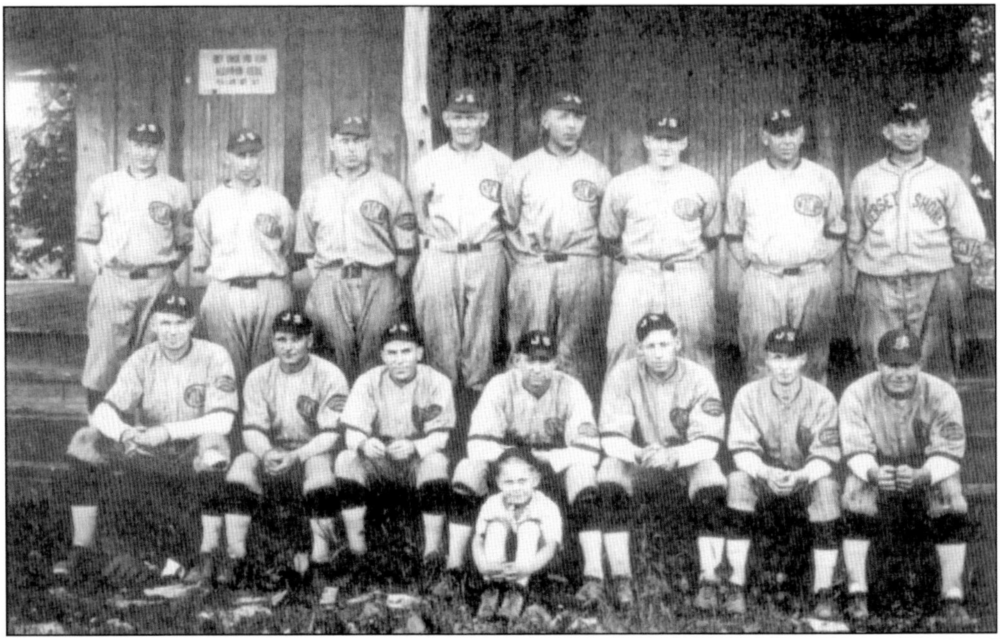

To build up local interest for the railroaders, Robert Cullivan organized his own brass band (Cullivan's Dark Town Band headquartered at the Allegheny House) and a baseball team in 1908. Here are members of the 1927 New York Central baseball team in a photograph taken at the old Gun Club, which was situated at the right field corner of Bailey Island Ball Park. This clubhouse washed away in the 1936 flood.

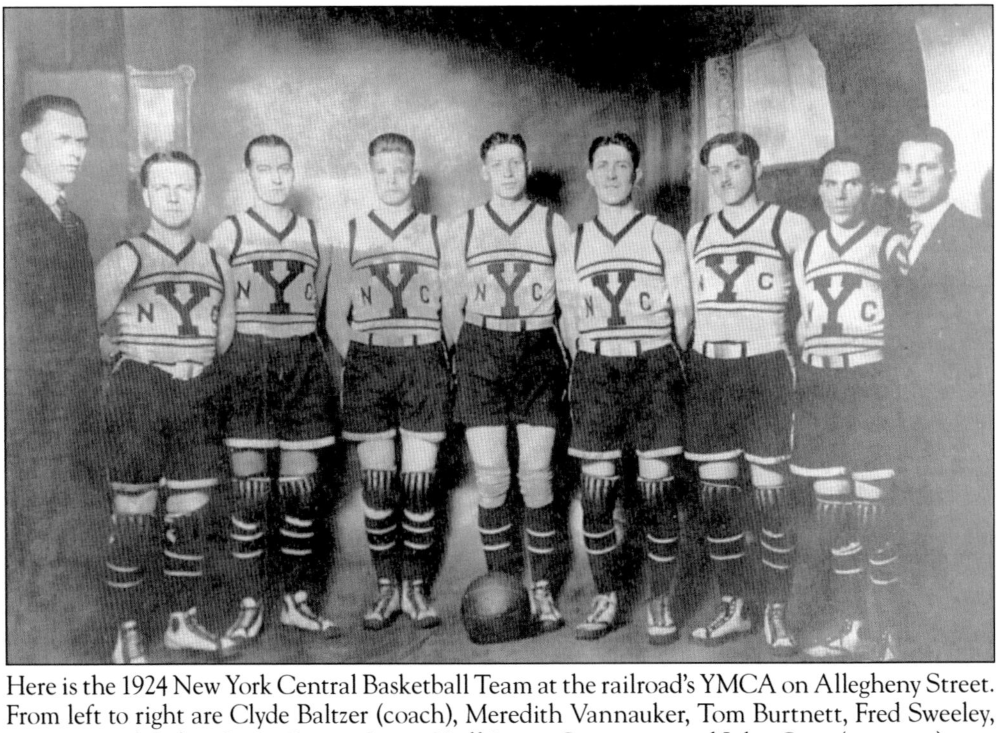

Here is the 1924 New York Central Basketball Team at the railroad's YMCA on Allegheny Street. From left to right are Clyde Baltzer (coach), Meredith Vannauker, Tom Burtnett, Fred Sweeley, Harry Stonebreaker, Bruce Bowes, Lewis Huff, Lewis Carpenter, and John Crist (manager).

Seven

UPTOWN JERSEY SHORE

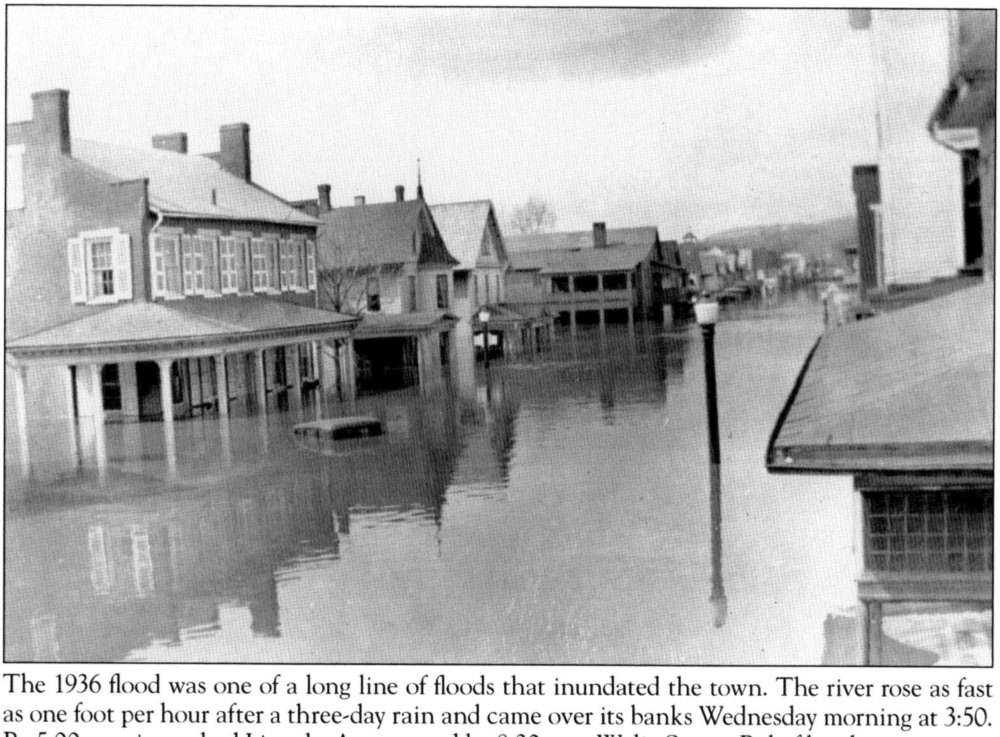

The 1936 flood was one of a long line of floods that inundated the town. The river rose as fast as one foot per hour after a three-day rain and came over its banks Wednesday morning at 3:50. By 5:00 a.m. it reached Lincoln Avenue and by 8:30 a.m. Wylie Street. Relief headquarters were set up at the high school and YMCA by members of the Works Progress Administration (WPA) and the Civil Conservation Corps (CCC).

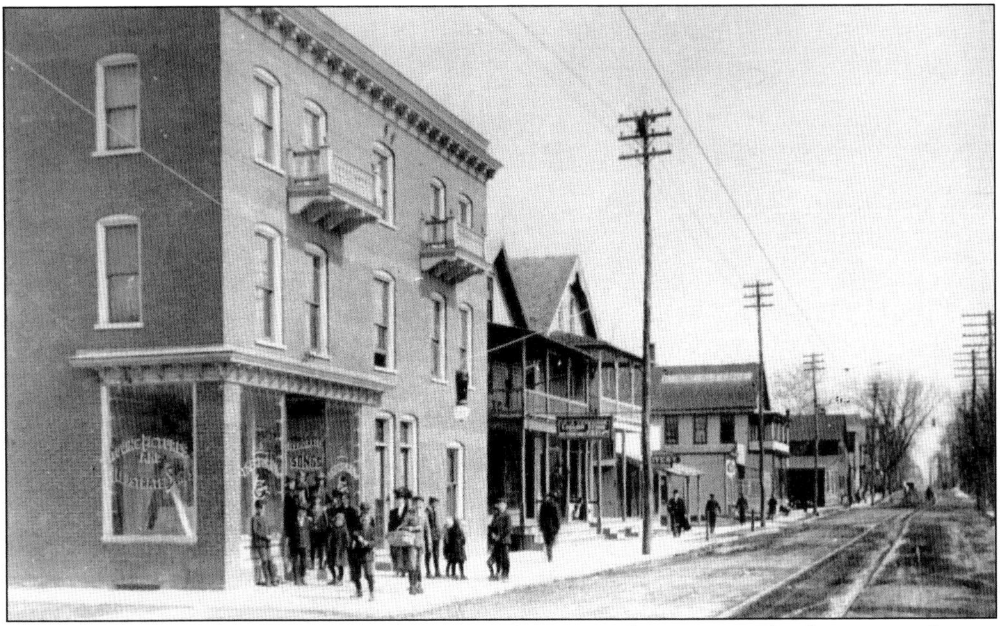

This is a view of Allegheny Street looking east from Lincoln Avenue. The first movie theater in town, the Electric Theatorium, was located here with a movie priced at 5¢ per person. This place was followed by Levegood's store, the old Shuman Livery, and the Frick Building built by John Irvin for Robert Camerer in 1898. Charles Frick bought the place in 1907 and opened a grocery store and dance hall. The Past Time Theatre was also located here. This place was torn down in 1944.

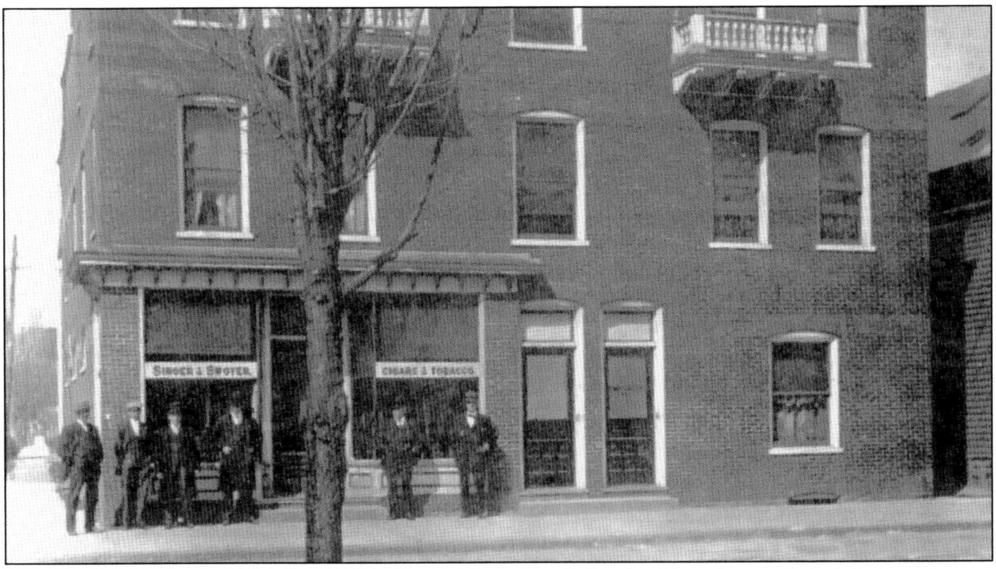

At one time there were five cigar factories in town, and this building housed the Nathan Singer and William Swoyer Cigar Factory, which started about 1902. Later Underwood Scherer opened an electrical appliance firm here, and in 1983 a fire resulted in the removal of the third floor. Other cigar manufacturers included Fillman, Herritt's Pittsburgh Stogie Factory, David Mick's Cigar Factory (established 1880), and Junod's on South Main Street. Mick's operation was in the old West Branch High School dormitory.

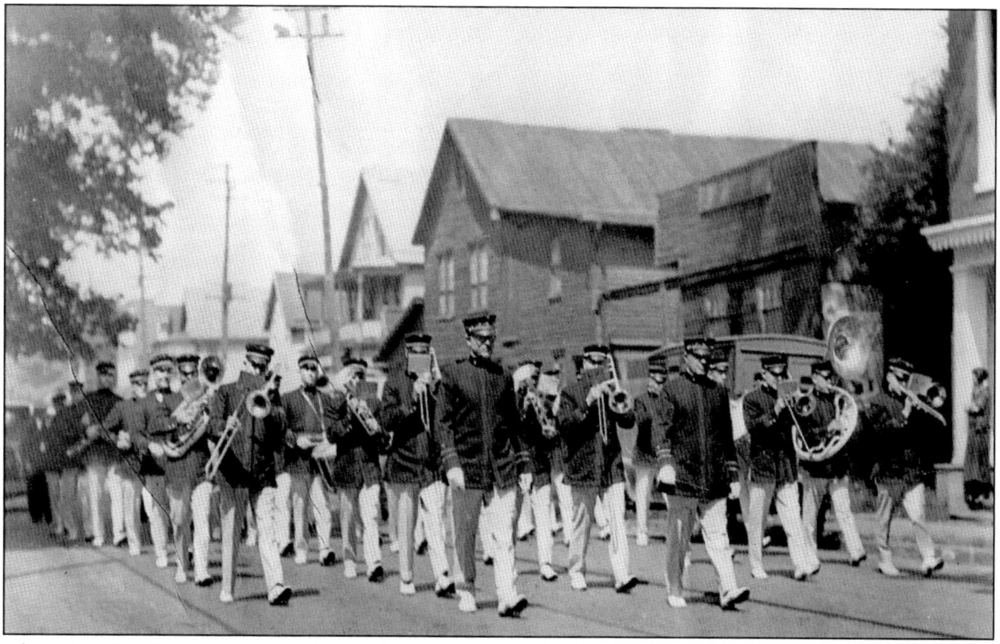

The New York Central Band marches past the old Camerer and Lambert Planing Mill on Allegheny Street. Robert Camerer was born in Germany in 1853, immigrated to America in 1867, and found his first work at this location when it was a tannery owned by L. R. Sponhouse. Camerer bought the place in 1884 and turned it into a planing mill. Window sashes, shutters, doors, and blinds were manufactured here.

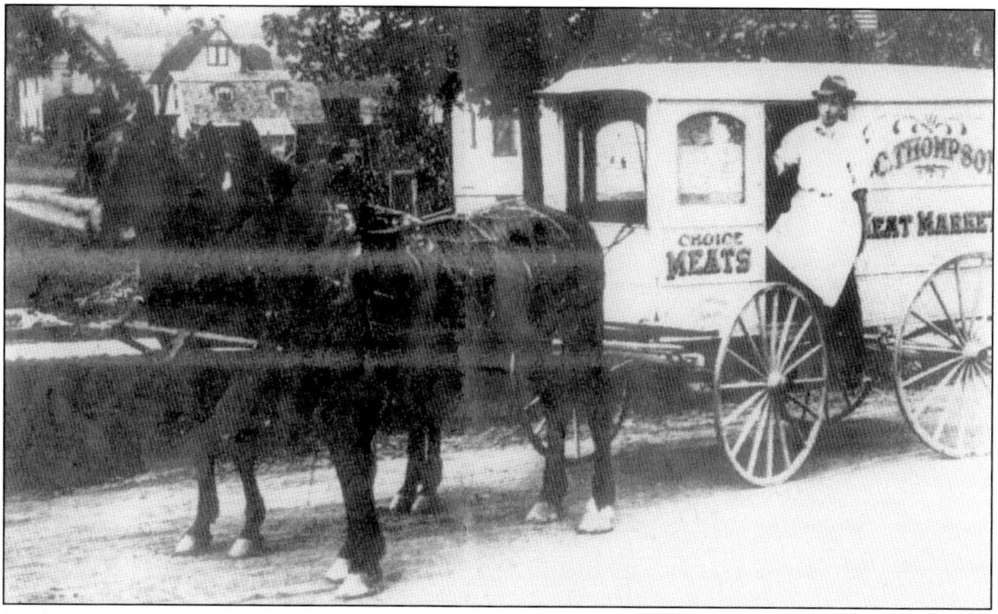

Leidy Curtin Thompson and brothers Howard, George, and Newt settled in Jersey Shore in 1887. After the great flood of 1889, they set up their first meat market in the old Junod building on South Main Street. Leidy's family lived at the old Bastress farmhouse at the top of Mount Pleasant Avenue and farmed all the land between Pfout's Run and Bastress Street. A delivery service was soon in operation, and a slaughterhouse was established at Denniston Hollow.

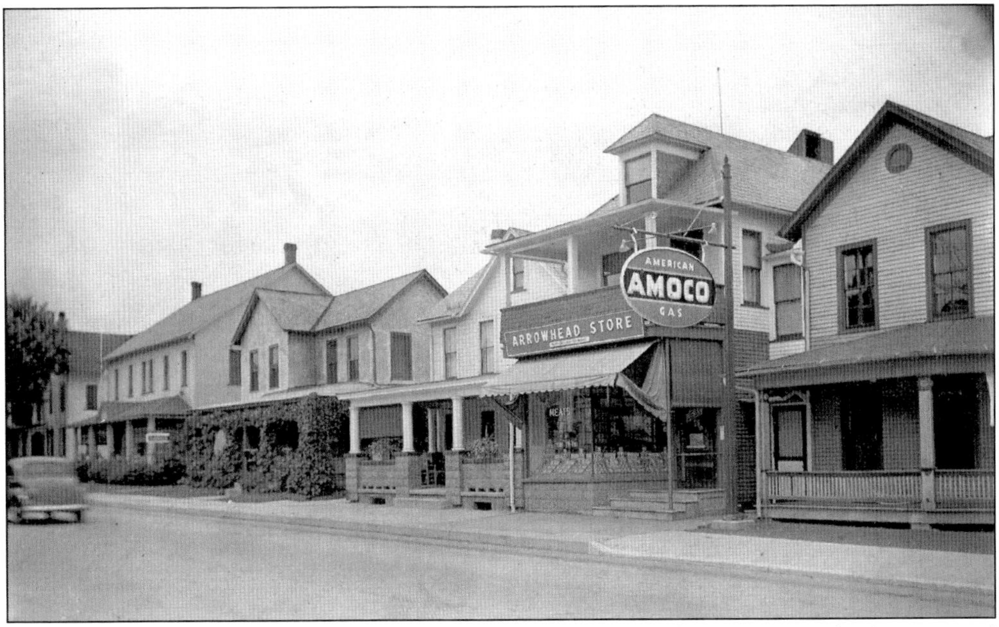

These buildings were on the north side of Allegheny Street between Lincoln Avenue and Calvert Street. From right to left were Eddie Elder's home (Elder's Restaurant), Clair and Annie Thompson's Meat Market/Thompson's Cash and Carry Market, the L. C. and Alice Denniston Thompson home, the Floyd Messimer home, Sarah Denniston and Harry and Dorothea Thompson's double house (Lee and Dot Heaton's later), and Selt's Harness Shop in the 1890s.

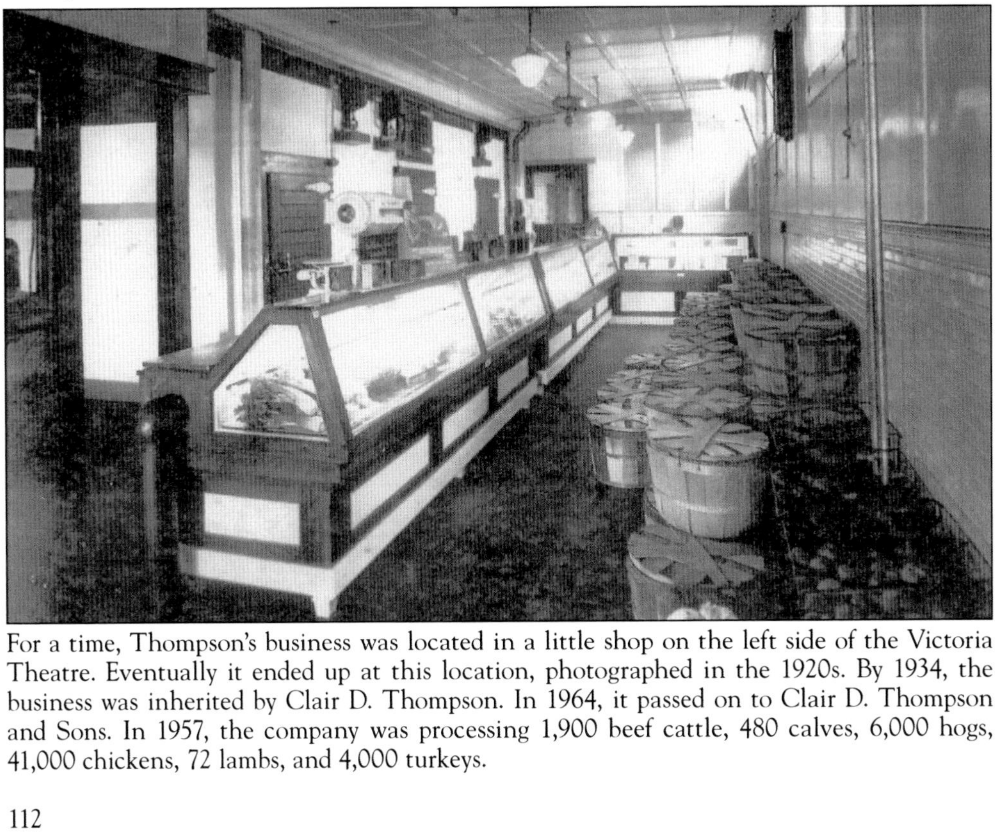

For a time, Thompson's business was located in a little shop on the left side of the Victoria Theatre. Eventually it ended up at this location, photographed in the 1920s. By 1934, the business was inherited by Clair D. Thompson. In 1964, it passed on to Clair D. Thompson and Sons. In 1957, the company was processing 1,900 beef cattle, 480 calves, 6,000 hogs, 41,000 chickens, 72 lambs, and 4,000 turkeys.

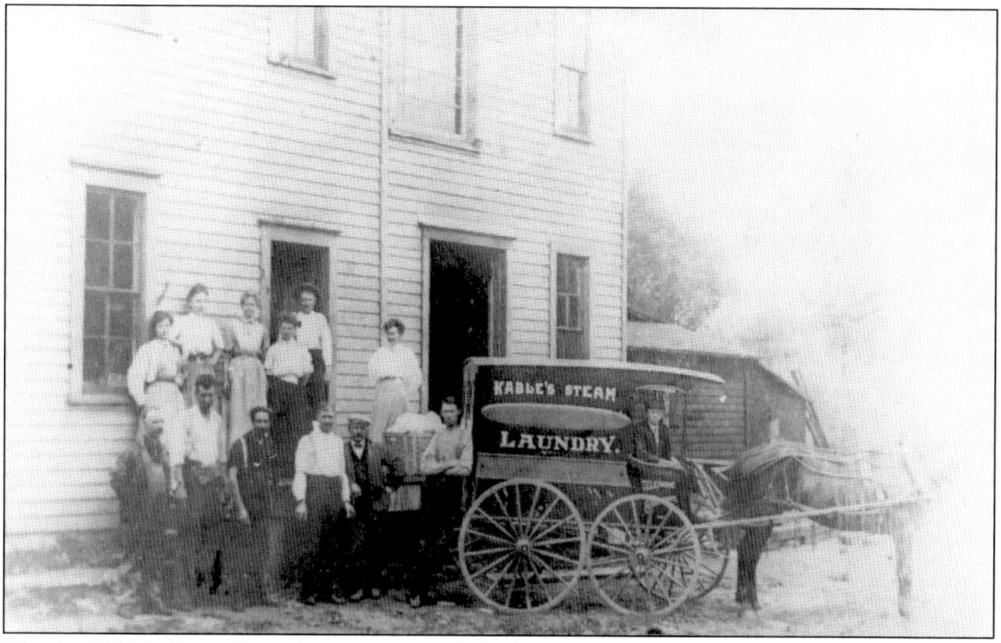

Charles Kable's Steam Laundry was on South Wylie Street behind where Berry's Packard Garage and home were later built. The Packard Garage was built on the site of a building used as an A&P market, which was moved across to North Wylie Street and operated by John Ryan as a used furniture store. This photograph was taken in 1906, and the "Perfection Laundry" burned down in 1926. Jersey Shore's first steam laundry was on Market Street.

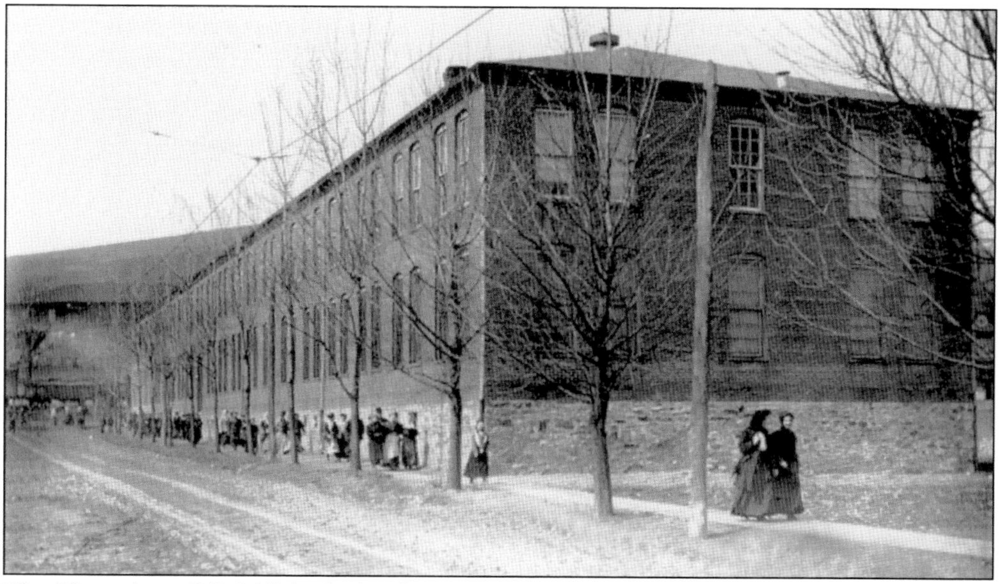

The Bloomsburg Silk Mill built this factory in 1902 at the west end of Washington Avenue. Above the west end of the building was located the New York Central freight station. The operation was taken over by Susquehanna Silk Mill in 1908. A 1913 employment advertisement guarantees $3.50 per week for learners, and the workweek has dropped from 58 to 54 hours. The mill employed between 500 and 700 people. The place closed in 1936 and was purchased by Central Cable in 1939.

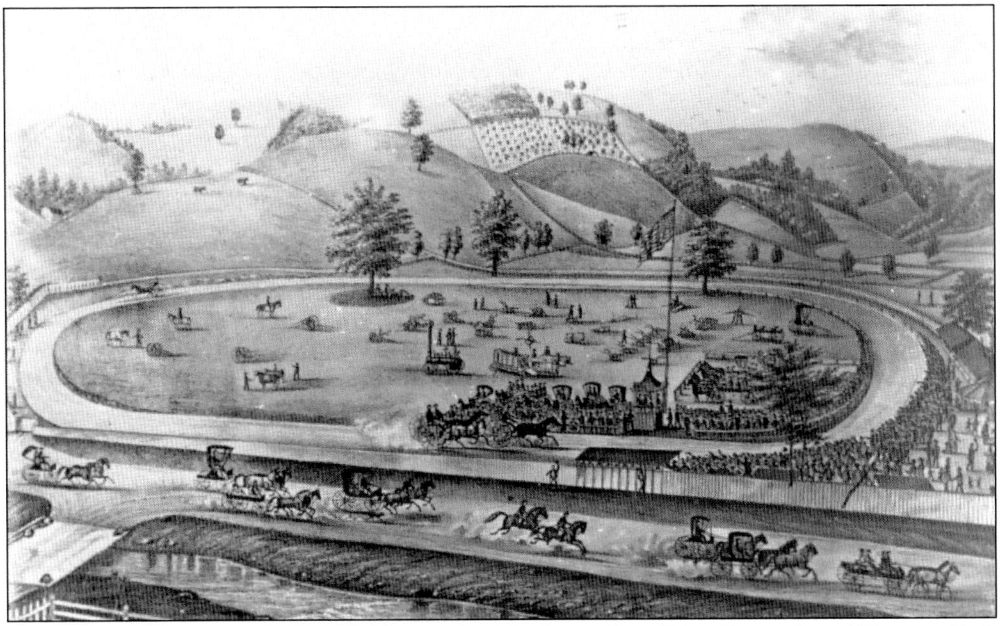

This is a view of the Lycoming and Clinton County Agricultural Fair Grounds and Trotting Park that was opened in 1875 and went out of existence by 1882. It was located on Allegheny Street between Arby's and the YMCA. An 1877 brochure advertises, "The grounds are conveniently located within an eighth of a mile from town and possesses one of the best half mile tracts in the state." The fair features contests for livestock, agricultural machinery, lumber, grain, vegetables, fruit, plowing, music, and shooting.

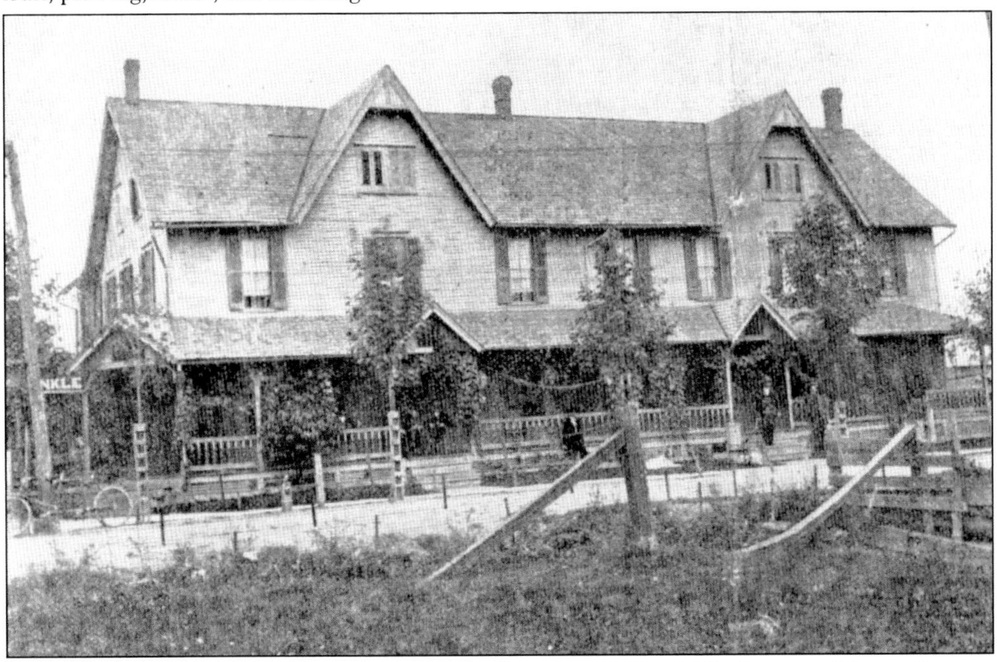

This was the Hotel Dunkle as it appeared in 1899 at the corner of Allegheny and Staver Streets. It was only two blocks from the New York Central Passenger Station, and the entire house and porch were illuminated with electricity. The rate was $1.50 a day.

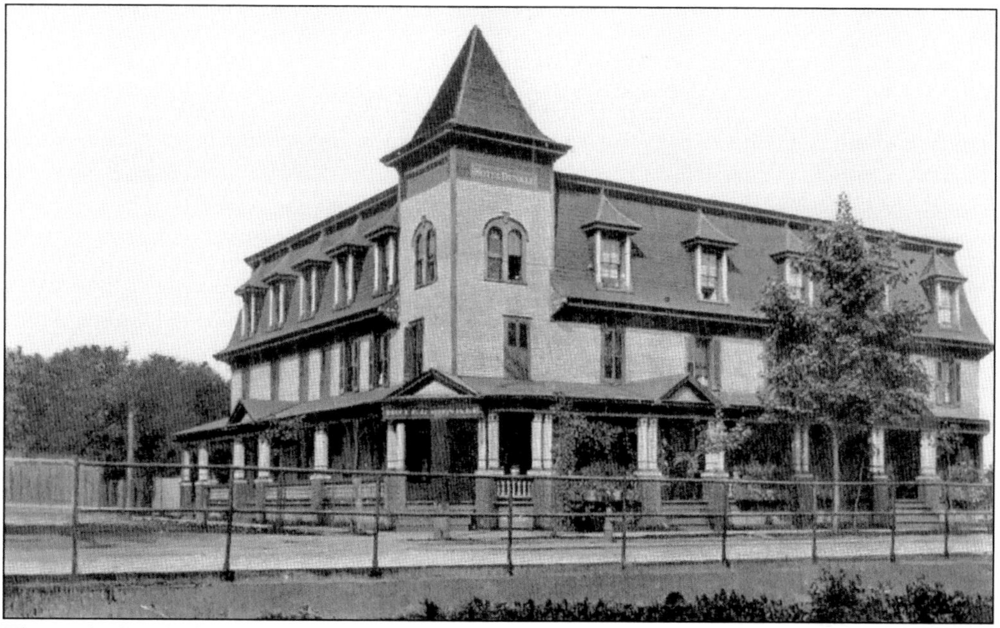

This is the hotel of Forest B. Dunkle after the old place was renovated. It was restructured again in 1931 to better serve as an apartment house. In 1885, there were 57 acres added to the borough including land from Wilson to Staver Streets and northwest of this hotel. Two hundred more people now lived in the borough, which was soon divided into two wards. Street names were being posted and street numbers painted on the houses, and a good sidewalk was laid to the race grounds.

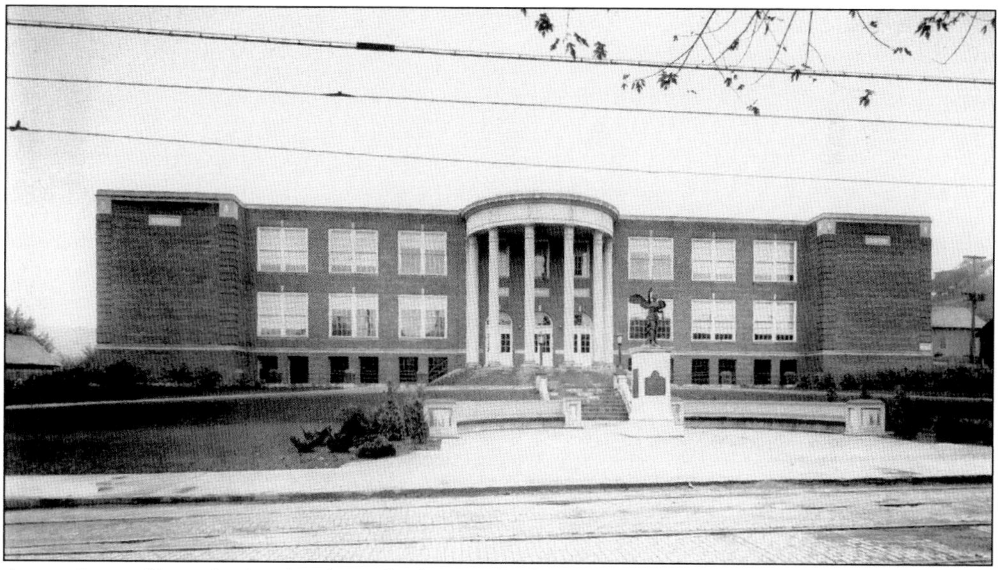

A new Jersey Shore high school was built on Allegheny Street to replace the Broad Street high school. Its cost was $250,000. An orchestra was started in 1922 and a band in 1925 by Charles Noll of South Williamsport. The first school newspaper, *Hillside Echoes* was replaced in 1939 by one called *Contact*, and the athletic field was completed by the WPA in 1936. Familiar school names include Painter, Grugan, Potter, Schoendorfer, Bardo, Bay, and Keiler.

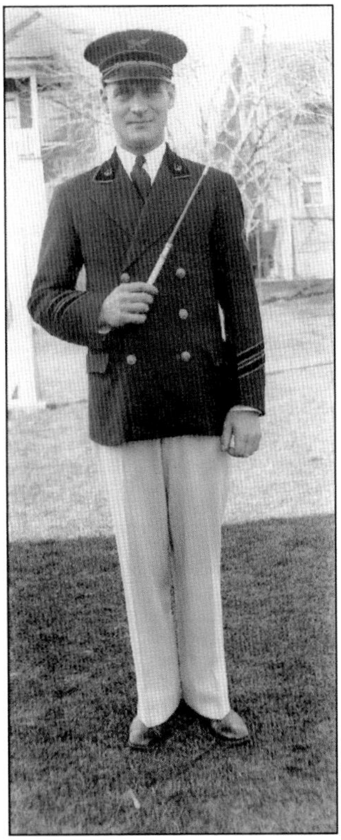

Frank L. Schoendorfer took charge of the Jersey Shore High School Band in 1930 and held that position until 1965. This band had an excellent reputation throughout his tenure. He helped organize the Pennsylvania School Music Association and was three times president of this organization for the Central District. Band students may well remember three marches he wrote, "The Uplifter," the "Celebrator," and the "Keystonian." One well-known dance band he played with was called the Pied Pipers, which included Bob Mencer, Charlie Vairo, Curley Hale, and Lou Piper.

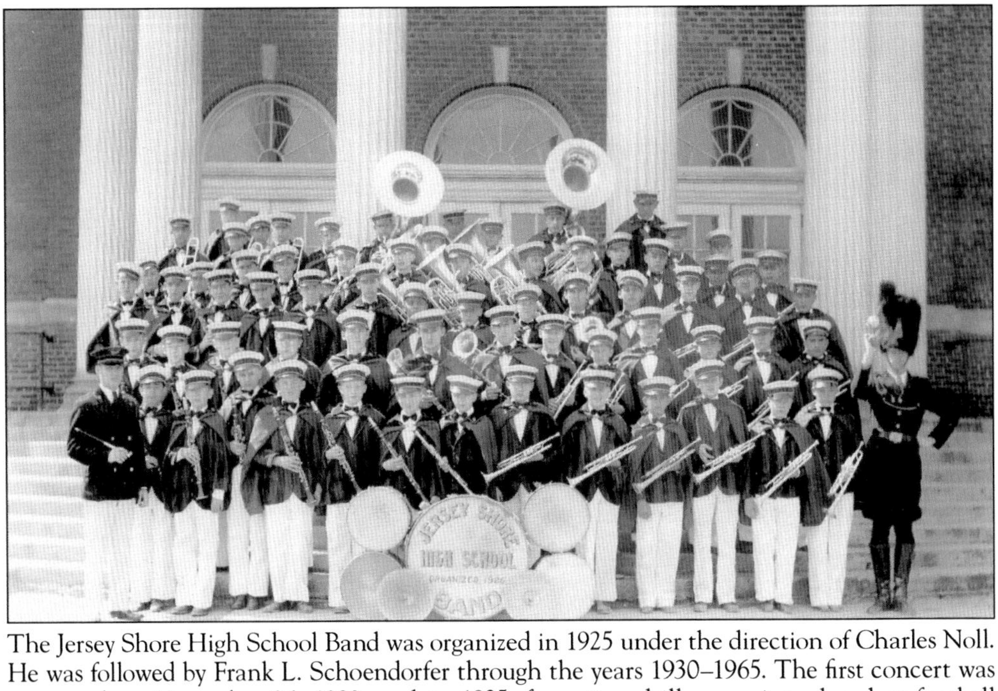

The Jersey Shore High School Band was organized in 1925 under the direction of Charles Noll. He was followed by Frank L. Schoendorfer through the years 1930–1965. The first concert was presented on November 26, 1929; and in 1935, formation drills were introduced at football games. Girls joined the band for the first time in 1937 and were allowed to play instruments in 1942. New band uniforms were purchased in 1938.

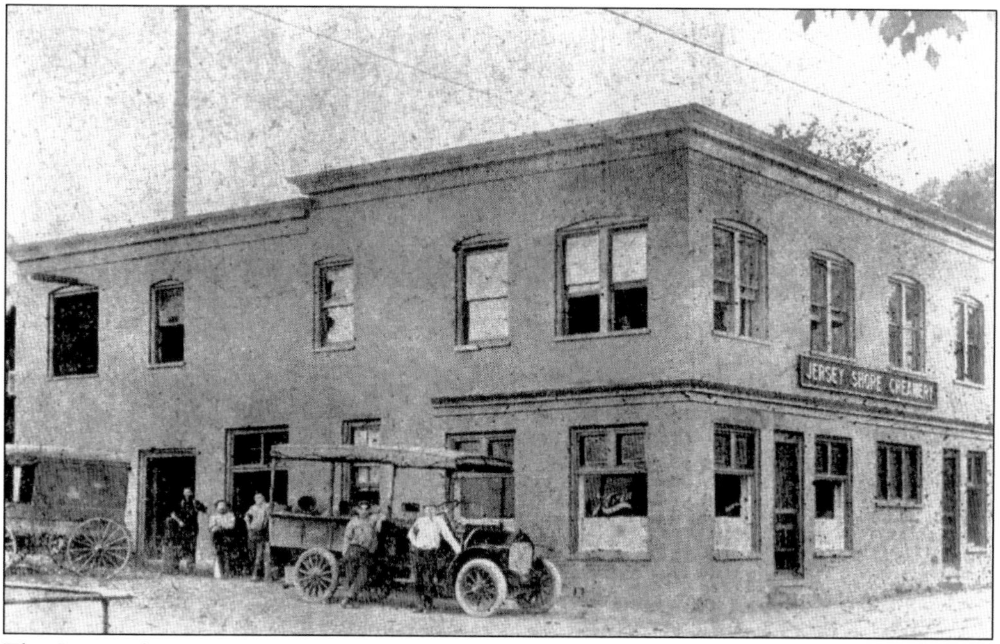

The Jersey Shore Creamery was constructed in 1912 by E. R. Wood of Williamsport, who operated the creamery until 1920. This picture was taken in 1913 and shows both the new delivery truck and old delivery wagon. The place produced milk, butter, cream, and Korvan Ice Cream. The brine freezers could produce 1,000 gallons of ice cream a day. By 1953, the output from this creamery was about 7,000 quarts of milk per day. The business eventually sold out to Valley Farms as did Dairylea and Hurrs.

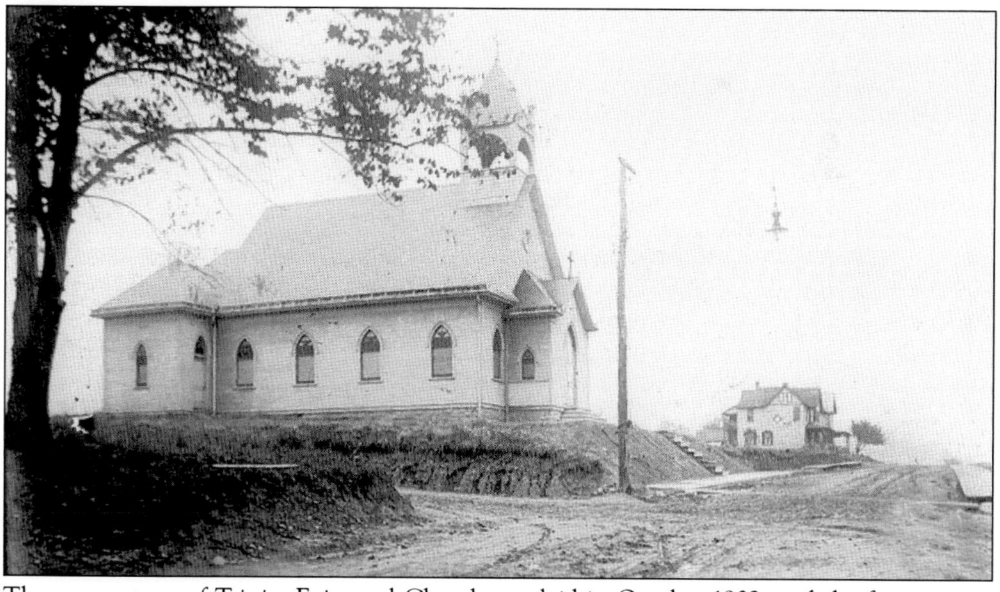

The cornerstone of Trinity Episcopal Church was laid in October 1902, and the first services were held in September 1903. The cost was $6,000. Mention of establishing an Episcopal church here dates back to 1823. Prior to this church building, services were held in the Williamson house on North Main Street and at the Masonic temple hall in the Sallada building. Note the unpaved streets, arc streetlight, wood sidewalk, and absence of the parsonage.

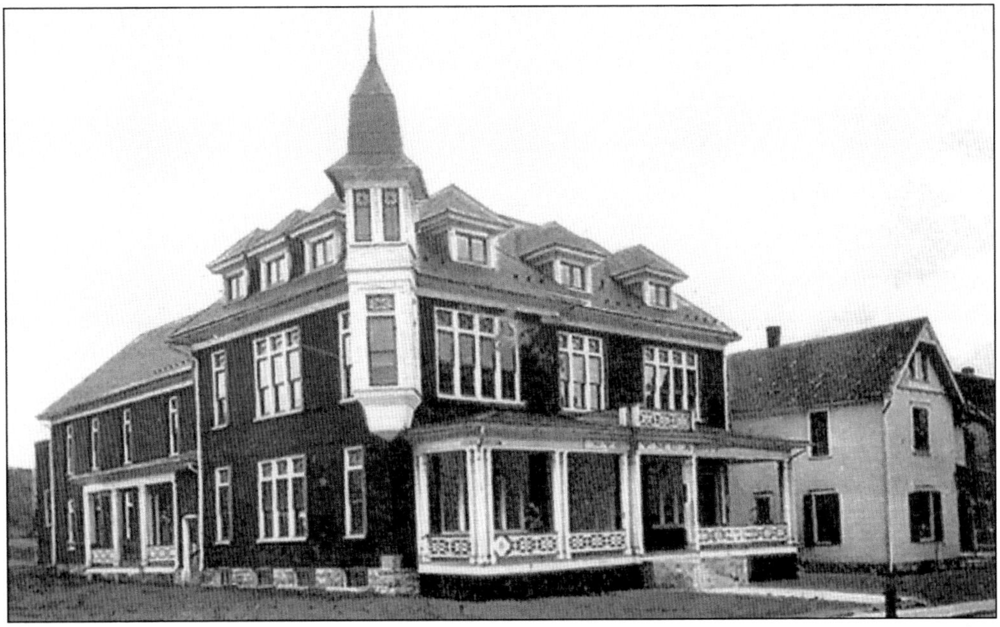

The charter for the New York Central's YMCA was granted by Judge William Hart on December 22, 1909, and the YMCA was built on Allegheny Street. A gymnasium and auditorium were added in 1912, and over time the place included a basketball court, bowling alleys, library, banquet hall, kitchen, and swimming pool (closed in 1955). Camp Cedar Pines opened in 1915, and Lewis L. Carpenter was director of the YMCA between 1927 and 1967. Louie was one of the best all-time athletes in Jersey Shore history.

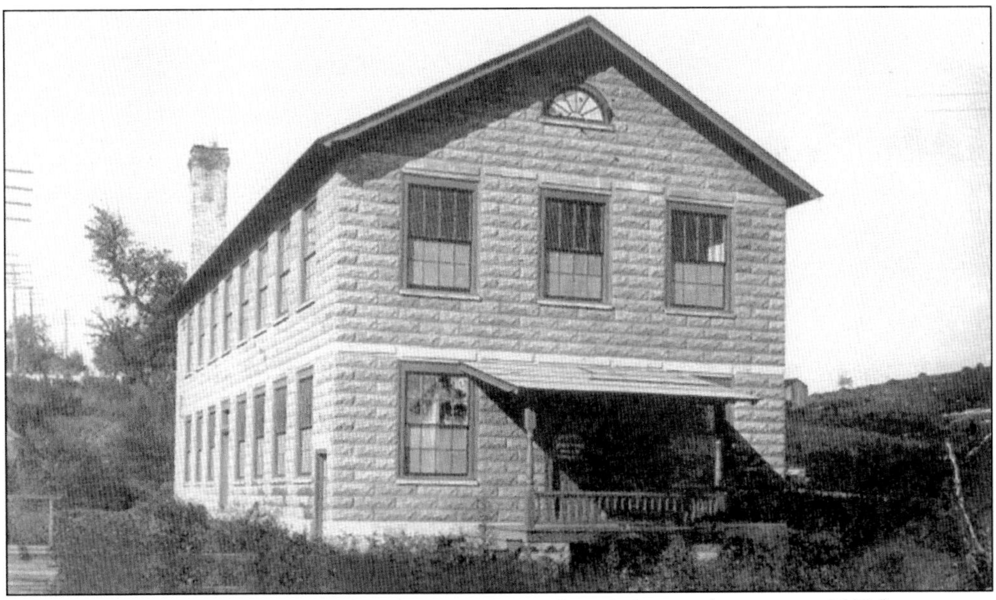

The local New York Central Railroad's YMCA was founded in early summer 1901 by a group of railroad officials, prominent among them was Donald Sommerville of Antes Fort. The first location of the YMCA was in New York Central House No. 3 at the railroad yard at the Junction. This building was formerly known as the "L. P. Van Wort House." A sign on the porch reads "Jersey Shore Knitting Mills."

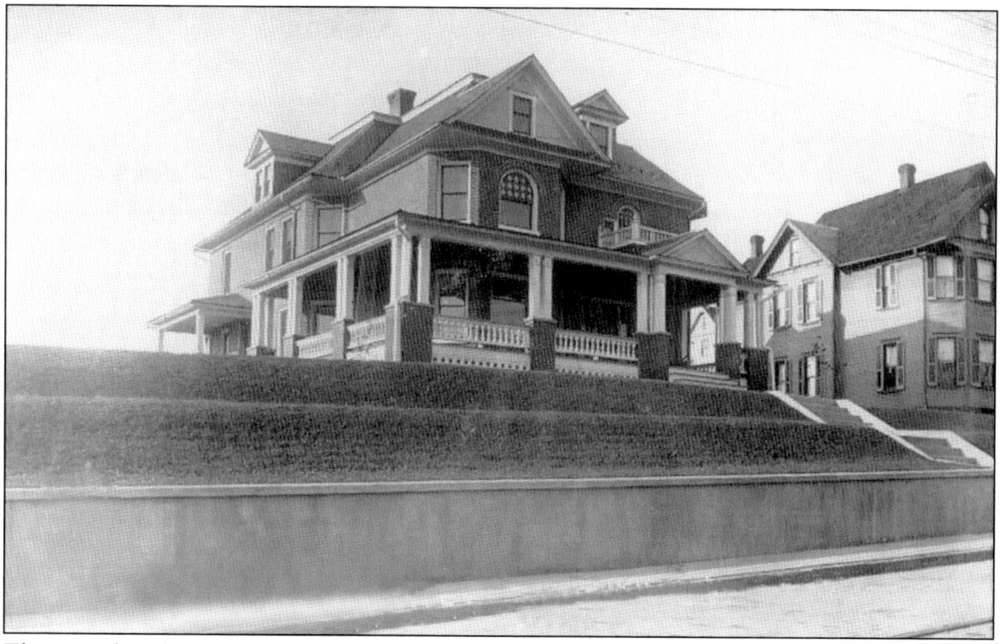

This was the Elmer C. Scheffer home at 943 Allegheny Street. Elmer came to Jersey Shore in 1902 and built many homes and businesses to accommodate the growth of the town due to the New York Central yard in Avis. This became Herritt's Convalescent Home in 1948 and was continued by William and Margaret Person in 1962. Their license was for 19 people.

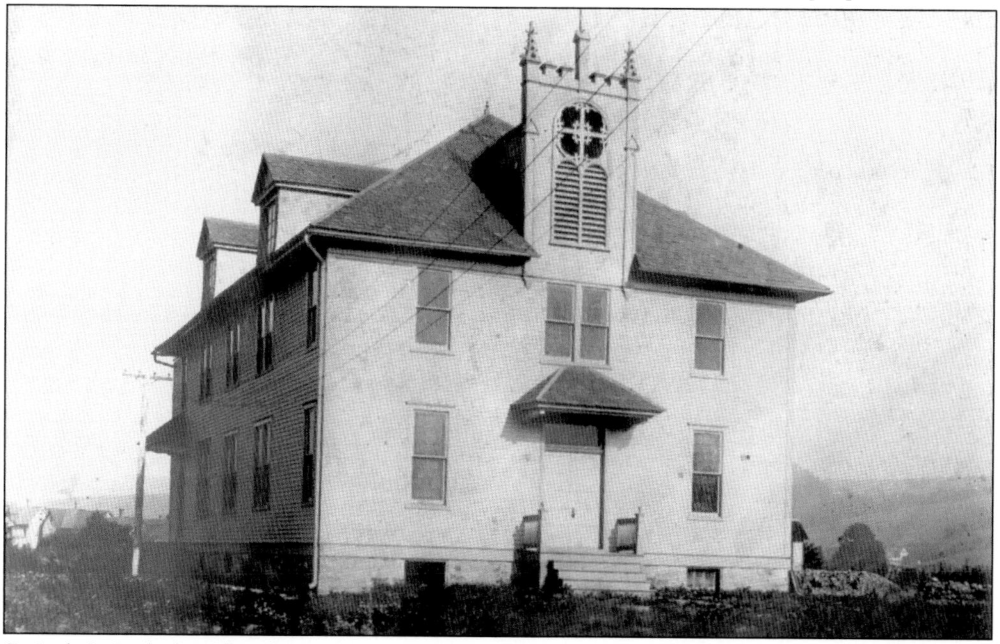

St. Luke's Catholic Church was built in 1904 and the rectory in 1908. The first Catholic service held in the Jersey Shore area was in 1882 at Antes Fort, and prior to the building of this church, services were held in either the Odd Fellows Lodge or that of the Knights of the Golden Eagle. St. Luke's was a mission of the Annunciation Church of Williamsport but was made a separate parish with the coming of Rev. Dennis Bustin. A new church was dedicated in 1969.

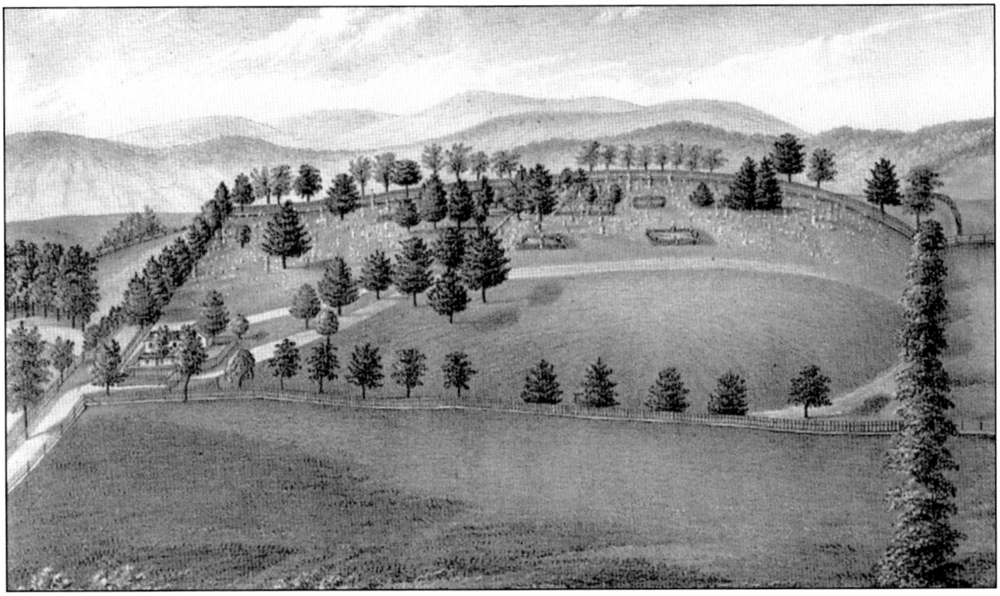

Land for the Jersey Shore Cemetery was laid out by Alexander McHenry, surveyor and civil engineer, on land donated by Mark Slonaker (432 lots) and Dr. Uriah Reed. The site was designated Mount Pleasant. This cemetery became incorporated on April 14, 1863, when interment fees were about $2. The original entrance to the cemetery was at Cemetery Street, and the chapel was built in 1926. In 1912, 69 graves were moved here from the Broad Street, or Richmond, Cemetery.

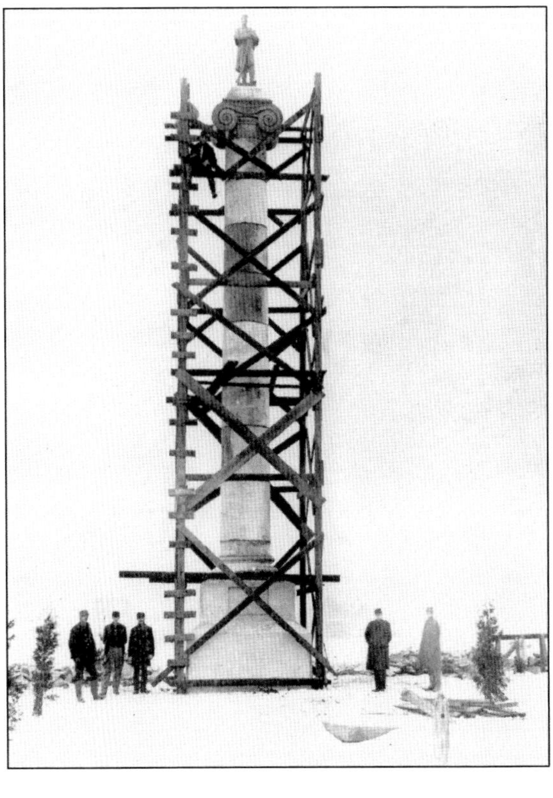

This was one of six pillars that came from the old Pennsylvania capitol building in Harrisburg that burned in 1897. This pillar was acquired by Mayor Peter Bricker and put in place by Adam Burger, a stonemason from Antes Fort. The monument was dedicated on May 30, 1908. Other columns were to be found at Lochabar Spring and Linnwood Cemetery, and two were at the north end of the Market Street Bridge in Harrisburg. The sixth column was lost by 1905.

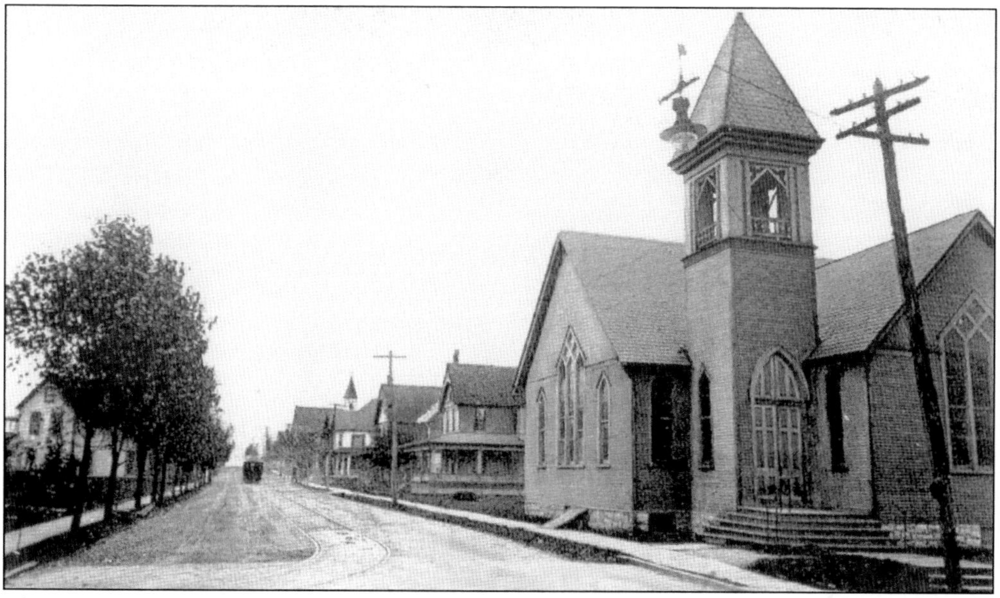

The Epworth Methodist Church was formed in 1895 with 27 charter members, and this site was purchased in 1897 for $2,850. The church burned on December 7, 1919, and a new brick church was built and dedicated on May 21, 1921. Today this building houses the Jersey Shore Public Library whose grand opening was on October 22, 2000. The state bank of Jersey Shore was on the other side of Oliver Street and was later purchased by Cap Wehler and Amos Dougherty and turned into the National Sporting Good Store.

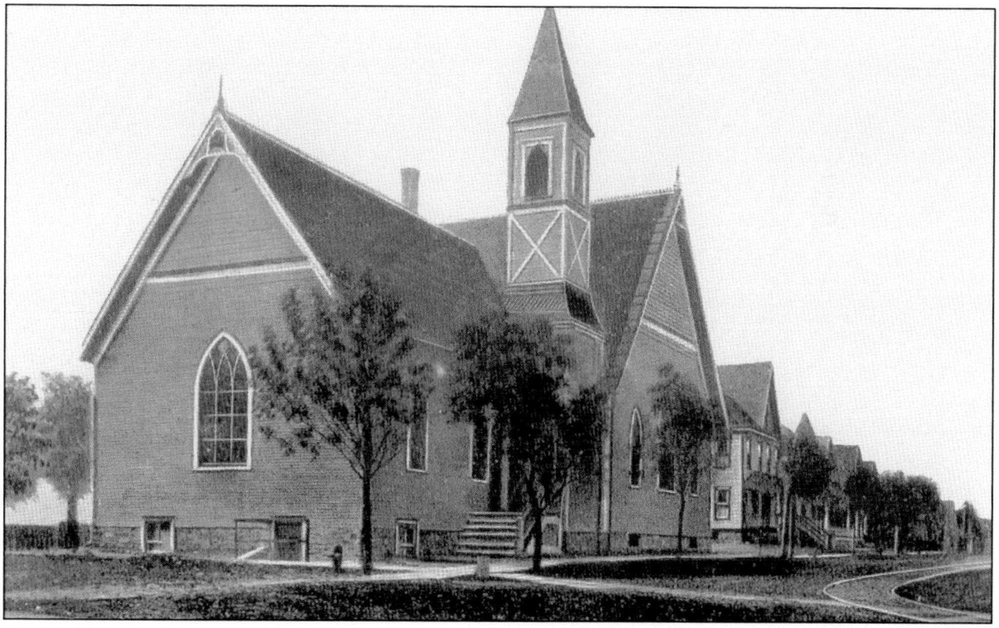

The railroad industry provided many jobs and stimulated growth of uptown Jersey Shore. By 1902, the First Baptist Church sponsored a mission church in uptown Jersey Shore and a lot (which was a cornfield at the time) was purchased at the corner of Oliver and Walnut Streets. The Walnut Street Baptist Church and parsonage were soon constructed. The church bell was purchased from the Jersey Shore Foundry at a cost of $5.

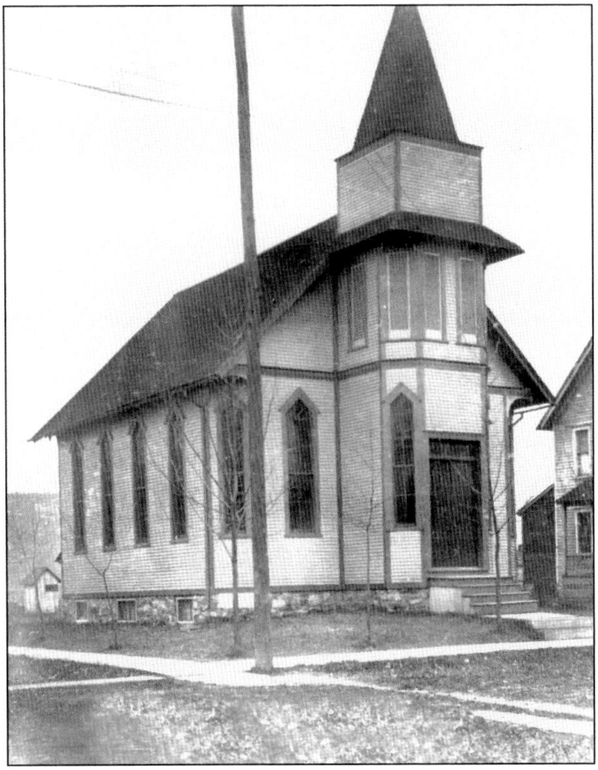

The Swedish Evangelical Lutheran Gustavus Adolphus Church of Jersey Shore Junction was chartered on October 23, 1895. A lot was purchased in 1896 from Ebenezer White for $1, and the church was built at the corner of Locust and Pine Streets in 1897. Sermons were in Swedish until around 1939. The first deacons were John Peterson, Aaron Peterson, and Charles Sundberg. This church closed in 1964 with the final sermon given by Rev. Donald Olson.

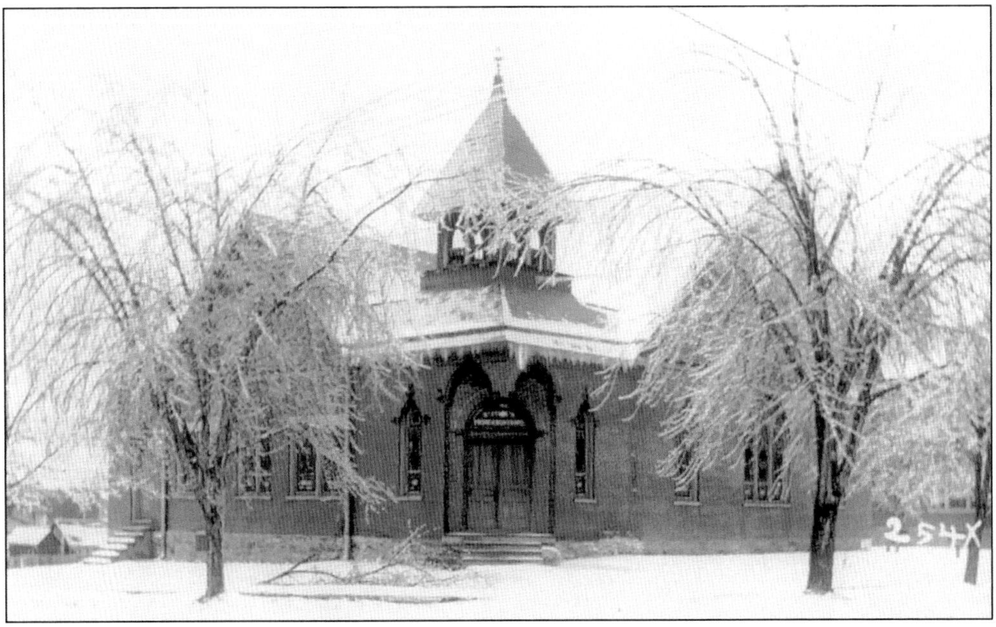

St. Paul's Chapel was an outgrowth of the First Presbyterian Church but not without controversy. The need for this third ward church was strongly promoted by the Presbyterian Chapel Aid Society, and as a result, the church was built and dedicated on February 26, 1905. The Church of God purchased this chapel in November 1926 through the efforts of Mr. and Mrs. George Ramer, who moved to Jersey Shore in 1900.

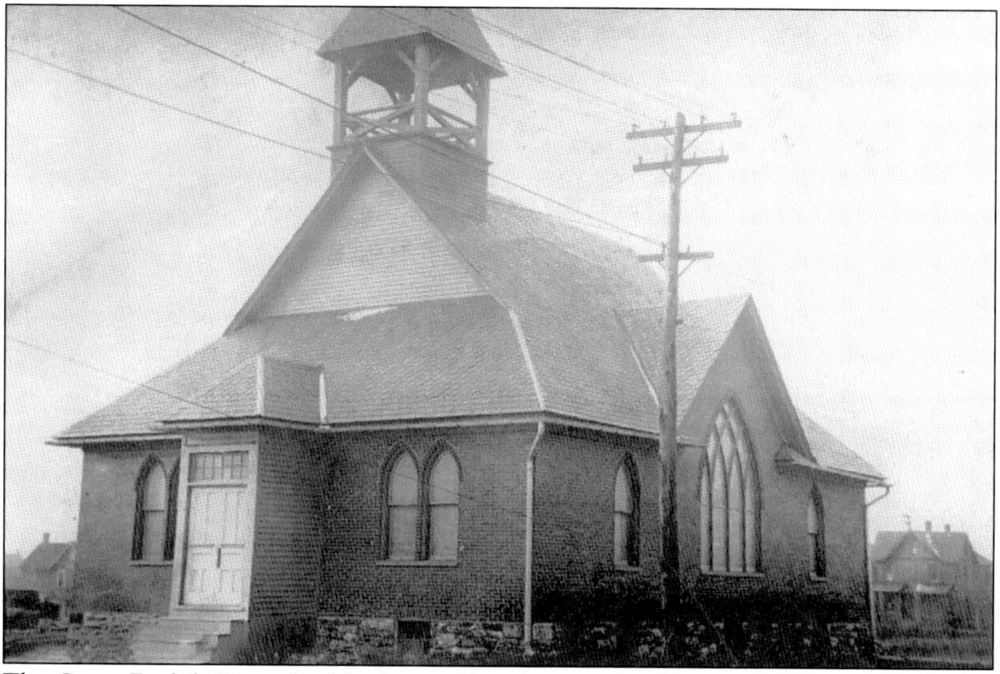

The Grace English Evangelical Lutheran Church was organized in 1905 after an 1899 start dissolved in 1902. After receiving a legal charter on June 18, 1906, 37 members decided to build this church on Maple Street. The cost was $4,500, and the dedication service was held on January 19, 1908. A Sunday school addition was built in 1956, and a new front was added to the original church in 1975.

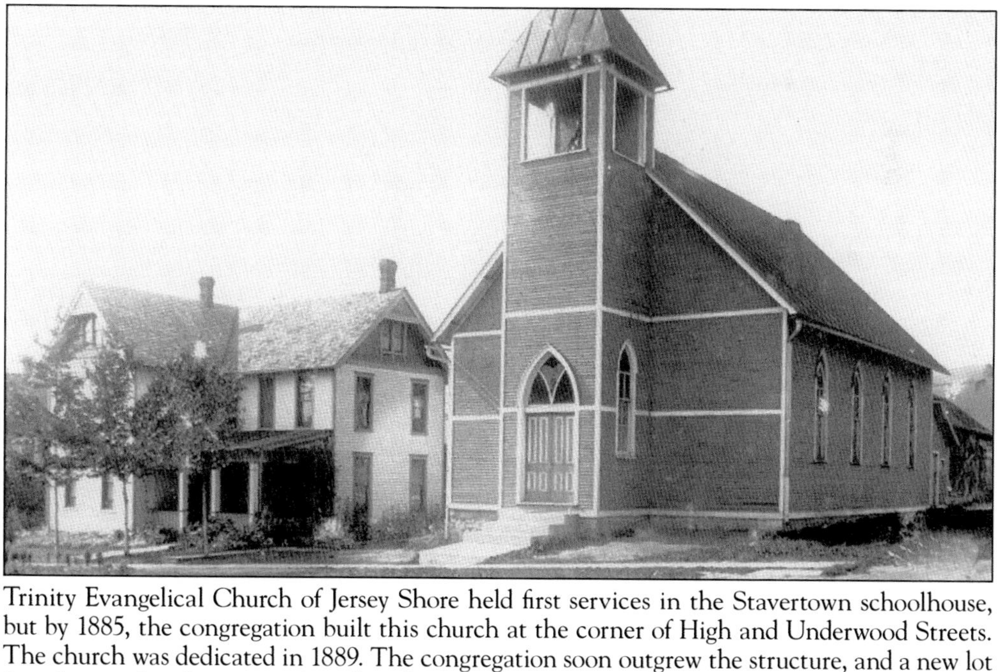

Trinity Evangelical Church of Jersey Shore held first services in the Stavertown schoolhouse, but by 1885, the congregation built this church at the corner of High and Underwood Streets. The church was dedicated in 1889. The congregation soon outgrew the structure, and a new lot for a bigger church was purchased at the corner of Allegheny and Glover Streets. The church was torn down in 1915.

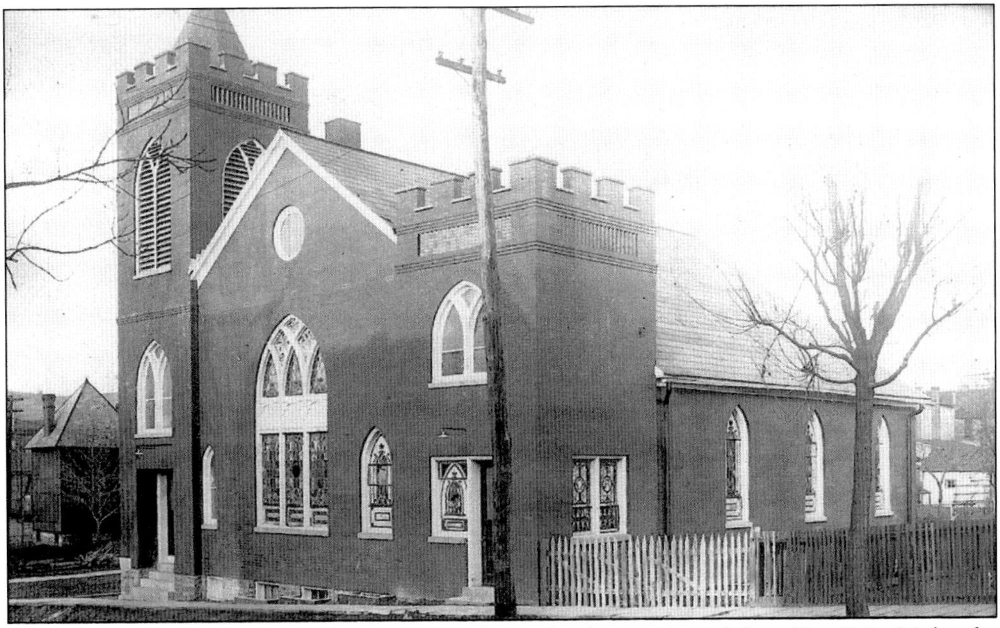

The new Trinity Evangelical Church was built on this lot purchased from Dr. C. L. Mohn for $800, and the building contract was given to Elmer Scheffer on June 3, 1912. The building was dedicated on February 13, 1913. A rapidly growing congregation resulted in the building of a large addition, which was constructed in 1916 and dedicated on May 7. Sunday school attendance was near 500 people at this time.

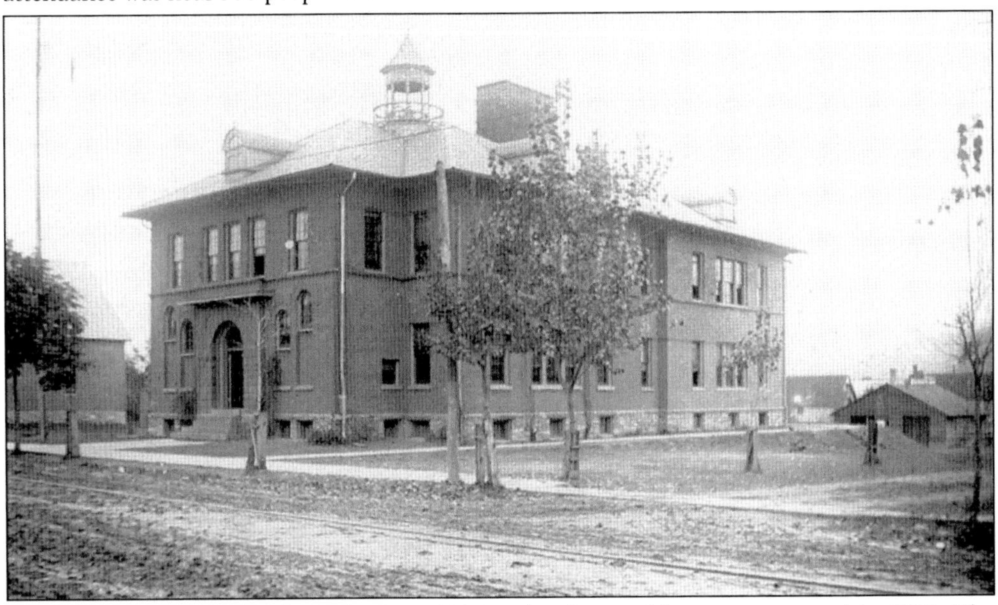

The Walnut Street School was built in 1886 with a large addition constructed in 1914. The number of students attending that year was 1,193. Leroy Keiler is a familiar name to education in Jersey Shore, having been in the profession for 43 years. He was principal of this school from 1925 to 1940, and principal of the Broad Street School from 1946 to 1967. He was also associated with the Boy Scouts and the YMCA for 35 years, and he was head counselor at Camp Cedar Pines for 28 years.

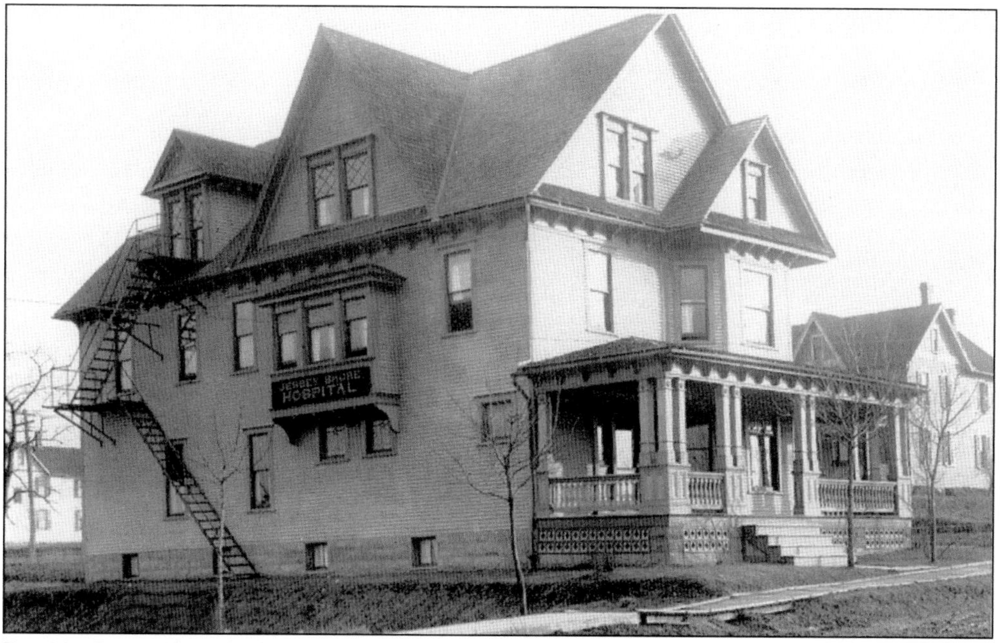

By 1909, Jersey Shore had an adequate supply of doctors but needed better hospital facilities. The home of L. D. Herritt, at the corner of Thompson and Howard Streets, was purchased in 1910, converted for hospital use, and opened its doors on October 11, 1911. Its capacity was 14 patients. A new addition and remodeling increased the patient capacity to 245 in 1924. The place was again enlarged when the Sanford Hospital merged with the Jersey Shore Hospital and became the Jersey Shore Community Hospital in 1938.

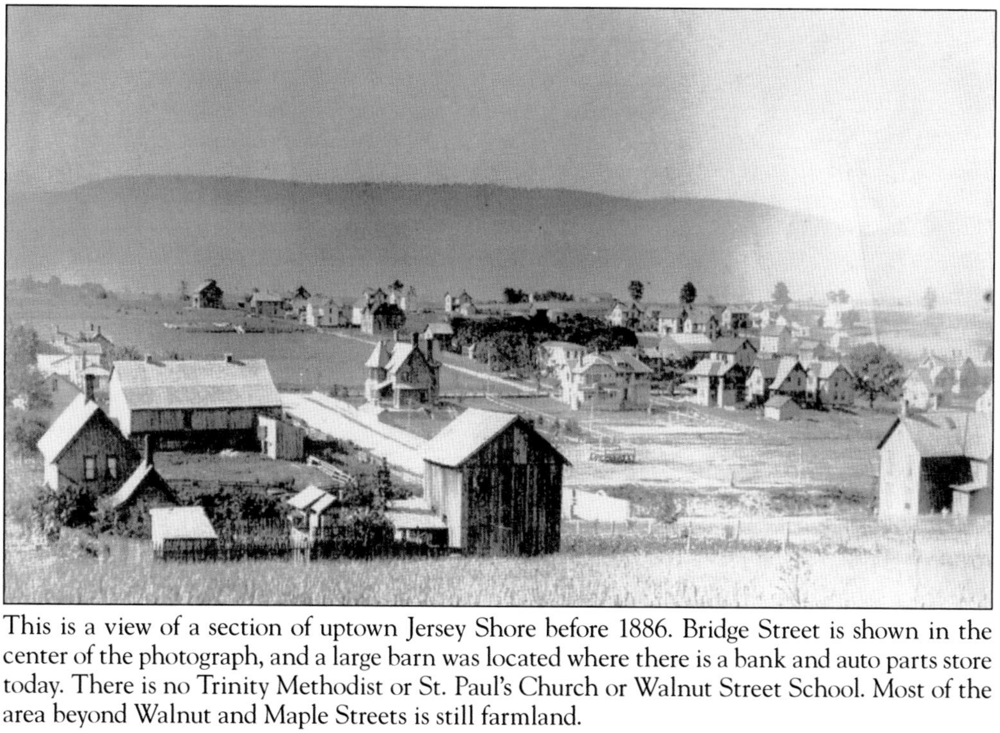

This is a view of a section of uptown Jersey Shore before 1886. Bridge Street is shown in the center of the photograph, and a large barn was located where there is a bank and auto parts store today. There is no Trinity Methodist or St. Paul's Church or Walnut Street School. Most of the area beyond Walnut and Maple Streets is still farmland.

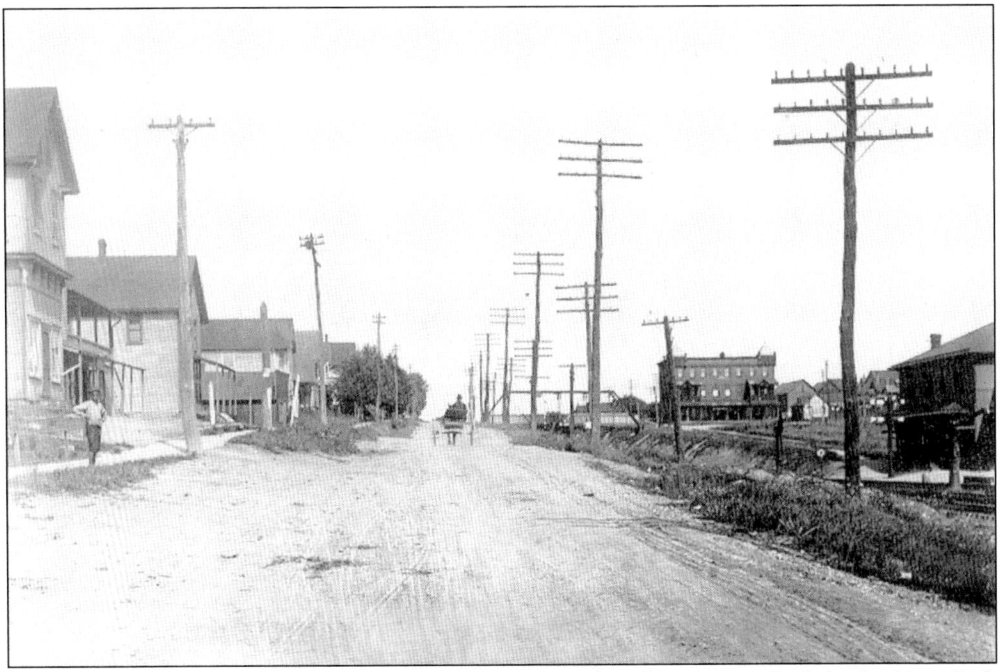

This view is looking east on Railroad Street showing railroad houses to the left, the New York Central office to the right, and the large Torbert Building on Bridge Street. J. William Miller ran a barbershop here, and William Fillman's Cigar Factory and poolroom was on the right side with Sallada Brothers Store in between; the Odd Fellows met upstairs. Today development of the Pine Creek Rails to Trails is again stimulating growth in this section of town.

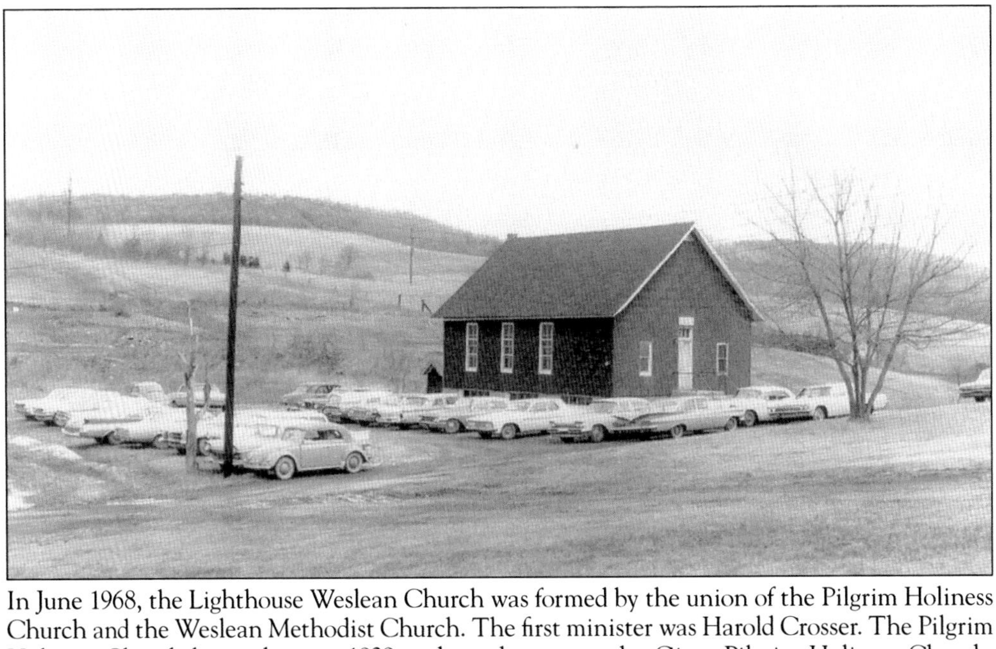

In June 1968, the Lighthouse Weslean Church was formed by the union of the Pilgrim Holiness Church and the Weslean Methodist Church. The first minister was Harold Crosser. The Pilgrim Holiness Church began here in 1939 and was known as the Gipsy Pilgrim Holiness Church. Meetings were first held in the American Legion building, the Stavertown Mission Hall, and by 1942 meetings were held in this schoolhouse.

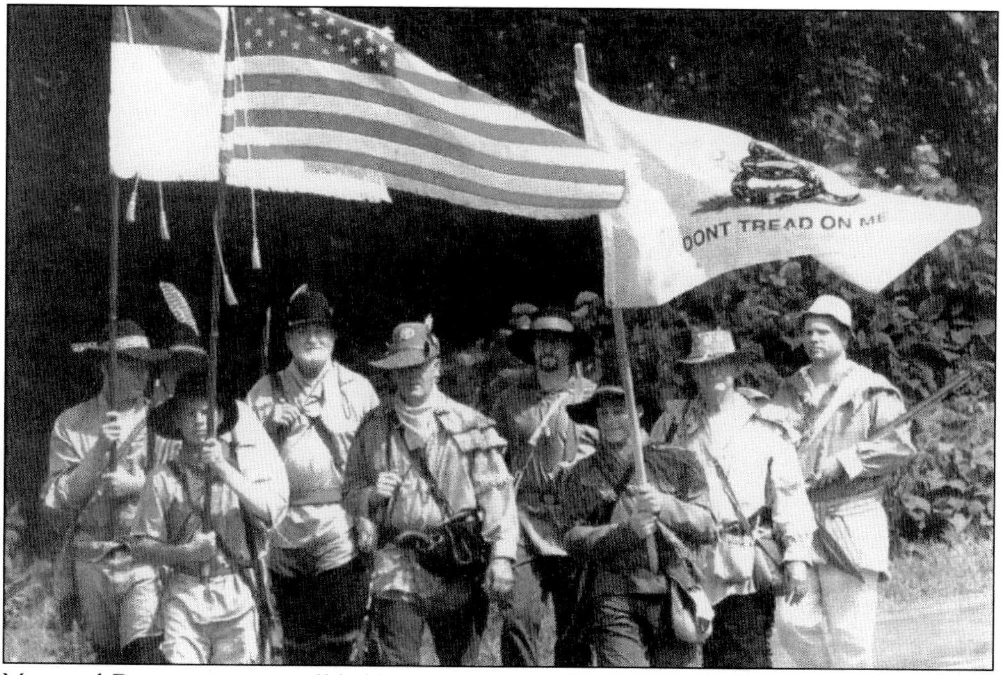

Memorial Day services are still held at the site of the Tiadaghton Elm and the signing of the Pine Creek Declaration of Independence from Great Britain on July 4, 1776. The event involves a brass band, military honor guard, a display of historical flags, a speaker, and the Fair Play Men. Prior to 1962, the ceremony was under the direction of the Sons of the American Revolution (SAR). It was taken over by the Rotary Club in 1962 and passed on to the Lion's Club in 2003.

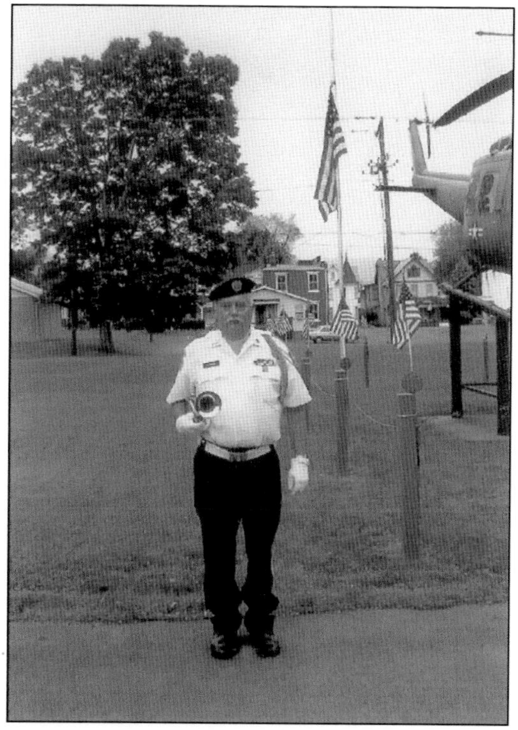

In recent years it has become increasingly difficult to find live buglers to play taps at grave sites of military veterans. A recording is used, if necessary, but Wayne C. Peer, who has been referred to as "Mr. Taps," thinks this is not right and has taken on this mission, ranging near and far, to play taps at the grave sites of military service men. This tradition began in 1862 during our great Civil War.